THE VERNACULAR ARCHITECTURE AND BUILDINGS OF STROUD AND CHALFORD

BY

NIGEL McCULLAGH PATERSON

© Copyright 2006 Nigel Paterson.
All rights reserved. No part of this publication may be reproduced, stored in a retrieval system, or transmitted, in any form or by any means, electronic, mechanical, photocopying, recording, or otherwise, without the written prior permission of the author.

Note for Librarians: A cataloguing record for this book is available from Library and Archives Canada at www.collectionscanada.ca/amicus/index-e.html
ISBN 1-4120-9951-x

Printed in Victoria, BC, Canada. Printed on paper with minimum 30% recycled fibre.
Trafford's print shop runs on "green energy" from solar, wind and other environmentally-friendly power sources.

TRAFFORD
PUBLISHING

Offices in Canada, USA, Ireland and UK

Book sales for North America and international:
Trafford Publishing, 6E–2333 Government St.,
Victoria, BC V8T 4P4 CANADA
phone 250 383 6864 (toll-free 1 888 232 4444)
fax 250 383 6804; email to orders@trafford.com

Book sales in Europe:
Trafford Publishing (UK) Limited, 9 Park End Street, 2nd Floor
Oxford, UK OX1 1HH UNITED KINGDOM
phone +44 (0)1865 722 113 (local rate 0845 230 9601)
facsimile +44 (0)1865 722 868; info.uk@trafford.com

Order online at:
trafford.com/06-1708

10 9 8 7 6 5 4 3

DEDICATION

To Kathy,

Jen, Ben and Mechelle,

Andrew and Gill

Mum and Dad (d.12-10-05),

Cover photograph: The Old Duke of York Inn, Chalford Hill.

ACKNOWLEDGEMENTS

There are many who have contributed to the information and development of the thoughts and opinions given in this book: particularly I would like to thank Ian Mackintosh, Lionel Walrond and Mike Hemming. Thanks must also go to all those who have allowed the viewing and photographing of their properties. Further detail on some of the buildings can be found in the archive of the Gloucestershire Building Recording Group, which is kept at the Records Office in Gloucester. Also, thanks to those who helped with selected photos/information, particularly, Juliet Shipman, Joan Tucker, Sonia Brown, George Edwards and Robin Harrison.

Thank you to Emma Stuart, who read the draft text and provided useful comment.

Finally, thanks must go to the many people, who have done something to help preserve the building heritage of the Stroud area.

PREFACE

The detail given in this book has been collected over the last thirty years, as part of an on-going interest in the historic environment of the Stroud area. Most of the information and personal observations have not been published before and therefore adds to the fund of local knowledge. It does refer in places to the work of others: I hope I have given them due recognition, if I have not – apologies. Credit must also go to members of The Stroud Preservation Trust, Stroud Civic Society and the Gloucestershire Buildings Recording Group, who have participated in some of the building investigations. One of my main aims in writing this book is to provide information to those interested in our rich local historic environment. It may not be classed as a 'good read', but it does contain much information gathered in the field by observation and analysis of a large number of buildings. Such information has not been published before for Stroud and Chalford and has been used to form a view of how the buildings and settlements have changed over the centuries. It will contain information, which some may disagree with and some will be proved wrong by later investigation. However, it is intended to provide food for thought and perhaps encourage further discussion and refinement of some of the views given.

In places, I have suggested ways/methods to repair/restore historic buildings. What I suggest is what I would do, not necessarily what you should do. If unsure about how to maintain/repair your own building, take advice, find out the views/experiences of other owners and read books. There are many good professionals/craftsmen in the area, they will be very happy to help you out.

I am grateful to Trafford Publishing for providing a means to get this sort of book published. I have paid for the publishing costs and recover these from the book sales. Local publishers are not interested in promoting this sort of book, as they say that the market is too limited: lets hope they are wrong. Another advantage of the Trafford 'print on demand' system is that the book will be available on a long-term basis and can be updated as more information becomes available.

CONTENTS

1. **INTRODUCTION** 11

2. **GEOGRAPHY AND GEOLOGY OF THE AREA** 15

3. **UNDERSTANDING COTSWOLD STONE VERNACULAR BUILDINGS** 21

4. **DETAILS OF VERNACULAR BUILDINGS IN THE STROUD AREA** 33

5. **CARE AND REPAIR OF STONE VERNACULAR BUILDINGS** 81

6. **VERNACULAR BUILDINGS OF STROUD** 99

6.1 Development of the Town   104

6.2 High Street – the early core of the Town   104

Earliest Buildings in the High St
       17th C Buildings in the High St
       18th C Buildings in the High St
       19th C Buildings in the High St

6.3 The Cross   127

6.4 The Top of the Town – the first expansion of the town in the 17th C   130

Parliament St
       Nelson St
Castle Street, Lower Street and Beyond
       Middle St
       Whitehall and Piccadilly
       Chapel St
Acre St

7. **WHAT HAPPENED TO STROUD BETWEEN 1960 AND 2003**   205

Chapel Street
The Ring Road
The Stroud Preservation Trust
58-62 High Street
Hill Paul Building

8. **VERNACULAR BUILDINGS OF CHALFORD**   225

8.1 Some Background   230

8.2 Development of Chalford Hill and Its Cottages   231

The Cottages
The Dry Stone Walls of Chalford
Descriptions of Some Cottages and Houses in Chalford Hill
Overview of the Development of Chalford Hill

8.3 Development of Chalford and Its Cottages, Houses and Mill Buildings   297

Buildings in Chalford
Mill Buildings
The Larger Houses in the Valley
Some Smaller Houses in the Valley
Cottages in Chalford Valley
Overview of the Development of the Settlement in Chalford Valley

9.   A COMPARISON OF THE SETTLEMENTS AT STROUD AND CHALFORD   329

10.   RECENT CHANGES AND THE FUTURE   333

11.   SOURCES OF INFORMATION   337

CHAPTER 1

INTRODUCTION

STROUD AND CHALFORD AS SHOWN ON AN 1831 MAP

INTRODUCTION

THE STROUD area has great natural beauty and a rich heritage of buildings of religious, domestic and industrial origins. The buildings are linked through their associations with the wool growing and cloth making industries. These industries developed in the area because it contained the necessary natural resources of land for grazing and power in the rivers for water mills. It also had readily accessible and suitable stone for building and water to support a developing and eventually large population of workers. Several books have been written in recent years about the local mills, canal and industry. There have also been many books of photographs showing how the area looked in the 20th C, when the area still retained its local flavour, with its individual identity and customs. However, only a limited amount of detail has been provided about the buildings themselves. This book sets out to fill this gap (in part at least).

I first saw the area from a train in the mid 1960's when going for an interview at Cardiff University. I didn't know where it was, but I found the intimate mixing of old industrial and domestic buildings attractive. I was also surprised by the apparent appearance of decay of the buildings, which was evident along the route followed by the train. I didn't think any more about the place for many years. After college, I was employed as a research scientist at the Coal Research Establishment, near Tewkesbury. We initially looked for houses in Cheltenham and Gloucester, but couldn't find anywhere we, or the mortgage company could agree on. The agents were dismissive of the Stroud area: the joke at the time in Cheltenham was that they propped up the dead in Stroud, to make it look inhabited! Luckily, we did look and immediately found the houses far more attractive, interesting, affordable and less pretentious. We found that Stroud and the surrounding villages had a genuine sense of place, with a built record of industries and ways of life that had nearly passed. We moved to Middle Street in Stroud. The house had had an improvement grant to bring it up to 'modern' standards, but this had only partially addressed the work that needed to be done to put the whole building into a good state of repair. I knew nothing about buildings, but was fairly handy and was prepared to have a go at most things and to employ builders when the confidence failed. There were also many empty buildings that you could just wander into to have a look. It was only after about a year that I realised that the Stroud valley was the one the train had come down on my way to college. By doing work and by being curious about the derelict buildings, I developed an interest in the history of the buildings: when they were first built and how and why they had changed over the centuries. There were issues concerning the plight of buildings in Stroud and the apparent uncaring attitude of the local council. Involvement with the groups who fought successfully to save buildings in Stroud helped to develop an understanding about individual buildings. The activities of these groups also resulted in the formation of the Stroud Preservation Trust, which subsequently restored buildings that could otherwise have been lost. We moved to Chalford Hill in the early 1980's where I continued to develop my interest in working on and understanding the local buildings. This activity has now taken me through the ownership and renovation of three houses in Chalford and into many, many local buildings. I have a lot of information in my head and now it's time to put it into print to record it for the future.

This is a book about the vernacular architecture of the area, with the major emphasis on Stroud and Chalford. The term vernacular refers to buildings built to a local style using locally available ma-

Chapter 1

terials. In this area we're talking about buildings that were built prior to approximately the mid 19th C and constructed in stone with stone tiled roofs. The vernacular period ended gradually with a transition from buildings that were dominantly 'local' in character to those that could be called mainly 'national' in their details. The transition must have started with the development of the transport links, which began with the canal in the late 1780's and continued with the railway in the 1840's. Both of these enabled materials to be brought into the area in bulk. 'National' details that were imported into the area include the use of Welsh slates for roofs, sash windows and coal burning grates. However, there was always a tendency towards national design in the homes of those who could afford it. National designs were interpreted and made locally, particularly in the internal wood fittings and fixtures and the classical detail used in the stonework.

The first five sections provide information on the vernacular buildings that can be applied to the whole of the Stroud area. They provide detail on the features of the buildings and how to identify the age and development of the building from the physical evidence in the structure. Section 5 is concerned with how to look after these buildings, as the youngest is now more than 150 years old. Let's be honest they were not built to last this time and their structures are fairly fragile. Having said that, they are easy to maintain, provided there are not great aspirations for generating something grand from what was intended as a simple dwelling. The last sections contain much detail on the buildings of the town of Stroud and the villages at Chalford. They both grew with the development of the cloth making industry in the area, but for different purposes and this is reflected in their buildings.

Many photographs are included: these have generally been taken from an adjacent road, lane or path, so they are the public view of the properties. They will therefore be easily recognised by those studying the buildings in the area.

I've enjoyed investigating and writing about the buildings, let's hope you will enjoy reading about them.

CHAPTER 2

GEOLOGY AND GEOGRAPHY OF THE STROUD AREA

Geology and Geography of the Stroud Area

The rocks of the Cotswolds were laid down between 130 and 200 million years ago in the middle of the Jurassic period. The sequence of rocks in the Stroud area is:

- Lias series (bottom)
- Inferior Oolite series
- Great Oolite series(top)

Each series is sub divided into strata of different types. The Lower Lias clays do not outcrop in the Stroud area, but do occur at the surface in the low-lying ground of the Severn Valley. The Middle Lias consists of clays, which are overlain by a narrow band of hard, resistant marlstone. The clay forms the floor of the Chalford valley. The marlstone varies in thickness and has previously been quarried, as a building material, in the Dursley area. It is not a particularly good stone, because the matrix is soft and prone to weathering. It contains many hard crystalline fossils (belemnites and bivalves), which are exposed by erosion of the softer matrix of the outer face of stone-walls. The Upper Lias is comprised mainly of the Cotswold Sands. These are porous and there is a spring line at their base, marking the junction with the Middle Lias clays. The Inferior Oolite forms the main escarpment of the Cotswold hills and is comprised of the lower, middle and upper Inferior Oolite groups. Each of these in turn is comprised of a number of formations, characterised by their morphology and fossil assemblage. Basically, they all consist of oolitic limestones, which are formed of calcium carbonate. The oolites are thought to have formed as submarine shoals, in tropical seas, where the wave energy and mineral salt content was high. The effects of wave energy show in the fossilised marine structures and these show that they were laid down in shallow water. The thickness of the beds is variable, but they can be thick, which suggests the deposition of material as large banks. Some of the limestones are pure and relatively fossil free and these form the best building stones (the freestones). Others contain varying amounts of sand and shelly material, which suggests they were laid down where the wave energy was less intense. The Inferior Oolite is succeeded by the Great Oolite Series. This consists of a variety of formations, which show a wide lateral variation. There are three main types of rock: clays, argillaceous and porcellaneous limestones and shelly oolitic limestones. The rock types are repeated in a vertical sequence and this seems to be associated with cyclical changes in the sea level and the nature of the sediments being washed in from rivers. The lowest member is the Fullers earth clay and this is succeeded by a variety of limestone beds, which, in this area, include weatherstones, tilestones, shelly limestone and white limestone. There is another spring line at the base of the limestone sequence, marking the junction with the clay. The limestone forms the top of the hills and this protects the underlying clay from erosion. However, where the hard layer of Great Oolite limestone is close to the valley side, it is subject to cambering. The limestone is inflexible, whereas the underlying clay is flexible and can creep. Towards the valley side, the Oolite can loose the support of the underlying clay and this causes vertical cracks to develop. The outer ends of the Oolite then dip towards the valley. The vertical cracks are known as lisomes and tend to fill with loose debris. They were used as a means for disposing of sewage and waste-water for many years, prior to the introduction of mains

Chapter 2

drainage. However, this use could easily contaminate the spring water supply and could have been the cause of outbreaks of disease.

The valleys centering on Stroud and the minor valleys, such as Toadsmoor and Marle Hill have been eroded along fault lines. The valleys are over deepened for the size of rivers they now contain and this reflects the conditions in the area at the end of the ice age (which ended abruptly about 10000 years ago). This over deepening has resulted in the valley sides being unstable in places. Many of the strata described above outcrop in the sides of the Stroud valleys. The valley floor at Stroud and along the Chalford valley to Chalford is formed of the Lias clay. This is overlain by the Cotswold Sands, the highest member of the Lias series. There is a spring line at the junction of the sands and the clays and it was common practice to build houses just above the junction of the clay and sands as the ground was well drained and there was a good water supply breaking out of the valley side. The Inferior Oolite series follow and these contain freestone beds that have been quarried in the area for building stone. The freestones do not have a marked bedding structure and are the best house building stone. They are easily cut into blocks when first quarried and have been widely used in the local buildings. They are not good for dry stone walls, as it decays when subjected to repeated freezing and thawing. They were used in the now badly decayed walls along Rack Hill at Chalford. Freestones are easily cut when freshly mined, i.e. when they are saturated with quarry sap (water with calcium carbonate in solution), but when they dry out a layer of crystalline calcium carbonate is deposited on the surface by evaporation. This hardens the surface and makes it more resistant to weathering. On no account should a Cotswold stone building be sand blasted as this will remove the protective layer and lay the building open to rapid stone decay.

Quarrying must have been an important industry in the Chalford area for several centuries and it is still possible to see the remains of the industry in the form of abandoned quarry faces **(Figures 2.1 and 2.2)**. Quarries and mines such as those under Coppice Ground (beside Brendan House) at Chalford, formerly worked the Inferior Oolite **(Figure 2.3)**. The Inferior Oolite is followed by a band of Fullers Earth and this is marked by the more gently sloping ground on the hillside and generally provides the better agricultural land (Pooles ground, Coppice Ground at Chalford). It forms an impervious band through the rock strata and hence there is another spring line above it. This would have been one of the factors that decided the siting of the ridge villages. The springs appearing in Chalford Hill, around Queen's Square and Commercial Road, are close to the upper junction of the Fullers Earth. The Great Oolite follows in the succession and this caps the top of the hills locally and has protected the softer Fullers Earth from erosion. The Great Oolite contains beds of Ragstones, which are harder than the freestones, as they contain more crystalline material, much of which is fossil remains. They are used in many buildings and dry stone walls in the Chalford Hill area. There was formerly a quarry between Dr Middleton's Road and Burcombe Road which would have worked the Great Oolite. Near The Camp, the lowest strata of the Great Oolite series are the Througham Tilestones and these provide material suitable for roofing slates. It contains a higher mica and sand content, which makes it more fissile.

GEOLOGY AND GEOGRAPHY OF THE STROUD AREA

Figure 2.1. Quarry face above Warehouse Mill.

Figure 2.2. Quarry face visible on Old Neighbourhood.

Figure 2.3. Former site of quarry on Marle Hill (in the wooded area).

CHAPTER 3

UNDERSTANDING COTSWOLD STONE VERNACULAR BUILDINGS

A derelict stone house (built in the early 1700's) in the Slad Valley: you could just wander inside.
(photo taken in the early 1970's)

CONTENTS OF CHAPTER

THE PURPOSE of this chapter is to help those who are interested in understanding more about Cotswold stone buildings. An approach is outlined, which is used to work out the different phases within a building and this is used to form a view on how the building has developed over the centuries. This is done by looking at the features that are present from the different phases within the existing structure. The use of the following features is given:

> Doors and other wood fittings
> Hearths
> Joists and beams
> Roof details
> Stairs
> Walling details

Understanding Cotswold Stone Vernacular Buildings

BUILDINGS ARE like three-dimensional puzzles. The key to their understanding is to collect individual parts of the puzzle and then build the pieces into a plausible view of the development history. This will be based on the collected evidence and may have to be altered as further evidence is found. Always be prepared to modify the view in the light of new information! Sometimes a view is better than none, since it provides something that can be tested and challenged and then refined. This sort of approach is necessary with the local vernacular buildings, because for many centuries, there has been a tendency to modify and add to, rather than replace completely. The reason for this is easy to see, as it is only with the advent of machines that the pulling down and removal of large volumes of building materials has become a practical option. The result of all this is that we have a large collection of historic buildings, very few of which have not been added to or altered on several occasions. Each of the stages of change is called a building phase, with the original build being the first phase. It is useful when interpreting a building to divide the building into structural blocks. Each block represents a structurally distinct part of the building, as happens when a new part is added to an existing part. A block may contain several phases of building, which show how the developing conglomerate of a building has been changed over the years. A phase can overlay more than one block. **Figure 3.1** shows a house where three structural blocks can be seen. The gable end of the central block shows three phases of development (as shown by the ghost roof slopes in the walling).

When working out the development of a building, start off by walking around both the outside and inside to get a feel for the place. Pieces of the puzzle are then collected by walking around the building many times and looking at the detail. You will begin to see the relationships between the different parts and the age of the individual features of the building. Look for details of building lines, fireplaces, beams, the detail of the roof structure, style of doors, windows, stairs, room heights, stone and coursing detail, roof pitch, wall thickness, existing and former room plans and redundant features such as blocked hearths, windows and doorways. Make notes, sketches and plans and take photographs, so that the details can be studied at leisure. Take the time to study and evaluate, before drafting out a view of the building development. Then go back and test it, re-look at contentious parts and develop the view as necessary.

The following notes should help in considering building details. Refer to the Chapter 4 to get an idea of how the detail of the features has changed over the centuries, which can give a guide to the dating of the various parts of the building. Also, make use of books such as 'Fixtures and Fittings in Dated Houses 1567-1763' by Linda Hall and N W Alcock, who provide valuable details of features in dated houses of the 17th and 18th C. Also, try and find old photographs of the building and its location. These can often reveal the detail of the changes that have occurred over the past 100 years or so. Unfortunately, they can also serve to highlight how the building may have been spoiled by poorly designed extensions and unsympathetic windows and doors. **Figure 3.2** shows two photos of a cottage in Chapel St, Stroud, that was renovated as part of the Chapel St redevelopment in the late 1970's. By standards of today, what was done would be classed as most unsympathetic (however, it has to be said that at least the building was retained).

Doors and Other Wood Fittings: Make a careful note of doors and wood fittings (such as skirt-

Chapter 3

ings, architraves, shutters and dado rails). This detail is most subject to the changes in fashion and is most likely to have been changed over the years. Therefore, the earlier the building the less likely the original wood detail is to have survived. Take note of the nature of the timber detail (type of wood, construction, mouldings, etc) and associated iron fittings (nails, hinges, locks, etc). These will enable the detail to be dated and therefore an indication of either the original build date or when the room was remodelled. Sometimes a room is found to contain detail of a consistent period, this is nice, but more often a mixture of dates of origin will be found showing how the room has been maintained/repaired over the centuries. The detail can be used to indicate what the room was used for by previous occupants. For instance, think about the contrast between the large open stone fireplaces that we like to see in our comfortable lounges and its original function as a working hearth, where all food was cooked by a combination of boiling, roasting and grilling and people huddled around to keep warm in winter. Food will have been prepared and eaten in the room and many other domestic functions performed. Two examples of wood detail are shown on **Figures 3.3 and 3.4**: a late 18th C two panel door and early 18th C panelling surrounding a window seat.

Hearths: The detail of the hearth can provide useful information about the history of a building. The earliest form of the hearth usually indicates the date of the original build, with the reservation that hearths can be inserted into a building in a later phase. A good example of this is the insertion of floors and hearths into a former open hall. Building lines usually show whether a hearth and associated flue have been added to an earlier building. All of the earlier hearths (i.e. those predating the widespread use of coal in the late 18th C) were wood burning and have large hearth openings, no draft control and large flues. Sometimes, they have been completely infilled, but their presence is indicated by an overthick wall, possibly a stepped chimneybreast and a redundant chimneystack. Although, sometimes parts or all of the structure have been removed. I've seen a ground floor hearth modified to create a doorway through to an adjacent cottage, a flue passing through a first floor flue opened up and converted to a cupboard and in another case converted to a first floor hearth. If wood burning hearths have been converted to coal burning, the hearth opening will have been largely infilled, but leaving the large flue above. Shine a torch up the flue from the hearth to see if there is a large flue associated with an earlier form of the hearth. Remove the plaster from the hearth wall, when investigating an infilled hearth, as this will enable the stages of the infilling to be identified. If an earlier form of the hearth is to be recovered, always ensure the both lintel and flue are intact, before starting work. Sometimes good luck tokens were put into the hearth when it was modified. Commonly, a coin was used and this provides an indication of the date of the infill. In at least one instance, a dried cat is known to have been placed in a sack and hung in a redundant flue, to prevent evil spirits entering the house! If a cast iron coal- burning grate is present, avoid the temptation to remove it, too many good examples have already been lost. The detail of the grate provides another means for dating that phase of the hearth. **Figures 3.5 and 3.6** show a late 17th C wood burning hearth and a late 18th/early 19th C coal burning fireplace.

Joists and beams: The detail of the floor structures provides information on the age of a building/phase and changes that have occurred. If original, the detail provides a guide to the date of the original building: such dates are not precise, but are a good guide. The details that provide the clues are the size and nature of the timber and the dressing, the style of the chamfer and stops (if present), the nature of the joists and their lodging with the beam and the detail of the junction with the wall. I've seen 16th C beams in a building resting on machine cut timber pads in the wall, which together with other evidence showed that the beams had been re-used and the build date was early 19th C, not 16th C. But, the presence of reused timbers indicates an earlier building has been removed and materials salvaged. Sometimes the floor joists have been renewed, leaving oversize/redundant beam lodgings. Again the detail gives the date of the change. Hearthstones set in the floor structure shows the location of hearths that may be blocked up in the wall and trimmed and infilled sections of floor show the sites of former accesses between floors (stairs and hatches). **Figures 3.7 and 3.8** show some 16th C joists with their original beam. The joists are laid flat and have chamfers and stops, which shows they were intended to be seen. The beam has a wide, flat chamfer and a draw stop, set off the chamfer. All these details are characteristic of early (i.e.16th C) work.

Roof Details: The roof structures of vernacular buildings are remarkably long lived and it is common to find the original structure, or major parts of it, in place in local houses and cottages dating from the 17th C. The detail of the structure can provide important information about the development of a building. As with walls, there seems to have been a tendency to adapt and modify roof structures, rather than replace them, unless they were weakened by decay. In the case of weakened structures, many additional timbers may have been added in an attempt to prolong the life of the structure and to avoid costly repairs. The details of roof structures are outlined in Chapter 4. When investigating a roof structure, start off by trying to decide whether the structure is original. Do this by considering its relationship with tie beams, building lines, the roof angle, the presence or absence of redundant peg holes and mortices and the nature of the timber and its preparation. Look for cut outs for windbraces and the nature of the simple timber joints. Roof structures were generally constructed in timber yards, and assembled on site. It is common to find the individual parts labelled to aid the re-assembly. Look for the labelling and see if it has consistency. The extent of a roof structure shows the size of the building it served. In a building of several phases, a change in the roof detail is strong evidence for the position of a phase change. In all periods there is a tendency to re-use wood, so be aware of the possibility that the redundant pegholes and mortices may relate to a different building. Also, reused timbers may be found in an 'original' roof structure, if something in the vicinity was demolished when the new building occurred.

Identify the nature of the way the individual members are held together. Structural timbers are generally fixed together using straight, wood pegs in vernacular buildings. Sometimes there is no true joint and the peg is simply driven through drilled holes in the timbers. The holes can be offset, so that the peg pulls the timbers together. Other widespread fixing methods are the pegged mortice and tenon, the fish plate and the face halved joints. The mortice and tenon joint is found joining the apices of the principal rafters and also joining the feet of the principals to the tie beam. The face-halved joint may be found joining the apices of the principal rafters. Look at the opposite faces of the apex of the truss to determine whether the joint is mortice/tenon or face halved: in the former the diagonal line of the joint is in the same direction on each side, whereas the directions are at approximately 90° to each other if it is a face halved joint. The fish-plate joint is found joining successive purlins, through the principal rafters, in later vernacular buildings and in replacement roof structures. The detail of the joints, and structure detail can be used to give an indication of the date of origin. Sometimes a precise dating is possible, as very occasionally, the builder/carpenter will have put their name and a date on one of the members.

Figures 3.9 and 3.10 show examples of a typical 'A' frame roof truss (this one 17th C) and the earlier form of the extended collar truss roof.

Chapter 3

Stairs: The stone treads of winder stairs will have become worn over the years and may have been overlain by timber treads. Look beneath the treads of ground floor timber winders to see if there is stone beneath, as the presence of a stone stair indicates a date before the early part of the 18th C. The upper timber section (if present) may have been rebuilt, often using pine. Often the whole stair has been removed and relocated elsewhere. A semi-circular recess adjacent to a hearth shows the former existence of a winder stair. This space may have been adapted as a cupboard or to gain access to an adjoining cottage. **Figure 3.11, 3.12 and 3.13** show some examples of stairs in local buildings. Figure 3.11 shows a late 17th C, stone winder stair in a cottage undergoing a sympathetic renovation. Figure 3.12 shows 17th C dog leg stair, in oak, retained in a house, which has had the original outer timber frame walls replaced in brick (in the 19th C). Figure 3.13 shows an early 19th C stair with a mahogany handrail surviving in a sadly neglected building.

Walling detail: This includes the stone, its coursing and mortar, building lines and architectural embellishments such as dripmoulds, string-courses and classical detail (pediments, porches etc). As a rule, the stone of an earlier phase underlies that of the later phases, with the exception of localised areas of rebuilding and blockings. There will be a building line between different phases, with a difference in the nature of the stone and its dressing, its coursing and its mortar, between the phases. However, bear in mind that if the phases are close in date, then differences in the stone and coursing may not be apparent, but the building line should still be visible. There could be vertical, horizontal or angled lines, sometimes all three if there have been major changes. The vertical line is usually the most obvious. This is because the corner of a Cotswold stone building is marked by a vertical line of quoin stones, which give structural integrity to the building. In many cases, when an addition is made, the new phase is butted against the corner of the earlier phase and the quoins become embedded as a vertical line of larger stones in the revised wall. The direction of the quoins indicates the earlier part. On occasions some quoins are removed and the new stone is knitted into the earlier walling, but the intermittent building line will still be apparent. An angled line occurs in gable end walls, where the number of storeys has been increased or half height walls added to an attic. They reflect the earlier roof slopes and occasionally where multiple changes have been made, there are likely to be several angled roof lines. These changes were generally made in the latter 17th and 18th C and did not seem to consider the absence of any meaningful foundations on these buildings. This may disturb a structural engineer, but the buildings still stand! Horizontal lines are present in the front and rear walls if the wall heights have been raised. They are more difficult to see, as there are no large stones marking the height of the original wall. One way of identifying where the change has occurred is to study the quoin stones, as quite often their nature changes at the point where the building phase changes. Once this point is seen then slight changes in the nature of the walling stone and the coursing may become more apparent.

The nature of the dressing of the stone and its coursing can be used to give an indication of date. Early (16th C) good quality stonework is finely dressed by hand chisel, the mortar lines are narrow and the coursing is regular. In the 17th C, the hand dressing is less good, the mortar lines are wider, but the courses are generally regular. Coursed rubble-stone walls are very common in buildings originating in this century. In the 18th C, the dressing can be poor, the stones less regular in shape, the mortar joints wide and the coursing poor. Also, jumper stones commonly interrupt the courses. I have to be careful not to be too definite here, as in each century, there is very good work and poor work, which may differ from the general points made above. Look out for machine cut stone (the cut marks are very regular), this will date from approximately the mid 19th C or later.

Figures 3.14 –16 show some examples of different walling details. Figure 3.14 shows some early hand dressed stone masonary blocks, possibly dating from the 16th C. Figure 3.15 shows 17th C, coursed rubblestone walling, typical of many houses and cottages in the area. Figure 3.16 shows a coursed rubblestone wall with jumper stones. The use of jumper stones seems to appear in the very late 17th C.

Chapter 3

Figure 3.1. Building Blocks.
(The Ferns, Chalford Hill)

Figure 3.2. Before and After.
(Cottage in Chapel St)

Figure 3.3. Late 18th C Two Panel Door.
(55 High Street, mid 1980's)

Figure 3.4. Early 18th C Window Seat Panelling.
(Laurel Villa, Stroud, late 1980's)

Figure 3.5. Late 17th C Wood Burning, Open Fireplace.
(The Orchards, France Lynch, early 1990's)

Figure 3.6. Late 18/early 19th C Coal Burning Fireplace. *(Tannery House, Leonard Stanley, late 1980's)*

UNDERSTANDING COTSWOLD STONE VERNACULAR BUILDINGS

Figure 3.7. Joists, Laid Flat and with Chamfers and Stops.
(former house in farmyard of Tann House farm, Frampton on Severn, early 1990's)

Figure 3.8. Beam with Wide Chamfer and Draw stop Set Off the Chamfer.
(same floor as Figure 3.7)

Figure 3.9. A 17th C 'A' Frame Roof Truss.
(Berrymore Cottages, N Woodchester, mid 1980's)

Figure 3.10. An Extended Collar Truss Roof.
(Salmon's Mill House, Stroud, mid 1980's)

Figure 3.11. Late 17th C Stone Winder stair.
(Cottage at Waterlane, late 1990's)

Figure 3.12. 17th C Dog Leg Stair.
(Haresfield Farm, late 1990's)

31

Chapter 3

Figure 3.13. Early 19th C Stair.
(Baytree House, Dudbridge, 2004)

Figure 3.14. Well Dressed Masonary Blocks.
(16th C house in Chalford Industrial Estate, 2006)

Figure 3.15. Coursed Rubblestone Walling.
(Church Court, Stroud, 2006)

Figure 3.16. Rubblestone Walling with Jumper Stones.
(Clematis Cottage, Chalford Hill, 1985)

CHAPTER 4

DETAILS OF VERNACULAR BUILDINGS IN THE STROUD AREA

A simple, late 17th/early 18th C vernacular cottage, near Besbury Common: until 1998, the outside earth closet was the only sanitation, the inside of the cottage was simple and showed how the owners lived until very recently with only the very basic amenities.

CONTENTS OF CHAPTER

THIS CHAPTER provides much information on the features of local stone buildings. It is not exhaustive, but gives information that can be used to identify and obtain an approximate date of origin for the features within buildings. This can then be used to work out the building phases and development of the building. Details are given of:

    Beams
    Doors
    Dripmoulds
    Floors
    Gabled dormers
    Hearths
    Hinges
    Joints
    Joists
    Lath and plaster partitions
    Lintels
    Mortars
    Mouldings
    Panelling
    Plans
    Plaster
    Roof pitch
    Roof structure
    Stairs
    Stonewalls
    String courses
    Stud and panel partition walls
    Timber frame walls
    Windows, window frames and glass
    Some differences between 18th and 19th C buildings

Details of Vernacular Buildings in the Stroud Area

In this chapter, the details of local vernacular buildings are discussed. Enough information has been provided to show how the detail of the features has changed over the centuries as the needs and fashions changed. There should be sufficient information here to enable a guide to the date of a particular feature in a building to be established. Refer to Chapter 11 'Sources of Information' if you wish to read more widely.

Beams

Timber beams are used to support floors and to provide a tie for the roof truss in many buildings of the vernacular period. The details of the beams can be used to provide a guide to the original build date and to the dates of subsequent phases of change. The beam details include the size, nature of the chamfers and stops, the detail of the joist lodging with the beam, the quality of the finish and the type of wood. In the 16th C and earlier, there was a good supply of timber and beams tended to be large in cross sectional area and of good quality. A slow decline occurred during the 17th C, as demand increased and supplies became depleted. In the 18th C, the timbers can appear to be fairly poor quality (in terms of both finish and scantling): however looks can be deceiving, as many have lasted over 200 years! Until the 19th C, the beams were cut by hand with a pit saw and/or an adze. After this time, they became increasingly machine cut and therefore very regular in appearance.

It is quite common to see beam surfaces covered in hack marks. This has been done at some stage to provide a key for a plaster covering.

Explanation of terms:

Chamfer: The angle between the vertical sides and horizontal underside (or soffit) of the beam can be cut at an angle to form a chamfer along the lower edges of the beam. The chamfer can be flat (most common in this area), hollow (concave), ovolo (convex) or a more complex profile. With flat chamfers, the width can vary: as a general rule, the wider the chamfer, the earlier the beam. The origin of the chamfer is not known with certainty, but it has been suggested that it originated with traditional naval carpentry. In ships, the headroom was limited on the lower decks and the chamfer was used to minimise the accident risk when banging into the structural timbers. The same logic also applies to low ceiling cottages and houses.

Stop: It was general to end the chamfer at a short distance before the beam became bedded in the wall of the building. A stop was used to merge the chamfer with the right angle formed by the beam edges and soffit at this point. Various styles of stop have been noted in the area: these include the draw (or runout) stop, triangular stop, scroll stop and geometric stop. Variations have been noted and these include the draw stop set off the chamfer or step stop (a small 90° step at the end of the chamfer, with the draw starting on top of the step, **Figure 4.2**) and the incorporation of a bar crossing the chamfer a short distance before the stop (e.g. scroll stop with bar, **Figure 4.1**). The presence of stops at either

CHAPTER 4

end of the beam is a good indication that the beam has been cut for the room it is in. If stops are only present at one end or absent, then the beam may be re-used or the walls may have been altered.

Scantling: The cross section of the beam, varies from large to small.

16th/early 17th C beams: Beams in 16th C buildings are generally of an excellent quality, straight and well finished. Oak is a commonly used timber, with elm also in widespread use. The chamfers are wide (approx. 125mm or wider) and generally flat in local buildings (Figure 4.2). There are variations in the style of the chamfer with concave and convex profile to the chamfer being observed over a wider geographical area. In timber framed buildings, the chamfers can become more complex, presumably because there was a greater involvement of carpenters in the construction of the building. The most commonly observed stop is the draw stop set off the chamfer, although the plain draw stop and the triangular stop have been noted. In these early buildings the joists are also large and generally laid flat. The nature of the joist:beam joint, can vary. Most commonly, the joist is jointed into the side of the beam, particularly in positions where it spans between an adjacent wall and the beam. Where it spans between adjacent beams, it is not uncommon to find the joist jointed into the side of one of the beams and lodging in a cutout in the top of the other beam. This must have facilitated construction, otherwise it would be difficult to assemble the pair of beams and set of spanning joists. In the 16th–18th C, the width of the building was limited by the length of the beams that were available. This set the maximum span of the roof truss. Most buildings fall in the 3.5 to 4.5 m range. Several examples of half beams (Figure 4.3) set against the end walls of the room have been noted, particularly across the front wall of the hearth. A beam across the front hearth wall removed the joist ends from the proximity of the flue and avoided problems with them smouldering and catching fire.

Mid/late 17th C beams: The use of elm for beams becomes more common, although oak was still used in the better buildings. Smaller trees must have been used, as the beams are less regular, sometimes they are rather waney, with some residual bark in places. Flat chamfers, up to 125mm wide are seen in buildings of the mid 17th C, although by the end of the century, they can be reduced in width to about 25mm. The scroll stop (**Figure 4.4**) becomes fairly common by the end of the century, although step stops and run-out stops are still seen (although reduced in size with the width of the chamfer). It is more common to see joist lodgings in the top of the beams, particularly in smaller houses (**Figure 4.5**). The side beam/joist joint is still seen in better quality work. Where joists lodge in the top of the joist, they can be fixed with a wood peg. Also, the lodging and its joist may be numbered (Roman numerals common): this shows that the timbers were prepared in a timber yard and brought to the construction site in a prepared state.

18th C beams: These generally do not have chamfers or stops and the finish can be rather rough (**Figure 4.6**). This is partly due to the poorer quality timber that was being used and also because they were usually intended to be covered with lath and plaster. Oak was seldom used, elm was common, with pitch pine being used in the later part of the century. The joists are invariably lodged in cutouts in the top of the beam. In the later part of the century, the cutouts can have a half dovetail shape and this matches a similar profile at the joist end. The dovetail stops the joist pulling out of its lodging.

19th C beams: Beams went out of use during the 19th C, except where they were required as roof ties and then they could be hidden above the ceiling level. The upper floors tended to be supported on the

Details of Vernacular Buildings in the Stroud Area

walls of the floor below. If beams were used, the timber was generally machine cut and very regular (**Figure 4.7**). Pitch pine was widely used for structural timbers.

20th C beams: This is strictly outside the period of this book. However, the Arts and Crafts movement of the early 20th C marked a brief return to vernacular building styles. Hence in these houses timbers having the details of earlier centuries can be found.

Doors (External and Internal)

The most common form of door construction in the 17thC was the plank and ledge door (**Figures 4.8, 4.9**). It is comprised of a series of vertical planks, which can be joined by a tongue and a groove, with a number of horizontal ledge timbers on the rear side to hold the planks together. The ledges and planks are fixed together with handmade iron nails, hammered from the plank side, through the ledges and the ends curled over. This is the door in its simplest form. Variations include recessing alternate planks and moulding to the sides of the planks. External doors may be comprised of vertical planks, backed with a complete set of horizontal planks, to form a double thickness door for added security. These are found on houses rather than cottages, and together with good quality iron fittings (strap hinges, knocker and a turnhandle for a latch) and perhaps regularly placed iron studs, provide an impression of status to the building. The doors are made of oak (higher status and external doors) or elm. Plank and ledge doors continued to be made in subsequent centuries, but their use slipped down the social scale, and by the 19th C were only used in workers cottages.

The second common form of door construction is the panelled door (**Figures 4.10-4.12**). These are comprised of panels, set in a frame made of vertical members (stiles) and horizontal members (rails). The panels may be flat or raised or raised and fielded (i.e. the raised panel had a chamfered edge). The inner faces of the stile and rails (that frame the panels) are generally moulded. Panel doors appear first at the higher end of the social scale and examples go back to at least the 16th C. They were appearing in small houses by the mid 17th C. Early examples are made of oak, with some in elm. It became the door style that typifies the Georgian period, generally constructed in pitch pine, but in hardwood for the best quality work. They were always painted in the 18th C and not left as exposed wood. The number of panels varied widely, depending on status and time. However, the 6-panel door typifies the form common in the first half of the 18th C. The design is classical and guided by principles laid down by Palladio. The upper pair of panels are much smaller than the middle pair, which in turn are slightly less tall than the lowest pair. Many variations exist and these include the amalgamation of an individual pair of panels to create a door with an odd number of panels and the use of 8, 4 or 2 panels. External doors may have the lower panels raised flush with the frame, to provide increased strength and to avoid traps for water. The doors became more substantial as the century progressed and, by the early 19th C, the number of panels became reduced to 2 or 4.

External doors were not glazed in the 18th C, although there are a few examples where the pair of upper small panels have been glazed with bulls-eye glass. Instead, fanlights were used to light hallways, where it was difficult to provide an external window. The use of fanlights over the main external door appeared in the mid 18th C and was very popular in the last part of the century (particularly in towns). They did not generally appear at the cottage level. They are basically comprised of an iron frame with applied tracery in cast lead. The composition could be complex with the design becoming more geometric as the 19th C approached. Fanlights had fallen out of use before the mid 19th C.

Chapter 4

Door furniture was simple and made in cast or wrought iron. In the 17th C, the door furniture was restricted to handmade strap **(Figures 4.13 and 14)**, butterfly, H or H-L hinges, together with a latch (in iron or wood) **(Figure 4.15)**. An external door could have a heavy knocker. In the 18th C, the external door would have a knob to the side of the centre rail, connected to a slide lock on the inner door face and perhaps a heavy knocker. Letter-boxes did not appear until the mid 19th C, when the postal system was fully organised, which, in turn, was accompanied by the numbering of properties (although the process was started several decades earlier). Brass fittings were not common in the 18th C, as it was too expensive. The use of the slide locks for external doors continued into the later part of the 18th C **(Figure 4.16)**, when mortice locks were introduced and gradually permeated down the social scale. Bramah introduced the first lock activated by a rotating barrel, rather than a sliding bolt: the great benefit of this was that it removed the need for a large and awkward key. Yale and Chubb further developed the rotating barrel concept in the first part of the 19th C.

Dripmoulds (also called Hoodmoulds)

These are found over the tops of stone mullion window frames. They consist of a horizontal length of moulded stone above the window, which has an angled upper surface and a concave underside. There are short vertical returns down each side of the frame, which are terminated by short horizontal sections **(Figure 4.17)**. They are formed of separate stones to the frame itself. Their purpose is to direct the water running down the wall away from the windows and therefore reduce the amount of leakage into the house through what must have been leaky windows. They occur in 17th C and earlier buildings, prior to the use of gutters. The use of leaded valleys appeared in the 18th C and dripmoulds went out of use. Dripmoulds made a comeback in some Victorian stone buildings, but here they are decorative and not functional (as these buildings have gutters). In the late 17th C and very early 18th C, the dripmould can extend over all of the windows of a floor, with the vertical returns at either end of the run of windows **(Figure 4.19)**. In some early and some late (and larger buildings), dripcourses (of moulded stone) have been noted to run around the whole building above the ground and first floor windows **(Figure 4.18)**.

Floors

The ground floor of a vernacular Cotswold cottage or house will usually have a stone flagged floor, laid dry and directly onto the underlying earth. Some of the flags may be large. The poorest cottages may only have had an earth floor. If a cellar is present, then there is usually a suspended wood floor, supported on a cellar beam. The earlier or later higher status buildings may have a stone vaulted cellar and this can support a flagstone floor. The upper floors are always of timber construction and consist of joists and beams. The detail of the structure, i.e. type of wood, size of components, nature of joints and detail varies with time. Refer to the relevant parts of this chapter for further information. **Figures 4.20 and 21** show late 17th/early 18th C floor structures in two cottages. Note that the undersides of the floor boards are lime-washed and the ceiling was therefore not originally plastered and that the beam has a narrow chamfer and does not appear to have stops. **Figure 4.22** shows an earlier floor structure. Note that the timbers are more substantial and regular, and that the beam has a wide chamfer with stops.

DETAILS OF VERNACULAR BUILDINGS IN THE STROUD AREA

GABLED DORMERS

The gabled dormer was used widely in the Cotswold stone houses of the 17th C, it went out of use in the 18thC. In this form of construction, the front and rear walls were continued up to the height of the ridge of the roof as gables. In small houses only one gabled dormer may be present in each of the front and rear elevations (**Figure 4.24**). In larger houses or groups of smaller houses, two or more gabled dormers are commonly present in each elevation (**Figure 4.23**). They are associated with a particular form of roof construction, known as the extended collar truss roof. Sometimes, there is only a gabled dormer in the front elevation: in this case the roof truss is a combination of extended collar to the front and conventional 'A' frame to the rear.

HEARTHS

In medieval open hall houses, heat was provided by an open hearth, placed near the centre of the hall and under the ridge of the roof. There was no flue and the combustion gases escaped through special vents in the gable ends or a louvre constructed above the ridge of the roof. In the late 15th and 16th C, it was common to insert a first floor in the open hall and to construct a hearth with a flue in the hall and sometimes on the new first floor. In this case, it is usual to see the inserted stack projecting through the roof and commonly off-centre from the ridge. The former presence of an open hall, in a building that is now floored, can also be indicated by the presence of soot stained roof timbers (if they have survived). A good local example of a former open hall, with soot stained roof timbers, is Daneway house at Sapperton. However, surviving examples are few in number and none have been found in Stroud or the area covered by this book. That is not to say they weren't present in earlier times, but they have not survived in an identifiable form. New buildings constructed from this time were floored and contained hearths and flues from their first build. It was usual to construct the hearths in the gable end walls (most common in this area) or in the rear wall with a chimney gable. The incorporation of this new type of hearth must have made a dramatic improvement to the quality of the atmosphere in the home. In simple terms, this type of hearth consists of an opening into the room with a flue above it leading to a stack, at a higher level than the ridge of the roof. There is a negative pressure drop across the flue and stack, together with a temperature gradient, which causes an upward flow of gases. The sides (jambs) of the fireplace opening were constructed of large, dressed slabs of stone, which are chamfered and stopped in 16th and 17th C houses. The lintel over the opening that supports the front hearth wall was either wood or stone. **Figure 4.25** shows a late 16th/early 17th C fireplace with well dressed stone jambs and an arched lintel. The fireplace seems to have had little use, despite being about 400 years old! If stone has been used, it should be deep, as in No 33 High Street in Stroud, otherwise it will have cracked over the years. A wood bressumer beam (oak or elm) was more commonly used. The rear side of the beam was flared to encourage the smooth flow of gases up the flue, and avoid turbulence behind the lintel. The optimum ratio for the size of the hearth opening into the room to the area of the opening at the top of the stack for these large hearths is said to be 7:1. The hearth openings are large and wood was used as the fuel. Depending on the location in the house, they could be used for heating or cooking. In the 17th C, the cooking hearths generally incorporate a stone lined bread oven in either the side or rear hearth wall. There may also be a seat to one side. Cooking hearths were probably left smouldering most of the time (otherwise the rate of depletion of the wood supplies would have been excessive). **Figure 4.26** shows a good example of a

Chapter 4

mid/late 17th C open fireplace with a timber beam (the original beam has been replaced). Note the large stone jambs, with chamfers and the bread oven in the rear hearth wall. **Figure 4.27** shows a late 17th C hearth in a fire damaged house (and threatened with demolition). The beam is original and only has a minor chamfer. **Figure 4.28** shows what is thought to be a late 17th C parlour fireplace, with a four centred arched opening and a high, stepped mantelshelf. In the late 17th C, hearths with semi circular backs and a smoke channel (**Figure 4.29**) were built, the channel directed the flow of gases up the rear hearth wall and this helped to minimise leakage into the room. The draft from these large early hearths must have been inconvenient and by the late 17th/early 18th C the dimensions of the hearth were becoming restricted. Large 18th C hearths (**Figure 4.30**) are not as deep as those of the 17th C. Also, in the 18th C, the use of chamfers and stops on the jambs and lintel was discontinued. Ash pits were also constructed in front of the hearth. The ash could be collected and used in the manufacture of soap. Over the centuries, the original large hearths became progressively infilled. This probably started in the late 17th C when hearths with semi circular backs are found built within the larger, earlier opening. Semi circular backs were not used after the early 18th C and earlier openings became more restricted in depth and width by later hearths.

In the mid 19th C there was a widespread and eventually near complete switch to coal as the fuel. Coal requires a completely different set of combustion conditions to those needed for wood burning. A large reduction in the area of the hearth opening and the introduction of a grate and throat in the hearth and the chimney pot on the stack were all generally necessary to ensure efficient and controlled combustion. Much has been written about the technology of coal combustion and on the designs of the coal burning hearths. The designs of the hearth inserts and grates of coal fires can be used as key dating points for the changes to a house. Cast iron hob grates were fitted into the reduced wood burning fireplaces and into new buildings constructed from the late 18th C onwards. In the earliest form of hob grate (late 18th C), the front plate has been cast in one piece, with the design with opposed semi circles for the fire-bed and undergrates areas being most common. Fire bars were incorporated in the area in front of the fire itself. The grate design developed in the late 18th/early 19th C, with the front of the grate being cast as two side plates parts, with a connecting apron and fire bars. The length of the apron and bars could be varied to fit different sizes of hearth. Each side plate usually had an ogee profile to its inner edge, such that the two 'ogees' of the side plates approached each other at the level of the grate (**Figure 4.31**). In the final phase of development of the hob grate (early 19th C onwards), the sides were cast as separate upright rectangular panels, with connecting apron and fire bars (**Figures 4.32 and 4.33**). The apron and bars could be bowed outwards. There were many designs cast into the side plates and aprons and these can be used to date the grate. Rococo designs became popular towards the mid 19th C. Manufacture of hob grates ceased around the mid 19th C. They all suffered from the disadvantage that there was no control of the undergrate supply of air, with the consequence that their burning rates were high and uncontrolled. Towards 1850, the register plate was introduced to control the flue draft and this formed the next stage in the development of coal burning hearths. The early designs of register grate had a conventional hob grate (**Figure 4.34**), with a front plate arching over the area above the fire. This incorporated a rear section that adjusted the size of the opening into the flue with an adjustable cast iron flap. This could be used to rather crudely control the burning rate, by adjusting the draught caused by the flue pressure drop. In the later part of the 19th C, the hob design was phased out, and new designs based on a fire basket were introduced (**Figure 4.35**). In these, the basket was set lower than in the traditional hob design and this allowed the eventual introduction of methods for controlling the undergrate supply of air. This was far more effective at controlling the burning rate. In the late 19th/early 20th C, the arched opening of the register grate was replaced with designs with a square opening, with internal splays (with tiles) and a hood over the fire itself (**Figures 4.36 and 4.37**). From the mid 19th C, cast iron ranges were increasingly available for cooking fireplaces. The use of coal burning hearths in the home continued through to the latter part of the 20th C. The basic combustion technology remained unchanged from the early part of the century, but the design of the fire surround changed radically (**Figure 4.38**). The last styles of coal burning hearth are now unloved and are disappearing quickly.

It was usual for the fireplace opening to have a separate surround. This may have been less common for the large open wood burning hearths, although the presence of a set of holes drilled around the front face of the opening, which are packed with wood pegs shows the former presence of a surround. The simplest example seen locally (at Watercombe House, Watercombe) consisted of flat planks of pine fixed to the jambs and lintel and a mantle shelf. This was thought to date from the late 18th C. In higher status houses, an ornate chimneypiece in wood or stone may have been present, although no surviving examples have been seen in the Stroud area. This type of chimneypiece can be ornately carved and incorporate a mantle shelf with a panel over it, which may be carved or contain a painting. Some good, but simple, late 17thC stone chimneypieces, with high mantle shelves were present in Little Britain Farmhouse at S Woodchester in 2002 (**Figure 4.28**). A bolection moulding in wood or stone around the fireplace opening became popular in the late 17th/early 18th C. An example of this was present in one of the buildings behind 23 High St, when it was investigated in 1985. With the introduction of coal burning hearths and the proliferation of hearths in a house, there was a large increase in the fire surround styles, particularly in the parlour and other 'best' rooms. In the vernacular period, Cotswold stone and wood were used, whereas, the use of slate became more widespread as styles became more national (**Figure 4.36**). 18th C styles can incorporate columns at either side with a frieze depicting a classical scene. In the late 18th C, fire surrounds can be in the 'Adam' style (such as those in Stratford Park Mansion). These can be constructed in wood, with applied detail in plaster. In the early 19th C, surrounds with reeded or fluted sides and top, with roundels in the corner blocks have been seen in several local houses (**Figure 4.34**). In the mid 19th C, designs became more plain and the mantle shelf deeper and supported on brackets (**Figure 4.37**).

Hinges

Hinges can be used to give an indication of the date of a building and when it has been altered. Up to approximately the mid 19th C, hinges were hand made and fixed with hand made nails. The heavy strap hinges, which rotate on heavy iron pins hammered into the exterior doorframe are found in 16th and 17th C houses (**Figure 4.13**). The hinge ends can have a variety of styles and these, by comparison of those on dated houses, can give a guide to the date of the building, but beware, they are durable and may have been re-used (check the door for additional shadows of other hinges and fixings) (**Figure 4.39**). In the 18th C, the large strap hinges are also found and can have base plates to fix them to the frame (**Figure 4.14**). Again, the ends show a variety of styles. Internal door and cupboard hinges are smaller and invariably fixed with handmade nails. Smaller versions of the strap hinges with base plates and relatively plain ends are found on plank and ledge doors (**Figure 4.40**). 'H' and 'H-L' hinges are the most common form of hinge on doors that have a panelled construction. These types of hinges are found from the mid 17th C through to the late 18th C (and perhaps a bit beyond). Dated examples of hinges are given in 'Fixtures and Fittings in Dated Houses 1567-1763' by Linda Hall. Hinges dating from the 19th C tend to be of a modern form, but made from thicker metal.

CHAPTER 4

JOINTS

Timber joints are an important structural element of the roof construction. The nature of the joints found in the stone buildings of the Stroud area are not high quality joints as are found in the timber frame buildings of the Severn valley. They are few in number and can be as simple as the rather crude pegging together of overlapping timbers. Prior to the mid 18th C, wood pegs were used to fix the joints, after this time the use of iron fixings (nails and bolts) could be used to secure timbers together and avoid the use of carpentry joints. The main positions in the roof structure requiring the use of a joint are:

- At the apex of the principal rafter truss
- To secure the feet of the principal rafters to the tie beam
- To join the collar across a pair of principal rafters
- To link purlins along the roof slope
- To fix the purlins to the principal rafters
- To fix the ridge timber to the truss
- To fix windbraces to the purlin and principal

Joint at apex of principal rafters: In some 16th C buildings, a vertical joint is found, although a diagonal joint may have been used instead. In 17th, 18th and 19th C buildings the joint is diagonal. There are 2 types of diagonal joint: the face halved joint and the mortice and tenon joint. The former type is more common in 17th C buildings. The type of joint can be identified from the direction of the diagonal. Where the joint is a mortice and tenon, the diagonal is in the same direction on each face of the truss (**Figure 4.41**), whereas, with the face halved joint, the diagonals go in opposite directions. Both types of joint are held by wood pegs.

Principal rafter/tie beam joint: Always a mortice and tenon joint.

Collar:principal rafter joint. In 16th and 17th C work, the collar is joined to the underside of the principal rafters with a pegged, mortice and tenon joint (**Figure 4.42**). The depth of the collar seems to reduce in the later buildings in this range. In the late 17th C, in lower status houses, the workmanship can get poorer and the collar can be simply pegged across one face of the truss. The use of both types of fixing for the collar continues through to the present time, with the mortice and tenon showing better quality work. Also, the use of iron fixings replaced wood pegs in the later part of the 18th C. Forelock bolts were introduced first, to be replaced by threaded bolts in the late 18th C (**Figure 4.43**). Nails were used for inferior work. The original collar has often been removed from the truss and replaced by another in a different position. The former position is commonly shown by the redundant mortices and peg holes.

Purlin/principal rafter joint: There are 2 main types of purlins depending on relationship between the back of the purlin and the back of the principal rafter. In the butt purlin type of roof (**Figure 4.44**), the purlins pass through the principal rafter, such that the back of each principal rafter is in line with the back of the common rafters. In the through purlin roof (**Figure 4.45**), the purlin is trenched into the back of the principal rafter and therefore, the backs of the principal rafters are not in line with the

DETAILS OF VERNACULAR BUILDINGS IN THE STROUD AREA

common rafters (the back of the principal is lower). The through purlin roof seems more common in the earlier stone buildings of the Stroud area.

Purlin linking joints: Successive purlins are joined at their junction with the principal rafter truss. In the earliest form noted in a 16th C building with through purlins, the ends of the successive purlins were cut at an angle across the backs of the principals, roughly overlapped and pegged in place (**Figure 4.47**). In this case, the row of purlins appear in line along the roof slope. In some 17th C roofs of the same type, the purlins are lodged in wide trenches, with the succeeding purlin placed above or below the previous one and pegged in place. The purlins are therefore not in line, but appear staggered (**Figure 4.48**). With butt purlin roofs, the purlins are usually cut back at the junction with the principal and they may be cut diagonally to slot through the aperture in the principal or they may be jointed with individual mortice and tenon joints (**Figure 4.44 and 4.46**). In roofs of the late 18th C and later, a fish plate type of joint has been noted in several buildings. A rectangular shaped cutout is made in the end of each purlin. The joint is made by placing the purlins end-on and inserting a closely fitting length of timber into the slot created by the cut-outs and pegging the whole together.

Ridge timber/truss: All of the buildings studied in the area have a ridge timber. In the 16th-18th C it is usually a square section piece of timber, set in a cutout or notch at the apex of the principal rafter truss (**Figure 4.49**). In the late 18th and 19th C, a timber board could be used and these could be fixed to yolks, nailed across the face of each truss (**Figure 4.50**).

Windbrace/purlin and principal joints: Winbraces are only seen in 16th C and earlier buildings. They are generally fixed by wood pegs in trenches cut in the backs of the principal rafters and purlins (**Figure 4.51, left side of 4.47** (windbrace cut out)). Usually, not many of the windbraces in a roof have survived. However, their former presence is indicated by the cut-outs and its angle shows the direction of the windbrace.

JOISTS

In 16th C buildings, the joists can be large (approx. 6 in wide by 4 in deep in 33 High Street) and laid flat (**Figure 4.52**). They generally have a tenon and shoulder cut at the end, where they locate into a mortice in the beam. They are cut from good quality timber (use of oak is common) and in better quality houses are generally straight. In lesser quality work, smaller scantling timber was used and the joists can reflect the shapes of the original trees. It is quite common to find that the joists have chamfers and stops of the same style as the main beams, but of a smaller scale (**Figure 3.7**). They were intended to be exposed in the ceiling: in No 33 High St, the underside of the floorboards was plastered between the joists. If the house had a parlour, then this ceiling may be ceiled beneath the joists and an ornamental moulded pattern may have been applied to the plaster.

Joists in 17th C houses are generally laid upright and are of smaller dimensions to those of the previous century. Sometimes they are almost square in section (**Figure 4.53**). Both oak and elm are used. They are not chamfered or stopped, although the evidence often shows that they were exposed in the ceilings. When later ceilings are removed, the joists are commonly found to have coatings of limewash on them. In more polite rooms, it is likely that they were ceiled from the initial build. They may have a tenon at one end to locate with the mortice in the side of a beam. Although plain ends are common and this type sit in cutouts in the top of the beam. The joists are often bent and reflect the shapes of the original tree.

Chapter 4

The style of the joists used in the early 18th C are similar to those of the 17th C. Oak was sometimes used, the use of elm and other woods was widespread. Limited evidence (limewash on joists and on the wall plaster between adjacent joists) has been found for them being exposed in the ceilings of some cottages, but not in larger houses. Later in the century the use of machine cut timber appears. Also the use of a half dovetail at the joist:beam joint was used to prevent the joist pulling out of its lodging.

19th C joists are machine cut and the quality of the timber varies with the status of the building. In cottages, the timbers can be of rather small scantling, which gives rise to springy floors. The joists can be fixed in their lodgings with nails.

Lath and Plaster Partitions

These appear in the late 17th C. They are a lower status type of walling compared to a stud and panel partition. They are found in cottages and lower status rooms in larger houses (e.g. attics). They replace wattle and daub partitions used earlier in this and previous centuries (**Figure 4.55**). They consist of vertical studs nailed to the ceiling and floor. In earlier examples they can be fixed in cutouts in the side of beams or collar (in the roof structure). The studs are fairly closely spaced (about 18 inches apart) and the timbers are not large (generally about 4x2 in or 3x3 in). In the simplest form, lath is only nailed to one side of the studs and this is plastered on both sides, therefore on one side there is a completely plaster covered wall, whilst on the other side there is plaster between the studs only (**Figure 4.54**). Later on, lath was nailed to both sides of the studs, so that completely plastered walls were formed on both sides. This form of wall continued to be used through to the mid 20th C, when alternative forms of wall boarding became available. The nature of the plaster used changed over this long period of use. In pre early 19th C walls, the plaster is white and lime based. With the advent of widespread coal use, coal ash was mixed in with the lime, and this gives the plaster a grey tone (the higher the carbon content of the ash, the darker it became, so wide variations are present between buildings). Also, the nature of the lath changed: early walls have hand split lath, fixed with handmade nails. With the introduction of machinery to cut the lath (later on in the 19th C) the lath becomes regular, with an obvious machine cut and mass produced nails were used. In 19th C cottages, it is not uncommon to find simple tongue and groove, timber partitions (**Figure 4.56**)

Lintels

These are used to support the walls over window and door openings. Stone mullion windows provide the support for the stonework above and so do not need a lintel. However, sometimes there may be either an overlying wood lintel or relieving arch in stone. A lintel is needed behind a stone mullion window to support the stones and rubble infill over the inner part of the window opening. Wood is used for these lintels. Early lintels in this position may be large, flat slabs of timber (**Figure 4.57**), which may be thicker on the ground floor than on the upper floors (as they support a greater weight of stone). It is also common to find the lintel formed of several lengths of timber. In later cottages, the lintel timbers may be timbers reused from earlier buildings (look out for redundant mortices and peg holes). Early lintels are hand cut (adze or saw), later ones are machine cut and regular. Oak and elm are commonly used in 17th C buildings. The use of pine became common in the 19th C. Wood window frames require an outer lintel (**Figure 4.58**). This may be wood, although this tends to rot and in an early cottage, they will probably have been replaced. More generally, a stone lintel was used in this position. If a single piece lintel is used, it will be deep, as these tend to crack under the downward load of the upper stonework and due to slight movement. In the late 18th C and 19th C, horizontal lintels in three pieces, the central one acting as a keystone were used to overcome the problem of fracture under load. An alternative way of using stone was to build a segmented arch lintel over the window, using dressed/semi dressed pieces of stone. This type of lintel is common in 19th C cottages. Lintels over doors have similar details to those over windows. The outer lintel is generally a single piece of stone, since the span is less than over a window opening they tend not to fracture. In 17th C cottages and houses, it will probably have a chamfer on its outer, lower side, which follows on down each door jamb to terminate with a stop. Chamfers fell out of use by the early 18th C, but they did come back into fashion with the Victorian 'Gothic' style of architecture. 18th and 19th C doorways generally had plain, stone lintels, the higher the quality of the building, the better the finish of the stone.

Wood lintels may be found over both door and window openings in cottages of all periods.

Mortars

In stonewalls, the bedding matrix is a soft clay/earth which was most likely just dug from the ground around the building. It just crumbles/washes away if exposed to the weather. The outer face of the wall was roughly pointed using a lime-based mortar. To give additional protection the wall could also be lime washed or rendered with roughcast. The lime mortar sets by the action of carbon dioxide in the atmosphere on the calcium oxide (the lime). This reaction is relatively slow and forms a soft, but durable mortar. Some buildings retain mortar, which has been in place for several hundred years. Lime mortar was also used as the bedding matrix in brick walls prior to the introduction of cement based mortars. Coal ash was added to the lime mortars after the introduction of coal, as a fuel, in the area. This probably occurred from the late 18th C onwards. See the section on 'Care and Repair of Buildings' for advice on how to maintain stone and early brick walls.

Mouldings

Mouldings used in the 17th C were used to decorate exposed structural timber and stone pieces, such as the chamfer and stop used on a beam or on a fireplace jamb. In higher status work, they were used to hide joints and visually intrusive transitions between different timber planes. As such they disguised areas where movement could occur and softened the change between light and shadow. These mouldings tended to be three-dimensional and could be heavy in appearance (**Figure 4.59**). In the early 18th C, the function of the moulding began to change. Initially, they were still used to hide intrusive joints and other features and as in the previous century, tended to be heavy in appearance. The bolection moulding was widely used in the late 17thC and early 18th C and these tended to be applied, rather than created from the structural feature. The concept developed in the early 18th C to use detail which adhered to the classical principles of architecture, and moulded details in timber, such as skirting boards, dado rails, cornices, architraves, were used. They were used to conceal the structural elements of a building, such as the actual door-frame, and tended to become flatter and lighter in appearance from the early part of the century. A range of decorative details on the timber came into use

CHAPTER 4

in the 18th C and these include fillets, quirks, reeding, fluting, ogee, concave and ovolo moulding and beading. As with most fashions they entered at the higher end of the social scale and moved down the scale as the century progressed. Some did not reach the humble cottage. Plaster mouldings were widely used after the first quarter of the century and many good ceilings with cornices and moulded patterns survive from this century. Complicated mouldings were easier and cheaper to replicate in plaster. By the end of the 18th C, mouldings in plaster were light, in low relief and Grecian in style (as used widely by Robert Adam). In the Regency period (early 19th C) plaster mouldings were simpler and less obtrusive **(Figure 4.60)**. Reeding (**Figure 4.61**) and square corner blocks became particularly popular in this period. In the Victorian period **(Figure 4.62)**, plaster and timber mouldings were still widely used, but their classical origins were forgotten, with the consequent loss of architectural effect.

PANELLING

Panelling seldom occurs as an original feature in cottages. In was used in the 17th C in the best rooms of higher status houses (e.g. manor houses and houses of well-to-do yeoman farmers and clothiers). It is generally constructed in oak and the panels are moulded, the degree depending on the status of the owner and the skill of the carpenter. In the first half of the 18th C, it is common to find fully panelled rooms, generally formed from pitch pine in houses of the relatively well off (eg. the owner of a typical good quality 18th C town house). By the middle of the century, it was restricted to use below the level of the dado rail, with the use of plaster and either paint or wall paper above. Panelling was not widely used in the 19th C.

PLANS (REFER TO FIGURE 4.63)

The vernacular cottages and houses originally had a limited number of basic plans. Over the centuries, modifications and additions will have caused the plan to become more complicated and for the original form to be disguised. However, it should be possible to unravel the structure to see the original form and hopefully the information given in this book will help the interested owner.

17th C Cottages: These may have one or two-storeys, plus an attic floor within the roof space. The single storey type is probably the earlier and may have one or two rooms on the ground floor. The main room will contain a large hearth, usually with a bread oven and an adjacent winder stair. There may be a closet on the opposite side of the hearth. The second room may be unheated. The original cottage at The Ferns, Chalford Hill is of this type. The two-storey type usually has one room per floor, with the ground floor containing the hearth with oven and winder stair. The closet is not generally present. The upper room may be unheated, although those dating from the latter part of the 17th C may have a small first floor hearth. This shows an advantage of the two-storey type in that it can share the chimneybreast with the ground floor hearth. The original cottage at Clematis Cottage in Chalford Hill was of this type (although without a first floor hearth). Late versions of the two-storey type may have low attic perimeter walls to increase the headroom and make the space more usable. In Chalford Hill and other ridge villages, it is common to find that the 17th C cottages are aligned at right angles to the bank, with the hearth at the damp (bank) end.

17th C Houses: These generally have two floors with attics, commonly with gabled dormers and two or three rooms on each floor. The ground floor rooms will be kitchen/hall and parlour or kitchen, hall and parlour. The kitchen will contain a large hearth, with oven and possibly a winder stair. The parlour (the best room) will also contain a hearth (but not an oven and probably not a stair). The central room (if present) represents the former open hall of the medieval house, but its function has changed and is a reception room. It contains the main entrance and is sometimes sub-divided to provide some small service rooms at its rear. It may also contain the stair, which can be a significant feature of the room. The upstairs rooms tend to mirror the ground floor layout. First floor hearths are usually present and share the ground floor chimneybreasts.

18th and 19th C Cottages: They tend to have similar plans to the 17th C cottages, although the later ones may have increased ground floor service rooms under a catslide roof to the rear of the building. They are generally aligned parallel to the bank and have gable end hearths.

18th and 19th C Houses: Again, the earlier houses in this period can follow the plan of the 17th C houses, but as time progressed the use of plans which followed a more national style were quickly adopted. For instance the houses plan became two-rooms deep, giving four ground floor rooms. A central entrance hall with stair was invariably present. All rooms were heated (apart from storage areas), once coal came into widespread use.

Plaster (internal and external)

In early stone buildings, bare, lime-washed, internal walls would have been normal in smaller houses and cottages, except where timber frame panels, infilled with wattle and daub were used for internal partitions. Plastered walls would have been reserved for the best rooms and for more general use in higher status buildings. However, as time progressed, the widespread use of plaster moved down the social scale and so by the mid 17th C its use would be commonplace. There are two types of plaster used for internal work: lime based and gypsum based plasters. The advantage of gypsum is that it is quick setting, could easily be cast into moulds and was used fairly widely in the 18th C and later, particularly for better quality work. Lime based plasters were cheaper. They are also softer and more flexible and are suited for use in stone vernacular buildings, which are subject to slight movement. Both types were mixed with animal hair (to bind it together) and applied either to timber laths or directly to stone walls. Up to the mid 19th C, the laths tended to be split timber, whereas after this time they tended to be sawn. Also, after the early 19th C coal ash was added to the plaster mixture and this gives the wall covering a light grey tone. This can be useful for dating purposes and also to show where changes have occurred in a building (as often original white lime plaster was patched with grey plaster) (**Figure 4.64**).

External renders were also lime based and have been used to cover masonary since very early times. There are several reasons why a building could be rendered and these include to cover inferior work, to provide a weatherproof outer skin and for decorative effect. Often buildings are not rendered because they do not need to be. The external dressed stone, with appropriate pointing, provides adequate weatherproofing. Stucco is a thin render, applied to a thicker base coat and can be marked to simulate finely dressed stone blocks (**Figure 4.65**). It became popular in the 18th C as a way of dis-

Chapter 4

guising poor quality or much modified stonework. Roughcast is a lime based render to which graded stones were thrown whilst still wet and became popular towards the end of the 17thC (**Figure 4.66**). Pebbledash (**Figure 4.67**) is a more regular form of roughcast and is now currently associated with cement based renders. Tyrolean render is modern and is a textured cement material (avoid its use on a vernacular building).

Roof Pitch

The pitch of the roof can be a useful guide to the age of the house. In the 17thC and first part of the 18th C, all houses were stone tiled. This roofing material requires a steep pitch (**Figures 4.68 and 69**) to avoid water leaks in windy weather. The added benefit of this steep pitch was that it formed useful attic spaces with generous headroom. From the late 18th C onwards, Welsh slates were available in the area and where these were used, the roof pitch could be lower (**Figure 4.70**), as this material forms a better barrier to water leakage under high wind pressures. In houses with slate roofs, it was possible to add a full second floor, with a roof space above.

16th C and earlier buildings also had fairly steep roof pitches. This may be because they were thatched, when first built.

Roof Structures

Explanation of terms:

Double roof: Roof with common rafters and purlins

Purlin: Horizontal timber that passes beneath the common rafters to give them added support. Purlins run between principal rafter trusses and between the end walls and the first and last trusses. Usually one or two rows per roof slope.

Principal rafters: Large inclined timbers, joined at their apices and to either end of a tie beam (if present) that form the trusses of the roof structure. They support the purlins and transfer the load of the roof to the outer walls.

Collar: Timber that joins opposing principal rafters part way along their length. They give the truss added strength and help to oppose the spreading of the roof.

Tie beam: Ties the feet of the truss together to form a triangular truss. This opposes the tendency of the roof load to force the walls outwards.

'A' frame truss: The roof truss formed by a pair of inclined principal rafters, with a linking collar and usually with a tie beam.

Common rafter: The timbers that support the roof covering.

Bay: The space between successive roof trusses. A building is described as 2 bays long if there is a single truss, i.e. 2 spaces, one on either side of the truss and the end walls, if there are 2 trusses it is 3 bays long.

Types of structure

DETAILS OF VERNACULAR BUILDINGS IN THE STROUD AREA

'A' Frame Roof: Roof structure formed by a series of 'A' frame trusses, linked by purlins. This is the most common form of structure found in the area and is found over the whole date range. There are many variations and these include:

- 'A' frames with 1, 2 or occasionally 3 rows of purlins, depending on the length of the roof slope. (**Figure 4.71**)

- 'A' frames sitting on low walls and no link to the tie beam (**Figure 4.73**).

- 'A' frames sitting on low walls and linked to a tie beam by vertical jointed posts

- 'A' frames without a collar, but with a tie beam. (**Figure 4.72**)

In 16th C roofs of this type, windbraces may be present. They strengthen the principal/purlin connection and prevent the racking of the building under high wind pressures. They are structurally necessary in timber frame buildings. However, they are not strictly necessary in stone buildings, as the stone gable end walls provide a good anchor for the roof structure. However, they have been noted in 16th C buildings in the area and are probably due to the carpenters following the earlier timber frame tradition of construction. They are seen in the 16th C stone and timber buildings, but are not seen in 17th C stone buildings. Examples in local stone buildings are at the Court House at France Lynch and Court Farm Barn at Kings Stanley.

Extended Collar Truss Roof: This type of roof structure is found exclusively in houses with gabled dormers. The collar of a normal 'A' frame roof truss is extended both forwards and backwards so that it is embedded in the front and rear gabled dormer walls. This transfers the roof load, via the extended collar to the gabled dormer walls, rather than down through the principals to the tie beam of the truss. This means that the section of principal below the collar becomes redundant and can be dispensed with, which in turn means there is a more useful space in the attic for use. In its earliest form, the upper part of the truss is left above the level of the collar and is seen in houses up to the mid/late 17th C (**Figure 4.74**). In its final form the upper part of the truss is dispensed with as well, leaving only the extended collars and purlins as the main structural members (**Figure 4.75**). However, the 4 valley timbers for each pair of gabled dormers were also strengthened and laid at an angle over the collars, such that they meet at the roof apex (**Figure 4.76**). This form of the truss is seen in late 17th C gabled dormer houses. Gabled dormers had ceased to be built by the very early 18th C, but made a re-appearance in the mid/late 19th C (but not in association with extended collar trusses). Some houses only had the gabled dormers on the front elevation, in this type, the roof truss is a mixed 'A' frame/extended collar truss (with only the front end of the collar being extended to the dormer)

Purlin Only Roofs: These are found in small cottages of one bay. The purlin timbers pass from one gable end wall to the other without an intermediate truss.

STAIRS

The detail and location of the stair varies with time and status of the building. Stone newel stairs are occasionally found remaining in 16th C buildings of moderate and high status. These are formed

Chapter 4

of well-dressed steps, which stack on top of each other to form a spiral stair around a central newel 'post' (**Figure 4.77**). The latter is formed of the inner ends of each tread and has been likened to the vertebrae of a spine. In smaller houses and cottages, until the early part of the 18th C, the stair is invariably located beside and forms a part of the hearth and stack. These are called winder stairs and are commonly constructed in stone from the ground to first floor/attic (**Figure 4.79**) and in wood (usually elm) from the first floor to attic (**Figure 4.80**). Stone winders were not built after the early 18th C, although the winder stair still occurs after this date, but wholly constructed in wood and not necessarily beside the hearth. Winder stairs are also found in larger houses of the 17th C, but the proportions can be greater than in smaller buildings. Alternatively, in larger houses a wood staircase may have been constructed towards the centre of the building. Here, it forms a significant architectural feature. Semi circular stairs, open well and closed well stairs (constructed in several straight sections of stair, with half landings), have been seen in this position, in buildings of the Stroud area. These stairs are well constructed, commonly in oak and have detail that can be used for dating (refer to the book by Linda Hall 'Fixtures and Fittings in Dated Houses'). The main type of straight flight stair is the closed string (tread ends hidden by a rising architrave). They may have either turned (a vase shape is common), twisted or flat balusters, which can be fairly heavy in their appearance and rise from the top of the architrave. Newel posts tended to be relatively plain and were capped with a finial, and the base of upper posts may have a pendant. Handrails were heavy and moulded. Mast newel stairs are found in some 17th C Gloucestershire houses (e.g. Upper Upthorpe Farm, Cam). Here, there is a central wood post, with solid wood treads running between notches cut in the post and the surrounding wall (**Figure 4.78**).

The staircase was an important feature of well-to-do middle class homes of the 18th C. The open string stair appeared around this time (the architrave is cut and the tread ends are exposed) and applied brackets were used to decorate the tread ends (**Figure 4.82**). Balusters rose from the treads and not the architrave. The closed string design was also used (**Figure 4.81**). The stairs became lighter in appearance as the century progressed to the Regency period, especially when compared with those of the previous century. Classical detail could be used in higher status work. In the early part of the century, the best woods were used (oak and imported hardwood), the balusters were turned and the handrail was sturdy. The detail of the turning on the balusters is not a guide to the date of the stair on its own, as similar patterns could be used over a long period. However, the combination of details (wood, size of members and other detail) does give a useful guide to the date of origin. Lower down the social scale, the stair would be more likely to be constructed in pine, but the other detail could be similar. Handrails tended to be formed from the best wood and could be ramped to accommodate the change in level at a landing. The handrail was terminated at a newel post. 18th C newels could be classical in their detail (e.g. to mimic a Doric column). The handrail could be wreathed around before terminating at the ground floor newel post. Early 18th C newel posts did not project above the handrail, whereas later in the century and in the 19th C, the newel was capped with a moulded finial. By the early 19th C, the balusters had become simple (e.g. with a square section) and pine was widely used. However, it is common to see mahogany used for the handrail. Later on in the 19th C, the stairs were of the closed string type and tended to be wholly constructed in pine. Both balusters and newel posts were turned (**Figure 4.84**).

The straight flight stair was widely used in cottages and smaller houses in the late 18th and throughout the 19th C. The detail is simple (**Figure 4.83**) and depending on position, the flight could be stepped around through 90°. The proportions were determined by the size of the building.

DETAILS OF VERNACULAR BUILDINGS IN THE STROUD AREA

STONEWALLS

Stone is by far the predominant building material in local vernacular buildings. There is an outer and an inner skin of stone with the separating space filled with rubble packing. The stones are bedded in a soft earth/clay mixture, dug from the vicinity of the building site. The outer stones can be inclined downwards very slightly to improve the draining ability of the wall. The overall wall thickness is about 24-26 inches in 17th C buildings and several inches less in 18th and 19th C stone buildings. There are always quoin stones at the corners of the building and these maintain the stability of the wall. They form the building lines in a wall, which has developed in several phases. They give valuable clues on the development of a building: the direction of the stones forming the building line shows the earlier part of the wall. The outer wall stone is usually dressed rubble (the quality of the dressing varies with the status of the building, quality of the stone and with the date of building) or well dressed masonry blocks. Some exceptionally well-dressed stone is found in some 16th C buildings. The gaps between the stones were traditionally, and should still be, pointed with a lime mortar. A coat of lime-wash was also applied to the outside walls. Over the years a significant thickness of lime wash could build up and this must have helped with the weatherproofing. Even though this practice ceased several generations ago, some walls still retain areas of flaking lime wash. The multi layered nature of these remains and the tones of the different layers give an insight into how the buildings were treated in the vernacular period. In rubble stonewalls of the 17th C, the stone is laid in groups of horizontal courses, with the height of the stones decreasing upwards within each group. A difference between 17th and 18th C walls of this type is that 18th C and later walls can have 'jumper' stones laid within the horizontal courses (**Figures 4.85 and 86**). A 'jumper' is a stone that has a greater height than the majority of the wall stones and can span 2 or 3 courses. They have not been observed in 17th C and earlier walls. Also, the 17th C stones are generally better dressed, although there are examples of 18th C buildings with well dressed stone in the front elevation (**Figure 4.87**) and less well prepared stone for the sides that were not seen. In walls of all ages, the regularity of the courses varies with the quality of the stone and of the building. In the later part of the 18th C, ashlar stone was available in the area and was used for the more prominent buildings, especially in Stroud. These are basically brick buildings with a skin of ashlar stone to face the walls that were seen. Machine cut stone was widely used from the second half of the 19th C (**Figure 4.88**).

STRING COURSES (ALSO KNOWN AS PLAT BANDS)

These are horizontal lines of dressed stone that project approximately 2.5 cm from the outer face of the wall (**Figure 4.89**). They generally reflect the floor levels within the building. They came into use in the 18th C and are generally regarded as typical of the Georgian period. They may function as a dripcourse, although their under surface is not shaped to drip water away from the windows or walling below.

STUD AND PANEL PARTITION WALLS

This is one of the forms of internal partition wall used in the 16th and 17th C. It consists of an upper member, usually a beam that also supports the upper floor and a lower member or sill. There are

Chapter 4

longitudinal grooves (about 25mm wide) cut along the underside of the beam and topside of the sill. A regularly placed set of studs and separating panels are slotted between the pair of upper and lower grooves. The panels are also located in vertical grooves cut in the sides of the studs. Both oak and elm has been noted in the construction of these walls. Not many examples have survived, but a set of early 17th C stud and panel partitions (in elm) was present in a farmhouse at Harescombe in 2003 (**Figure 4.90**). The former presence of this type of wall is shown by the grooves in the underside of the ceiling beam e.g. at Borough Farmhouse at Kings Stanley (**Figure 4.92**). Sometimes an intermediate rail (horizontal member) (**Figure 4.91**) was included part way up the wall.

Timber Frame Walls

Timber framing was used in the construction of the upper storeys in some of the 16th C buildings identified in the High Street in Stroud. There are other examples in Stonehouse and Painswick. A good surviving example is the Post Office in Painswick and this gives a good impression of how the High Street buildings will have looked. It is not known with certainty why the buildings were of mixed timber and stone construction, however several possibilities have been proposed:

- Timber framing was regarded as a superior form of building and was favoured for the parts of the building that were visible. The carpenter's art was well developed and it gave the opportunity for some embellishment to the public face of the building.

- The 16th C marks the start of the widespread use of stone for the smaller buildings and it is possible that the stone building craft was not fully developed. Perhaps the use of a lighter weight timber structure for the upper floors was considered to be more stable.

- The use of a timber frame enabled the roof structure to be fixed to the frame, which would be necessary if a lightweight covering (thatch) was used. In a stone building, there is not much holding the roof in place, apart from the shear weight of the stone tiles.

The two main types of framing are square panel and close studding. The limited evidence available suggests that the close studding type was used in the Stroud area in the 16th C. There are many examples of both types away from the stone belt on the lower slopes of the Cotswold escarpment and in the Severn Valley. Whichever type of framing was used, the spaces within the frame were infilled with wattle and daub panels. A groove was cut along the bottom member of the panel to be infilled and regularly spaced holes were drilled in the upper member. Vertical staves were then fitted in each hole by forcing them along the lower groove. Split Hazel laths were then woven around the set of staves to create a wattle panel. This was then smothered with the daub coating, which was then flattened with some sort of wooden float. It is not uncommon to find timbers in later buildings with the groove of the regularly spaced holes, which have no apparent function. This shows that they have been re-used from a timber-framed structure.

Timber framing was also used for internal partitions in the 16th and 17th C (**Figures 4.93 and 4.94**). It is mostly of the square panel type and the method of infilling was the same as for the exterior walls. Close studding was occasionally used in the 16th C for higher status internal partitions.

Windows and Window Frames and Glass

Early buildings (16th C and before) may have had fairly heavy wood window frames. These would have been comprised of a series of vertical mullions, separated by a fairly narrow width of light and jointed within an outer wood frame, held together by wood pegs (**Figure 4.95**). They were unglazed and had inner shutters to minimise draughts and provide some security. Rooms tended to be cross lit, i.e. there were windows in opposite walls, the idea being that the best light could be obtained at different times of the day and also the effects of wind could be reduced by only opening the shutters on the downwind side. There are no known survivals of this type of window in the local buildings, although the remnants of one were found in No.33 High Street in Stroud.

There are also examples of stone window frames from the 16th C. These have stone surrounds and the window is usually divided into lights by mullion posts. Each light may have either a flat or an arched head. If the latter type is present, then the area beside each side of the arch (the spandrel) may be recessed. Because of their durability, there are several examples of 16th C stone window frames in the area (**Figures 4.96 and 4.97**). In these earlier forms of stone mullion window, the dressed stone that forms the side members of the frame, also forms the internal splay of the window opening and each side of the frame is commonly formed of several pieces of stone. It is probable that these were cut on site, as the side member is closely jointed to the coursing of the bulk wall stone.

Stone window frames were almost the universal form of window in 17th C buildings in the Stroud area (**Figure 4.98 and 4.99**). They all have flat heads to the openings. There are many examples of 2 and 3 light windows with the individual lights being separated by a mullion post. This post transfers the load on the upper part of the frame to the lower part, so there is no need for a lintel above the window frame. Although, there are some that have either wood lintels or relieving arches above the stone frame. A few 4-light windows have also been found (e.g. in the rear addition to Baimbridge house and in the earlier part of Stratford Park Mansion) in which the central mullion post is made larger (called a king mullion) (**Figure 4.100**). In 17th C buildings, the parts of the frame are comprised of straight cut stone pieces (probably cut at the quarry), with the openings (lights) framed with either plain chamfers or recessed (also called rebated or reserved) plain chamfers. In the latter type, the mullion posts and the inner part of the window sit within an outer frame, all cut from the same pieces of stone. These are the dominant forms, although, other forms of chamfer with ovolo (convex) (Stratford Park Mansion) and concave chamfers have been noted in the area. Generally the number of lights decreases in the upper floors, so it is common to see a 3-light ground floor window, with 3 or 2-light first floor and 2 or 1-light window in the roof gable. Each window frame is surmounted by a dripmould (also called hood mould), which as well as being attractive, is also functional. Originally, these houses did not have gutters and the dripmould ensured that the water running off the roof was diverted away from the windows. Up to the late 17th C there was one dripmould per window, however a variant appears in the late 17th C in which the dripmould is continuous over all the windows on each floor. This also includes the entrance on the ground floor. This type of dripmould may terminate at the outer sides of the windows situated at the extreme sides of the elevation or continue to the actual edge of the elevation. In some higher status and earlier 17th C buildings a continuous dripmould around the whole building has been noted (e.g. some houses at Througham). Dripmoulds went out of use by the early 18th C. Possible reasons for this include a wider overhang at the eaves (and the construction of a lead gutter on top of the eaves) and the introduction of string-courses (or plat bands) to direct the water flow down the face of the wall. In the late 17th C, an enlarged form of the stone window frame was used in some of the larger houses (there are examples in 33 and 50 High Street, Stroud). These

Chapter 4

are called 'cross' windows as they have a transom in the upper part of the window, together with a mullion post, which enabled the height of the window and area of the lights to be greater. 'Cross' windows are also seen in some early 18th C buildings, however, the members have become much lighter in construction (as in Laurel Villa in Nelson Street, Stroud). In the Georgian period, this type of window was superseded by sash windows, which fitted in a similar shaped opening.

17th C and later stone framed windows were glazed. The glazing consisted of glass rectangles (or sometimes diamond shaped) set in lead cames in the 17th and 18th C. In the 17th C, each leaded light was tied to a pair of vertical iron bars (square in section, but set diagonally). These have now generally been removed, but their former presence is indicated by the infilled holes in the top and bottom frame members. The lights were also probably sealed around the edges with lime mortar. In the 18th C, the fixing bars for the glazing were horizontal, of smaller section and greater in number. In this case, their former presence is indicated by infilled holes in the side members of each light. There are a few examples of wood mullion windows in the 17th C (**Figure 4.101**). Opening lights were present in the 17th and 18th C houses and consisted of a frame formed from flat iron bar, with the leadwork fixed to it. The frame opened on pin hinges, with the maximum extent of opening set by an iron quadrant. The light was closed in place with a latch that could be ornate in the 17th C, with a pair of turnbuckle handles being used in the 18th/19th C. In some cases, the iron opening light closed in a small rebate in the stone around the light, in other cases (possibly later/higher status) the opening light closes against a fixed iron frame. Some dated examples of window fittings are given in the book by Linda Hall. It has been noted that the area of each light (the glass) is greater in 18th C than in 17th C buildings. The reason for this is not entirely clear, but the larger area did provide more light for the building. It may also be associated with improvements in glass making technology and perhaps the reductions in the price of glass.

The use of wood frame windows became more common in the 18th and 19th C, although the stone mullion frames were also used. The two and three-light wood mullion windows are widespread in the area (**Figure 4.102**). The frame members are not particularly heavy looking and usually had either a bead moulding or a flat chamfer around the inside face of the lights. One light usually has an opening iron frame, which is similar in detail to those used in 18th C stone window frames. Sash windows also became widely used in the 18th and 19th C (**Figure 4.103**). They are far more common in houses and in areas where keeping up with the fashions was important (i.e. in the commercial areas of Stroud). Sash windows are not particularly common in cottages, where the stone window frame continued to be used through to the late 19th C in parallel with simple wood frames. The 18th C and later sash windows are double hung (i.e. both upper and lower parts can be slid vertically) and are multi paned, with the windows divided up by slender glazing bars (the inside face of these is profiled. Lambs tongue and ogee profiles were popular, whereas the outer face had simple rebates to accept glass). The six over six (i.e. two rows of three-lights per sliding member) and eight over eight light were the most common forms in the 18th C. They were not made to standard dimensions. The horizontal members of sash windows are called rails (top, bottom and meeting rails). The meeting rails are the bottom of the top sash and the top of the bottom sash and are where the sash fasteners were fixed. The side members are called stiles. Early sash windows have their whole sash box frame exposed and this was nearly flush with the outside wall surface. However, after the 1709 and 1774 Building Acts, the sashes were set back by at least 100mm and the sash box was mainly set behind the surrounding stone or brick wall. These changes were made as a precaution to prevent fire entering the building through exposed woodwork. In the Victorian period, the use of glazing bars declined and the large pane sash window became widespread (four over four and two over two). Again, improvements in glass making technology enabled this development. However, the removal of the glazing bars and the increasing weight of glass weakened the sliding window and this seems to be the reason why horns were added to the upper sash light in 19th C windows to increase the strength of the corner joints. Cottages generally had the simple casement type window frame in the 19th C and these had arched segmented lintels in the early part of the century (**Figures 4.104 to 4.106**). There are many examples in the area, although they are being lost fairly rapidly through replacement with inappropriate plastic frames.

The above notes describe the main types of window, however, in addition there are smaller windows providing light to the stair. In 17th C cottages and smaller houses, the stair is generally in the gable end next to the hearth and it is common to find single light stone framed windows lighting the stair, possibly at intermediate levels between the ground and attic floors. These generally show similar detail to the main windows. In larger houses with perhaps an open-well or dog-leg stair, larger windows are used to provide light. Sometimes a series of windows are present that ascend with the stair.

In late 17th C cottages and houses with gabled dormers, 'owl' windows may be found at the apex of the dormer. Evidence from dated houses suggests that they were not used prior to this time. Their function is not known with certainty. One suggestion is that they provided ventilation to the attics of the house, where goods and raw materials were stored. Another is that they enabled owls to get into the roof spaces to keep the rodent population under control. Some good examples can be seen at Borough Farm at Kings Stanley and on some of the gabled houses in Stroud.

The windows in local vernacular buildings seem to have been glazed from at least the 17th C. Until the early 20th C all glass was made by hand. Broad sheet glass is the earliest form and was made by blowing an elongated balloon of glass, cutting off the ends, whilst hot, and then opening out the truncated balloon to form a sheet. The glass was thick and the panes small. Broadsheet glass was developed into cylinder or muff glass. This was made by forming a blown globe of molten glass and swinging it over a pit to lengthen it. The ends were cut off and the cylinder split down one side. It was then re-heated on a sand covered metal plate so that the split cylinder flattened out to form a sheet, which was then cooled and cut into panes. Crown glass was made by blowing a balloon of molten glass and spinning it, until it formed a disc, about 1.5m diameter. Once cooled the disc was cut into panes, which generally had a maximum size of approximately 25 x 36 cm. The central part was also used and this is now referred to as bulls-eye glass. Crown glass was regarded as being superior to cylinder glass. It seems likely that cylinder glass was used in most local buildings. Crown glass and cylinder glass were the only types available up to 1832. Only relatively small panes of glass could be produced by these methods and therefore windows either had leaded lights or timber glazing bars. In 1832, a revised cylinder glass manufacturing process was introduced to the UK by Lucas Chance, which enabled increasingly larger panes of glass to be manufactured. This meant that windows could be produced without so many glazing bars or leaded lights. The cylinder glass could be polished, initially by hand and later by machine to form better quality, plate glass. In the early 20th C, the flat drawn glass process was introduced, which together with mechanised polishing, meant that large flat sheets of glass could be produced economically. In 1959, the float glass process was invented, at Pilkington's, St Helens. In this process the molten glass was floated on a tank of molten tin to produce a very uniform sheet of glass. Virtually all glass is produced by this process now and only a very few specialist companies produce glass by the Crown glass method for special work.

CHAPTER 4

SOME DIFFERENCES BETWEEN 18THC BUILDINGS AND THOSE OF EARLIER CENTURIES

There are important internal and external differences between the style of the 18th C buildings and those of the earlier centuries. Outside appearance became more important and windows, doors and other features were generally arranged more symmetrically in the main façade (**Figures 4.109 and 4.110**). The use of gabled dormers with their associated extended collar truss roof structures disappeared very early in the century. The eaves of the roof began to overhang more and sometimes an eaves cornice is present. In the second part of the century, overhanging eaves were superseded by the use of parapets, sometimes with pediments to adorn the main elevation. The presence of the parapet with a leaded valley gutter behind was probably introduced to enable the control of the water flow away from the front of the building (iron gutters are a 19th C invention). The exit from the leaded valley was into a cast lead rainwater funnel and into a lead downpipe. These have occasionally survived to the present time (e.g. on 43/44 Middle St, Stroud).

In towns and larger country houses, the style of the window frames developed from the stone mullion with dripmould (that was almost universally used in the 17thC) to cross windows (that can be in either wood or stone) and then to sash windows. These window forms are taller and narrower than the 17th C windows. Both cross and sash windows could have a stone surround in the early/mid 18thC. The profile of the surround varies and a 'Bull-nose' section is characteristic of early 18th c work. In cottages, the stone mullion window was still used, but the area of glass was increased (**Figures 4.107 and 4.108**)

The use of bricks, bedded in lime mortar became increasingly used for the less visible parts of the buildings (in party and rear walls and for some internal divisions). Bricks do not appear to have been used much in 17thC buildings in Stroud. The stone used in the front elevations (and other prominent parts) of substantial buildings was good quality ashlar. A few buildings were constructed entirely in brick from early in the century (e.g. Bank House in the High Street, Stroud).

Internally, the use of chamfers and stops on beams and hearth surrounds was discontinued and timbers are less well finished (but still cut by hand). The structural timbers were not intended to be seen and many were covered by lath and plaster. Fireplaces were still wood burning, but the hearth itself was less deep. If there was a stone lintel over the opening, then it would generally be made in several pieces. Sometimes 2 stones arranged in a slightly arched position, or 2 outer stones and a central keystone. Pitch pine was almost universally used for the timber fixtures (windows, doors, shutters, architraves etc). This wood has a high resin content, which makes it very durable, so many 18th C buildings retained much of their early timber features (until they received the attentions of insensitive late 20th C builders). Internal doors were generally of panelled construction (6 panels were common), although the use of the plank and ledge door continued to be used in cottages and low status rooms. Door hinges were handmade of the H or H-L type for most of the century, with the modern type of hinge appearing late on. Plain strap hinges with a mounting plate were generally used on the plank and ledge doors. Iron thumb latches could be used on all types of door, although turn handles and slab locks were increasingly used as the century progressed.

There are significant differences in the nature of the roof structures of 17th and 18th C buildings. Elm was widely used in the 18th C, together with other local woods. Oak is seldom seen. Generally, the structural timbers are less substantial and became more regular in their cut towards the end of the century. The roof pitches are lower, so the roofs were less tall. 'A' frame trusses were still used, but the detail can be different. The collar can still be jointed to the underside of the principal rafters, but may be pegged or nailed across the side faces. The use of threaded bolts to fix the collar appeared late in the century. Prior to this an earlier form of fixing, known as a forelock bolt was sometimes used. These consist of an unthreaded bolt, with a longitudinal slot cut in the outer end of the shaft, this is placed through holes drilled in the pieces of wood to be fixed. A triangular wedge of iron is hammered through the slot and the end turned over to secure the joint. Purlins were joined across the backs of the principals or through the principals. The purlins may be cut back at the junction with the principal and sometimes (later on in the century) a fishplate is used to physically join the successive purlins together in a row. The rafters are fixed to the purlins with iron nails.

Chapter 4

Figure 4.1. Scroll stop with bar (17th C).
(location not known)

Figure 4.2 Wide flat chamfer and draw stop set off the chamfer (16th C).
(Derelict building in farmyard of Tann House farm, Frampton on Severn, early 1990's)

DETAILS OF VERNACULAR BUILDINGS IN THE STROUD AREA

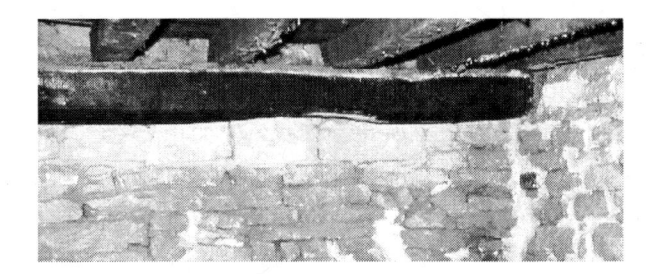

Figure 4.3. Half Beam.
(Late 17th C cottage in Nelson St, Stroud, 2005)

Figure 4.4. Scroll stop and narrow chamfer, late 17th C.
(12 Whitehall, Stroud, 2000)

Figure 4.5. Joists lodging in cut-out in top of beam (left side of beam).
(Late 17th C cottage in Nelson St, Stroud))

Figure 4.6 Early 18th C beam, without chamfer or stop.
(Old Duke of York Inn, Chalford Hill, 2006)

Figure 4.7. Machine cut beam (late 19th C).
(Old Duke of York Inn, Chalford Hill, 2006)

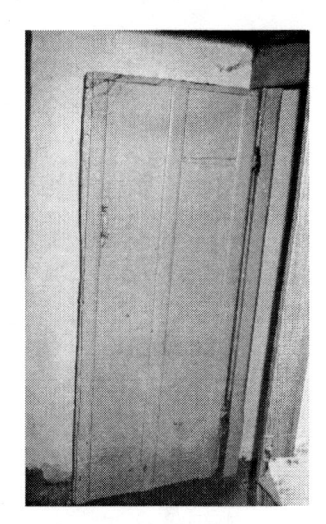

Figure 4.8 Plank and ledge door (mid/late 17th C).
(Berrymore Cottages, North Woodchester, 1988)

CHAPTER 4

Figure 4.9. Plank and ledge door (19th C), showing ledges and strap hinges.
(Elm Tree Cottage, Haresfield, demolished, 1998)

Figure 4.10. Four panel door (19th C).
(Westview, Brownshill, demolished, 1998)

Figure 4.11. Two panel door (early 18th C).
(Hillside Farm, France Lynch, 1991)

Figure 4.12. Six panel door (early 19th C).
(Watercombe House, Waterlane, 2001)

Figure 4.13 Strap hinge (pin type, 17th C).
(location not known)

Figure 4.14. Strap hinge with base plate (17th C).
(location not known)

DETAILS OF VERNACULAR BUILDINGS IN THE STROUD AREA

Figure 4.15. 17th C Door with original strap hinge and drop handle.
(Little Britain Farm, Woodchester)

Figure 4.16. 18th C slide lock in wood case. *(Reused in Old Duke of York Inn, Chalford Hill, 2006)*

Figure 4.17. Single dripmoulds (17th C).
(Teekles Court, Haresfield, 1998)

Figure 4.18. Continuous dripmould across wall.
(The Mount, Chalford, 2006)

Figure 4.19. Continuous dripmould over group of windows (late 17th C).
(Nailsworth, 1996)

Figure 4.20. Joist : beam lodgings (late 17th C).
(Cottage in Nelson Street, Stroud, 2004)

63

CHAPTER 4

Figure 4.21. Floor structure (early 18th C). *(Cottage at Waterlane, late 1990's)*

Figure 4.22. Floor structure (late 16th/early 17th C). *(Church farm, Harescombe, 2003)*

Figure 4.23 Triple gabled dormers (late 17th C). *(Borough Farmhouse, Kings Stanley, 2001)*

Figure 4.24 Single gabled dormer (mid/late 17th C). *(Berrymore Cottages, N Woodchester, late 1980's)*

Figure 4.25. Dressed stone hearth with four centred arch lintel (late16th /early17th C). *(Church Farm, Harescombe, 2003)*

Figure 4.26. Open stone fireplace with timber lintel (not original) (mid 17th C). *(The Ferns, Chalford Hill, 1990)*

Details of Vernacular Buildings in the Stroud Area

Figure 4.27. Open stone Fireplace, with timber lintel (late 17th C).
(Brookside, Leonard Stanley, 2005)

Figure 4.28. Moulded stone fire surround (possibly late 17th C).
(Little Britain Farm, Woodchester, 2001)

Figure 4.29. Reconstructed fireplace, with semi-circular back with smoke channel (Late 17th C).
(33 High Street, Stroud, 1984)

Figure 4.30. Wood burning fireplace, with two piece stone lintel (early/mid 18th C).
(Old Duke of York Inn, Chalford Hill, 2006)

Figure 4.31. Coal burning hearth, with early hob grate (late 18th C).
(55 High Street, Stroud, 1985)

Figure 4.32 Simple coal burning bedroom hearth (mid 19th C).
(Cottage at Oakridge Lynch, 1991)

Chapter 4

Figure 4.33. Mid 19th C coal burning hob grate in a plain stone surround.
(Westview, Brownshill, demolished, 1999)

Figure 4.34. Transitional hob type grate, with register plate (mid 19th C).
(Watercombe House, Waterlane, 2001))

Figure 4.35. Register grate with arched opening (late 19th C).
(Little Britain Farm, Woodchester, 2001)

Figure 4.36. Fireplace with splayed sides, hood and undergrate air control (missing here) (late 19th C).
(Cottage at Oakridge Lynch, 1991)

Figure 4.37 Similar to 4.36, with plain cottage surround. (late19th/early20th C).
(Westview, Brownshill, demolished 1999)

Figure 4.38. Not vernacular, but a now unfashionable, late style, coal burning hearth (mid 20th C).
(Elm Tree Cottage, Haresfield, demolished, 1998)

DETAILS OF VERNACULAR BUILDINGS IN THE STROUD AREA

Figure 4.39. Strap hinge with pin (late 17th C.
(reused in Old Duke of York Inn, Chalford Hill, 2006)

Figure 4.40. Strap hinge with baseplate (18th C).
(Old Duke of York Inn, Chalford Hil, 2006l)

Figure 4.41. Mortice and tenon joint at apex of principal rafters (late 16th/early 17th C).
(Church Farm, Harescombe, 2003)

Figure 4.42. Collar to principal joint (late 16th/early 17th C).
(Church farm, Harescombe, 2003)

Figure 4.43. Collar to principal joint (Early 19th C).
(Clematis Cottage, Chalford Hill, 1984)

Figure 4.44 Butt purlin roof (16th C).
(Court Farm Barn, Kings Stanley)

CHAPTER 4

Figure 4.45. Trenched (through) purlin (late 16th/early 17th C).
(Church Farm, Harescombe, 2003)

Figure 4.46 Butt purlin roof with cut back purlins (mid 19th C).
(Oakridge Farm, Far Oakridge, 2005)

Figure 4.47. Early form of purlin link joint (16th C).
(Oakridge Farm, Oakridge Lynch, 2005)

Figure 4.48. Staggered purlins (late 16th C).
(Upper Upthorpe Farm, Cam, 2003)

Figure 4.49. Ridge timber supported in a notch in the principal (late 16th C).
(Upper Upthorpe Farm, Cam, 2003)

Figure 4.50 Ridge timber supported on a nailed yolk (mid 18th C).
(Old Duke of York Inn, Chalford Hill, 2006)

Details of Vernacular Buildings in the Stroud Area

Figure 4.51. Windbraces (16th C or earlier).
(Ram Inn, Wootton under Edge, 2000)

Figure 4.52. Joists laid flat (16th C).
(33 High Street, Stroud, 1985)

Figure 4.53. Square section joists (latter part 17th C).
(The Ferns, Chalford Hill, 1990)

Figure 4.54. Lath and plaster partition with exposed studs (late 17th C).
(50 High Street, Stroud, 1995)

Figure 4.55 Wattle and daub panel partly replaced using studs and lath (16th C (wattle) and 19th C (lath).
(33 High Street, Stroud, 1985)

Figure 4.56 Tongue and groove timber partition (mid 19th C).
(Westview, Brownshill, demolished, 1999)

CHAPTER 4

Figure 4.57 Timber lintel (late 17th C).
(The Ferns, Chalford Hill 1988)

Figure 4.58 Timber Lintel (19th C).
(Nailsworth, 1985)

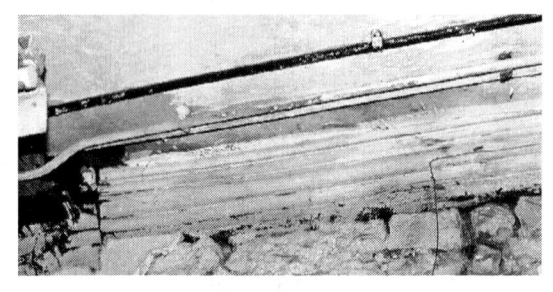

Figure 4.59 Moulding forming ceiling coving (17th C).
(Frogmarsh Mill house, 1999)

Figure 4.60. Applied plaster moulding to timber fireplace surround (late18th/early 19th C).
(Stratford Park Mansion, 1995)

Figure 4.61. Reeded moulding and applied moulding to shutter panels (early 19th C).
(Watercombe House, Waterlane, 2001)

Figure 4.62. Ceiling rose (19th C).
(Stratford park Mansion, 1995)

Details of Vernacular Buildings in the Stroud Area

Figure 4.63. Floor Plans.

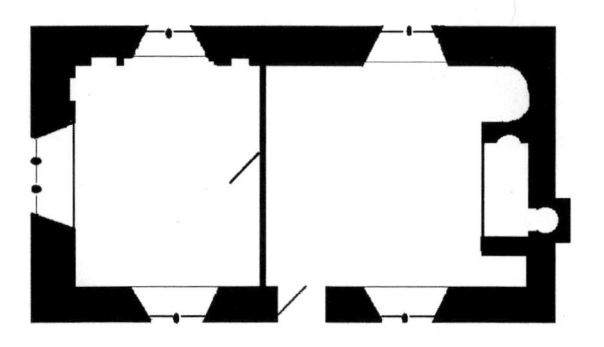

17th C, single room cottage (ground)

17th C, two room, single storey cottage

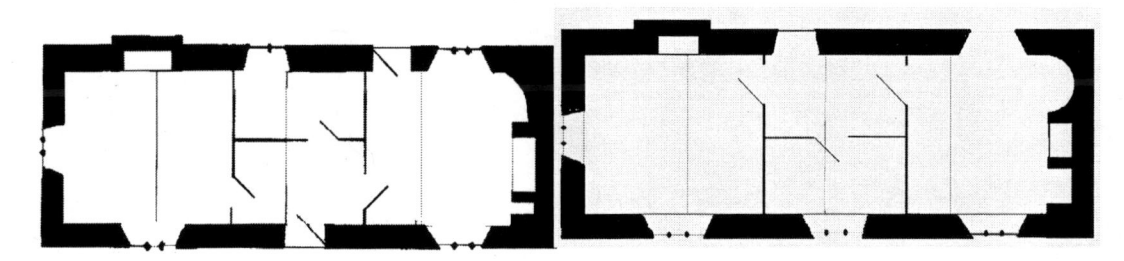

Late 17th C, three-room house (ground)

Late 17th C, three-room house (first)

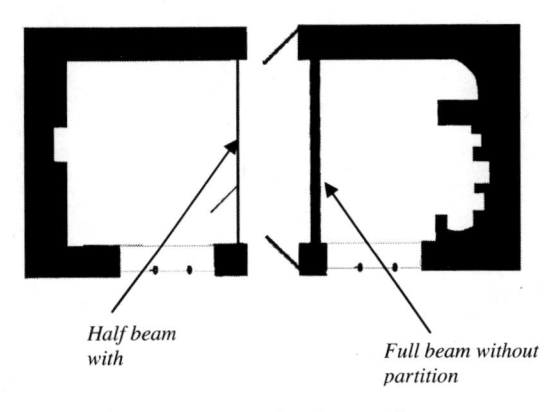

Half beam with

Full beam without partition

Tie beam

partition with door

Early 18th C, two-room plan (ground)

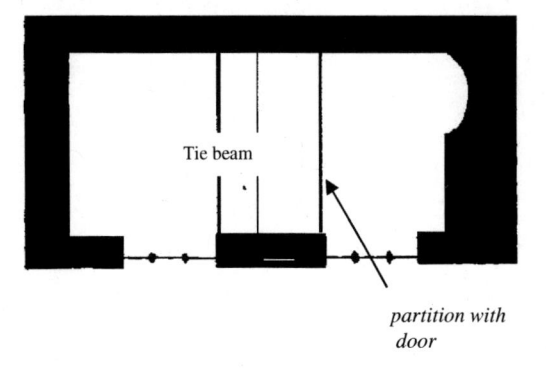

Early 18th C, two-room plan (first)

71

CHAPTER 4

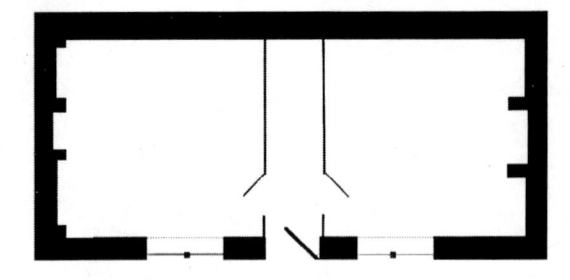

Early 19th C, two-room cottage (ground)

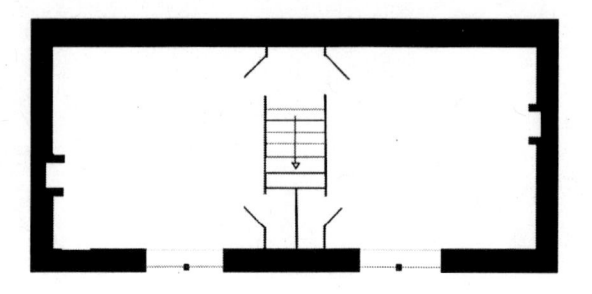

Early 19th C, two-room cottage (first)

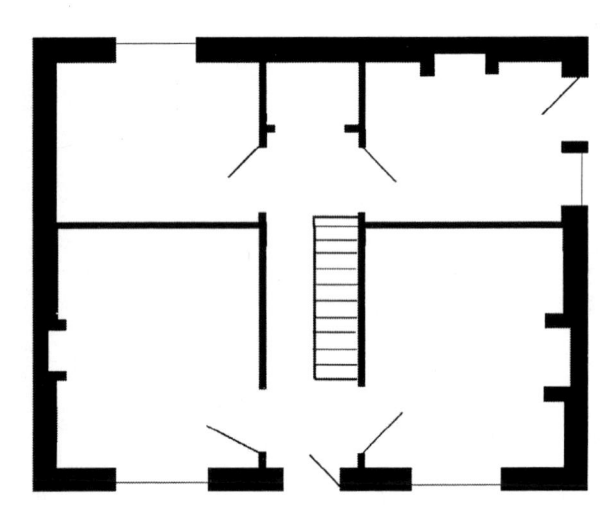

Mid 19th C house

Note that the relative dimensions within each plan are approximately correct, but not between plans

DETAILS OF VERNACULAR BUILDINGS IN THE STROUD AREA

Figure 4.65 Stucco effect (late 20th C).
(12 Whitehall, Stroud, 2000)

Figure 4.64 Change in plaster colour showing that walls have been raised (early 18th and mid 19th C).
(12 Whitehall, Stroud 2000,)

Figure 4.66. Lime based, roughcast render (late 17th C).
(Frogmarsh Mill house, 1999)

Figure 4.67 Pebbledash render (20th C).
(43 Middle street, Stroud, 1974)

Figure 4.68 Steep roof pitch (early 17th C). *(Church Farm, Harescombe, 2003)*

Chapter 4

Figure 4.69 17th (middle), 18th (left) and 19th C (right) roof pitches.
(Chalford hill, 2004)

Figure 4.70 Shallow roof pitch (mid 19th C).
(Westview, Brownshill, 1999)

Figure 4.71 'A' frame truss with collar (mid/late 17th C).
(Barton End Grange, Nailsworth, 1998)

Figure 4.72 'A' frame truss, without collar (late 17th C).
Hillside Farm, France Lynch, 1995)

Figure 4.73 'A' frame truss, with collar, sitting on low wall (early 18th C).
(Steepways, Chalford, 1990)

Figure 4.74 Extended collar truss (early form (early 17th C).
(Salmons Mill House, Stroud, 1990)

Details of Vernacular Buildings in the Stroud Area

Figure 4.75 Extended collar truss (later type (late 17th C)
(Cottage in Nelson St, Stroud, 2004)

Figure 4.76 Extended collar truss, later type (late 17th C)
(Borough Farm, Kings Stanley, 2001)

Figure 4.77. Newel stair, in stone (16th C).
(Court farm Barn, 1989)

Figure 4.78. Mast newel stair (16th C).
(Upthorpe Farm, Cam, 2003)

Figure 4.79. Stone winder stair (late 17thC).
(Cottage at Waterlane, late 1990's)

Figure 4.80. Wood winder stair (early 18th C).
(Foxes farmhouse, Bourton, 1997)

CHAPTER 4

Figure 4.81 Closed string, dog leg stair (late 18th C).
(55 High St, Stroud, 1985)

Figure 4.82. Open string stair (late 18th C).
(Tannery House, Leonard Stanley, 1990)

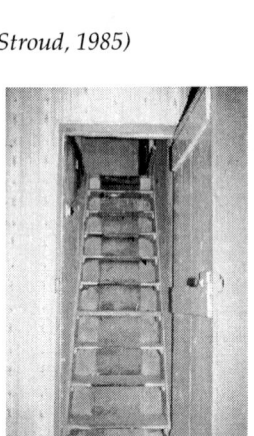

Figure 4.83 Simple cottage, ladder type, stair (late 19th C).
(Westview, Brownshill, demolished, 1999)

Figure 4.84 Closed string stair (late 19th C).
(The Ferns, Chalford Hill, 1990)

Figure 4.85 Coursed rubblestone walling (17th C).
(rear of Market House, Stroud, 2006)

Figure 4.86 Rubblestone wall with jumper stones (18th C).
(Old Duke of York Inn, Chalford Hill, 2006)

DETAILS OF VERNACULAR BUILDINGS IN THE STROUD AREA

Figure 4.87. Masonary block wall (early 18th C).
(Old Duke of York Inn, Chalford Hill, 2006)

Figure 4.88. Machine cut stone (late 19th C).
(Old Duke of York Inn, Chalford Hill, 2006)

Figure 4.89. String course (early 18th C).
(Old Duke of York Inn, Chalford Hill, 2006)

Figure 4.90. Stud and panel partition (late 16th/early17th C).
(Church Farm, Harescombe, 2003)

Figure 4.91. Stud and panel partition with rail (late 16th C).
(Yew Tree Farm, Brookthorpe, 1996)

Figure 4.92. Groove in soffit of beam for stud and panel wall (late 17th C).
(Borough Farm, Kings Stanley, 2001)

Chapter 4

Figure 4.93. 17th C square panel partition wall.
(Barton End Grange 1990)

Figure 4.94. 17th C square panel partition wall.
(Salmon's Mill House, 1990)

Figure 4.95. Early wood window.
(Yew Tree farmhouse, 1993)

Figure 4.96. Late 16th C stone window frame.
(Church Farm, Haresfield, 2003)

Figure 4.97. 16th C stone window frame.
(Chalford industrial estate, 2006)

Figure 4.98. Mid 17th C stone window frame.
(Cottage at Waterlane, late 1990's)

DETAILS OF VERNACULAR BUILDINGS IN THE STROUD AREA

Figure 4.99. Late 17th C stone window frame. *(43 Middle St, Stroud, 1980)*

Figure 4.100. Four light stone frame with king mullion. *(Stratford Park Mansion, 1995)*

Figure 4.101. 17th C timber mullion window. *(Tanglewood, Thrupp Lane, 2005)*

Figure 4.102. Late 18th C timber window, with iron opening light. *(Cottage in Nailsworth, 1980's)*

Figure 4.103. Early 19th sash window. *(Newnham House, Newnham, 2005)*

Figure 4.104. Cottage casement window frames. *(Marle Hill, Chalford, 1990)*

Chapter 4

Figure 4.105. Horizontal bars to support leaded lights (early 19th C).
(55 High Street, Stroud, 1985

Figure 4.106. Cottage casement window (early 19th C).
(Cottage in Chapel Street, Stroud, demolished 1979)

Figure 4.107. 17th C stone mullion window.
(Cottage in Nelson Street, Stroud, 1980)

Figure 4.108. 18th C stone mullion window.
(Old Duke of York Inn, Chalford Hill, 2006)

Figure 4.109. Mid/late 17th C cottage.
Cottage on Thrupp Lane, 2005)

Figure 4.110. Early 18th C cottage.
(Cottage at Oakridge Lynch, 2002)

CHAPTER 5

CARE AND REPAIR OF STONE VERNACULAR BUILDINGS

A late 17thC, simple vernacular cottage being sympathetically restored at Waterlane. The derelict cottage was used as a set for the TV version of Cider with Rosie in the mid 1990's.
(photo taken in 1999)

CONTENTS OF CHAPTER

IN THIS chapter some basic advice is given on how to look after a vernacular, Cotswold stone building. The most useful advice is to leave well alone and do not do work which cannot be undone in the future. Certainly avoid the temptation to make a 'posh pad' from a simple cottage.

What I suggest in the chapter is what I would do, not necessarily what you should do: if in doubt seek professional advice. Information is given on:

> Roofing materials
> Stone walls and pointing
> Window frames
> Chimneys
> Roof timbers
> Beams and joists
> Plaster ceilings
> Ceiling heights
> Floors
> Internal fixtures and fittings
> Hearths
> Internal partition walls

THE YOUNGEST vernacular building is now about 150 years old and they have withstood the ravages of time remarkably well. It is, however, the attentions of owners, builders and authorities in recent decades that has resulted in the greatest damage and they still represent the greatest threat to the survival of their essential character and contribution to the historic environment. They were built to provide a fairly basic suite of human needs: somewhere to work, sleep, cook and be reasonably secure. The buildings described in this book have satisfied these needs well for many generations. They were looked after by straightforward builders and craftsmen, who tended to replace like with like and who re-used wherever possible. They passed on a rich heritage of historic buildings to the 20th C. However, the Cotswolds is now an affluent area and we have become a high tech society in which people have aspirations, which go far beyond the basic human needs. There are those who desire to live in the historic environment, but also expect the features of the high tech world and of course, the trappings of the current lifestyle fad, whether it is a gym, pool, sauna, games room, wet room, boot room or whatever other 'need' can be created for a change hungry society. It is not easy to contain these 'requirements' within the fabric of a historic building, without having a detrimental impact on the building. Because the technology and fads are transient, it also means that there will be a more regular perceived need to change the systems with a consequent impact on the building. This can be seen in various TV shows such as 'Grand Designs' where some historic buildings can be seen, being subjected to these rather drastic sorts of changes. The over-riding philosophy should be to only do things to a vernacular building that are reversible, so that it can be returned to its earlier form in the future, without further damage to the essential character and fabric of the building.

I'm clearly giving a personal opinion in making the above comments and many will disagree with them. Their view might be that, the buildings were not constructed in the first place to survive for so long and they are now of such an age that major expenditure is a necessity if they are to survive for the next centuries. To make the buildings attractive to the 21st C buyer, they have to be able to meet the current lifestyle desires. Like most things in life, opinions vary and the future will judge which approach has been best (and even that judgement will depend on the values and aspirations that are current at that time). So, what I give here is my view on what should be done to maintain a historic building in something close to its vernacular form and with the least damage to its historic value.

ROOFING MATERIALS: Stone tiles **(Figure 5.1)** were the universally used local vernacular material from the 17th c onwards. However, many stone tiled roofs have been re-laid during the 20th C, with a range of manufactured tiles or with Welsh slates. So there are now only a relatively low number of stone tiled roofs remaining. This has resulted in a dilemma for owners and planners: should these be retained at all costs or should the most sympathetic artificial stone tile be used. The problem is that stone tiles are very expensive and beyond the resources available to many owners of vernacular buildings. This means that buildings with stone tiled roofs can be left to deteriorate.

New Cotswold stone tiles are now being produced again in limited quantities, but they are very expensive. They are usually mechanically split, rather than being frost split and this does cause problems. The mechanical method does not always split the stone along its natural fracture and they can split further on the roof in frosty weather. Reclaimed tiles are sometimes available, but the costs are exorbitant and their quality can be dubious as they are already old tiles. This has stimulated a black-market in stone tiles, which has led to the increasing frequency of their theft from more isolated buildings. Another issue with using either new or reclaimed tiles is that there is usually a requirement to felt the roof, before laying the tiles. This means that the weight of the tile is supported by a nail at the relatively thin neck, and this is weak. In a properly laid stone tiled roof the underside of the roof is torched with lime mortar or plaster and this fixes the tiles firmly in position, but this cannot be done if the roof is felted. It means that the re-laid stone tiled roof will not be as durable as the original roof or a roof with an alternative type of tile covering. There are some very good artificial tiles on the market and these should be allowed to be used, when an existing stone tile roof is time expired, even if the building is listed. A compromise might be that the stone tiles should be reclaimed and just used on the most sensitive elevation, but only if the tiles are in a suitable state. It is better that the building has an adequate roof to protect the rest of the structure, rather than left to deteriorate following problems with the planners over stipulations about using stone tiles. Always use oak pegs (if available), copper or stainless steel fixings for replacing stone tiles, avoid the use of iron or galvanised nails. Also, when repairing a stone tiled roof try and match the detail of the tiles, as they can vary quite widely from different sources.

It is possible that thatch was used to roof some of the early vernacular buildings in the area, but none survives now. This could be due to the local availability of good roofing stone. There are however, some examples of thatched buildings at Tarlton and over towards Wiltshire, which reflects the absence of good tiling stone there and the availability of thatching material. Always replace thatch with thatch and don't substitute with a modern material.

STONE WALLS AND POINTING: Many local vernacular buildings are built without footings: what you see is what you get. If the building is constructed on clay, then slight movement over the years can be expected and the walls may not be vertical and may bulge. Outward facing bulges can also be a result of the slight spreading of the roof, if the ties are not adequate or have failed. Inward bulges can be a result of the pressure exerted by an earth bank behind the wall. They do not necessarily need to be repaired if they have stabilised, but if unsure, seek the advice of an understanding builder or structural engineer. If some of the stones have perished in the wall, they can be removed and replaced with stone that matches that of the building (many houses have a pile of stones around the property, which will probably be suitable). Bed the replaced stones in lime mortar. The nature and integrity of the pointing is very important to the well being of Cotswold stonewalls. In recent years, much damage has been done to walls by the use of inappropriate cement based hard mortars, the so-called 'ribbon pointing' is particularly damaging **(Figure 5.2)**. The problem is that the stone is porous and soaks up rain. The water will seep downwards through the stone to the boundary where it should seep into the mortar and away from the stone. However, the use of hard mortar prevents the effective drainage of the stone. If water builds-up and then freezes, it can cause the stone to spall or break up **(Figure 5.3)**. This seems to be more of a problem with the Inferior Oolite than with the more crystalline (and less porous) Great Oolite. The only solution is to rake out the inappropriate pointing and re-point with a soft lime-based mortar **(Figure 5.4)**. Never use a disc cutter to remove hard pointing, careless use leads to much damage to the stone. Builders are not keen to use the lime mortars as they take longer to set and need to be kept moist during setting, otherwise shrinkage and cracking will occur. There are some local suppliers of the materials to prepare lime-based mortars. Also, some builders have started to use them in recent years. It is an easy job to do yourself, provided care is taken in using the materials (lime is hazardous) and keep safety in mind when working from a ladder or scaffolding.

CARE AND REPAIR OF STONE VERNACULAR BUILDINGS

A useful compromise when re-pointing stonework is to use a lime mortar, with a small amount of cement added: the mixture is 6 parts white sand, 3 parts stone dust, 2 parts hydraulic lime and 1 part cement. It sets in a different manner to the pure lime based material. An initial set is provided by the cement/sand/water reaction, this prevents cracking during the slow secondary setting caused by the lime/atmospheric carbon dioxide reaction. The set mortar has a creamy colour and is relatively soft. I used this mixture on a stone house 14 years ago and there is no sign of deterioration after this time. Do not allow the mortar to sit proud of the stone and avoid the temptation to do a ribbon effect: it is the stone that should be admired, not the pointing. Spread the mortar in the gap between the stones with a knife (I find the early 20th C knives with the flat blade very suitable), then tidy it up with the knife, let it set a little and then finish off by brushing with a paint brush or a floor brush.

Never have a Cotswold stonewall cleaned by blasting with sand or other solid material. The blasting can remove the outermost layer of the stone and this can cause severe damage to the wall. The reason is that when stone is first brought out of the ground, it is saturated with quarry sap. The sap is water saturated with dissolved calcium carbonate (the stone is made of this chemical compound). In this form the stone is easy to dress by chisel or with a saw. As the water evaporates out of the stone, it deposits crystalline calcium carbonate in the outermost pores of the stone. This makes the stone harder and therefore more resistant to weathering and also makes the stone more impermeable to water. Without this layer the stone buildings would not have lasted so well. Sand blasting can remove this outer layer and this reduces the resistance of the wall to weathering and water and can lead to the decay of the wall.

Some outer faces of stone walls were rendered from their build date, some have been rendered subsequently and others (the majority in the Stroud area) have never been rendered. If un-rendered, the stone would have been formerly limewashed to provide a degree of weather resistance. This practice ceased many years ago, but the remnants of the limewash coatings can be seen in more protected areas of stone-work. It is also found under rendering in buildings that were not rendered from first build. Lime washing is not generally practised now, probably because it required doing regularly. Prior to the 20th C, all of the cottages and houses would have been limewashed and the settlements must have looked somewhat different to now. I suspect that complaints would be received if everyone started limewashing again, as it is the colour and warmth of the Cotswold stone that we have learnt to appreciated in more recent years.

If the building has been rendered with hard cement rendering in the 20th C make sure that it has not cracked as this can allow water penetration behind the rendering. This can cause unseen damage to the underlying stonework and a source of damp to the inner walls. However, care must be taken in removing such renders as this can itself cause damage, particularly if the stone is soft or damaged **(Figure 5.5)**. Some buildings have been rendered because the stone has perished. Remove small sections at a time by hand and certainly not with a jackhammer. If re-rendering is required use a soft lime based render, seek advice on the best mixture to use or have it done by a builder experienced in their use.

WINDOW FRAMES: Never have plastic window frames installed in a vernacular stone building **(Figure 5.6)**. They are inappropriate and are not permissible if the building is listed. If you have a building, which already has them fitted, seriously consider having them replaced, as they are becoming a negative selling point. They are not as long lived as the manufacturers wish their customers to believe. Having said that, the providers of double-glazing do make life easy for their customers (at a cost) in terms of arrangements and installation. Also, avoid using modern style replacement wood frames **(Figure 5.7)**. It requires more effort on the part of the owner to find a carpenter/metal worker to make

Chapter 5

up windows of a suitable style for a vernacular building, but it can be done and is well worth the effort. Stone mullion window frames do not need much maintenance and they are long lived. However, the rear wood lintels may need replacing. Always replace with another wood lintel (try and use the same type of wood), never use a concrete or steel lintel. In the 17th and 18th C, the stone frames would contain leaded lights, supported on either vertical or horizontal iron glazing bars. However, this type of light has generally been replaced with large glass pains, perhaps with a central, horizontal glazing bar, over the past 200 years. If you have leaded lights try and keep them, there are local craftsmen who can repair/restore them **(Figure 5.8)**. The glass forming the light (either leaded lights or plain glass) can be bedded into the shallow rebate in the stone surround, using lime mortar (this adheres to the stone better than the ordinary window putty). There is usually one opening light in each stone mullion frame. Originally, this would be made from flat iron bar, forged to the correct shape and hung in the opening on pin hinges **(Figure 5.9)**. There would be turnbuckle handles to secure the light and a quadrant to prevent it opening too far. A leaded light would be fixed to the iron frame using some form of copper or lead rivet/tie. The opening lights were not exactly draft proof and many have been replaced with simple wood frames, with an opening wood light. These tend to rot and require more regular replacement than the original iron frames. There are specialist companies that will prepare metal window frames that are made to order **(Figure 5.10)**. These have a slender metal frame and a hinged opening light and this type should be considered when replacing opening lights in stone mullion windows. These new metal frames are more draught proof than their predecessors and can take double glazing.

Wood window frames are present in many local vernacular buildings. The earliest forms, which survive in reasonable numbers, date from the late 17th/early 18th C. There are cross windows (early 18th C) and mullion windows that seem to copy their stone counterparts, but the individual parts are more slender. Also, sash windows became popular in Stroud by the middle part of the century. In the late 18th C, a two and three-light wood frame windows that copy the larger 18th C stone frames are also common, particularly in the more rural settlements. In the 19th C, the cottage casement window was widely used, either with the segmented arch lintel or with a flat wood or stone lintel. The problem with these frames after several hundred years is that they will have decayed to some degree. Two options are available: either get them repaired by a carpenter or have replica frames made, ideally using the iron fixtures from the original window. Please avoid going down the plastic frame double-glazing route. There are several specialist manufacturers of period window frames who provide an excellent service for owners of period homes.

CHIMNEYS: Chimneys give balance to a building and it is important that they are not removed **(Figure 5.11)**. The stack also performs an important function in helping to anchor the building. However, many chimneys and stacks are now not in use, because of the widespread installation of central heating systems. If the flue is not in use have a ventilated cap installed on the chimney to prevent water getting into the flue wall. If chimney is original, it will be built of stone, keep the pointing in good condition and have any perished stone replaced by a professional. Ensure that a proper flashing is present and in good condition: replace defective flashing with lead and do not use synthetic alternatives or bitumastic paints (they are generally not effective). The problem with stone chimneys is that they were operated using coal as the fuel for many decades and sulphur from the coal attacks Cotswold stone, particularly at the low temperature of the chimney. This is the reason why many chimneys have been rebuilt in brick or cement based blocks. If money allows, consider having such replacement chimneys replaced in stone, this has a very positive impact on the appearance of the building **(Figure 5.12)**. Tasks such as this are definitely for the expert craftsman.

Roof timbers: If the roof structure is in good condition, leave well alone and never have the original timbers replaced unless there is a structural necessity. Even in the latter situation, have the timbers repaired or reinforced in preference to replacement. This will probably be cheaper anyway. Don't worry about woodworm decay, in many cases the damage is less severe than may be thought. If it is active get it treated, but clearly take advice from a professional on the structural integrity of the affected members. Death-watch beetle decay is a different issue. Timbers can be far more damaged than the outside appearance may suggest, as the beetle eats away at the heartwood of oak timbers. It can literally eat the middle out of large structural beams. Ideally, remove all affected timber and burn it. For sensitive timbers that are not structurally weakened open up the whole member and thoroughly clean and treat with lashings of timber paste (this penetrates better than the fluid) **(Figure 5.13)**. Again cut out sections and repair, rather than replace whole members if possible. If replacing important structural timber, replace them with the same type of wood, with similar jointing detail. A good touch is to date the repair.

Beams and Joists: The same repair/conservation strategy should be used as described for roof timbers. It is often the case that the beams survive better than their joist set, probably because the better timber was used for the beam. In many cases the beam will have rotted near the junction with an outside wall, graft in repair sections or use a steel support, rather than replace the whole beam. Always use the correct wood for the repair section. Always use the existing joist lodgings, when replacing joists. Modern timbers can be used if they are concealed above a plastered ceiling. If the joists are exposed always try and replicate the type of timber and the detail **(Figure 5.14)**.

Plaster ceilings: In the 1960-1990 period, it was fairly usual to replace the ceilings when 'restoring' an old property. An exception was the ornate plaster ceilings of early houses, but these tend not to have been installed in the smaller houses and cottages described here, although nationally, there are horror storeys of fine ceilings being removed by developers. In local buildings, in the 18-early 20th C period, ceilings were made from the lath and plaster. The plaster was generally plain, although there may be a more ornate coving around the edge. The problem with them is that over the years the plaster cracks away from the lath and starts to bow downwards and in the extreme collapses. Nowadays, these ceilings can be saved and re-attached to the laths. Use non ferrous or galvanised fixings when re-securing the plaster work and add lime-putty behind the plaster to form a bond between the laths and original plaster. Plaster mouldings can be copied fairly easily when restoring a moulded ceiling, using a rubber squeeze mould. This can be expensive when employing a specialist, but is recommended for large areas or if mouldings are to be restored. Small areas can easily be done by a competent owner, if they are prepared to spend time on doing a careful piece of work. Seek specialist advice to find out how to tackle this sort of work (e.g. from English Heritage or the local authority conservation department). The fully plastered ceiling was widespread from the early 18th C. Before this time it was common practice to leave the joists exposed and either fill in between the joists with plaster or leave the underside of the floor boards exposed. The whole could be limewashed. Laths were nailed to the underside of the boards to provide a foundation for the plaster. Examples of joists that were exposed in early 18th c ceilings have been found: although fully plastered many years ago, a clue to the earlier form is that the wall plaster continues up between the joist ends and is lime washed **(Figure 5.15)**.

Ceiling Heights: Some cottages have low ceiling heights: these are an integral part of the character of the building and should be respected. Avoid the temptation to either lower the floor or raise the ceiling.

Chapter 5

Floors: In cottages and houses built prior to the late 19th C, it would be usual to have a stone flagged ground floor. These were laid directly onto the earth, without pointing. If they have survived and the floor is dry, leave well alone **(Figure 5.16)**. If the floor is damp, have them carefully lifted and re-laid on a damp proof membrane. The usual method is to dig out the subsurface and lay a concrete floor on top of the membrane. Then lay the flags back onto the concrete, bedding them with a weak sand/cement mixture, so that the original level is maintained. There are alternative ways of damp proofing and always seek advice if unsure how to proceed. If a cellar is present, then there will generally be a suspended floor, in wood, built over it, although in good houses, there may be a stone vault overlain by flagstones. This floor will be dry and flagstones should be in reasonable condition. A wooden floor will probably have been attacked by wood boring beetles and damp, particularly if the cellar has not been well ventilated. It is common to find that the ends of the cellar ceiling beam have been re-supported, because the beam ends have rotted. Sometimes the repairs are rather crude **(Figure 5.17)**. In extreme cases the beam will need to be replaced, in others the beam end can be cut away and new support provided using a steel cradle embedded in the wall. Upper floors will be usually free from fungal attack, but will have been attacked by wood boring beetles. In the case of woodworm, where the timber has not been over-weakened, checks should be done to see whether it is active. If it is, it will need to be thoroughly treated. If the timber is weakened, it will need to be replaced: again preserve as much of the original material as is feasible. If the attack is by Death-watch Beetle (it has larger flight holes than woodworm), then the timber should be replaced. In the case of beams, where replacement is not easy, the timber should be fully exposed and cleaned and treated with a penetrating timber paste. Take note of the type of timber used for the floorboards. Do not replace early boards unless they are weakened and in this situation patch them if possible. Early boards will either be oak 16th, 17th and early 18th C) or elm (used until the mid 19th C) and may be wide. The type of nails will give an indication of when they were last disturbed. Always look in the floor spaces when boards are lifted as it is common to find items lost by previous occupiers **(Figure 5.18)**. Pitch pine floor boards will post date the early 19th C, when nationally available materials were being imported into the area. Stripped and polished boards make an attractive feature in vernacular buildings and many commercially available treatments are available to enhance their appearance. But, beware of the effects of over excited dogs with sharp claws and women with small-healed shoes: they cause damage.

Internal Fixtures and Fittings: These include doors, cupboards, hinges, handles, staircases and skirtings. Over the past decades many vernacular buildings have lost their internal fixtures and fittings during renovation work. Unfortunately they also have a significant resale value and there is a tendency for builders to remove them for salvage. Theft of fittings from empty buildings also occurs. Smaller houses and cottages of the 17th C are simple in their detail, being limited to heavy door frames, plank and ledge doors (or panel doors for the better rooms), limited ironwork (latches and hinges) **(Figure 5.19)**. These should always be retained, with repairs as necessary. It is common to find that the ground floor doorframes have rotted where they rest on the damp floor. The frame may be repaired, by grafting in a piece of frame: try and use the same wood as the original frame. 18th and 19th C housing has an abundance of pitch pine fittings. Pitch pine was imported and has a high resin content, which makes it very durable and it will last far longer than modern pinewood (which is more porous). Timber fittings may be wormy or have been decayed by fungus, but it should be salvageable. Retain as much as possible and have replica items made by a carpenter to match the original if repair pieces are needed. If the timber has been attacked by dry rot, it must be removed and burnt and the surrounding structure thoroughly treated to kill the fungus. New timbers must be thoroughly treated with preservative to limit the chances of a further attack. Be careful when stripping paint from 18th and 19th C woodwork. The paints were lead based and if they are heated, they release lead containing vapour, which is poisonous. Always strip paint with a liquid remover or have them done professionally in a caustic bath. Commercially available liquid removers 'burn' skin, so always wear rubber gloves when handling and protect your eyes. Removing paint in a caustic bath is very effective, but great care is needed, because of the large volumes of fluid and its nature **(Figure 5.20)**: always use a professional stripper! If plank and ledge doors are stripped in a caustic bath, always ensure they are subsequently dried out on a flat surface and keep them weighted down, otherwise they can bow. Also, caustic-treated timber needs to have the residual alkali in the wood neutralised, otherwise it leaches out and causes a white alkaline deposit to form. Colourless vinegar solution is effective as a neutralising agent. Ironwork should have lasted well and can easily be weld repaired if broken. Missing items can be obtained from reclamation companies **(Figure 5.21)**. Ironwork can be stripped using liquids, however an effective alternative method for small parts is to leave them in a fire to burn away the paint. The ashes from building site bonfires used to be a good hunting ground for vernacular ironwork, with the benefit that it came out ready stripped **(Figure 5.22)**! If the ironwork is unpainted, coat it with wax polish to prevent rust formation (warm the item so that the wax melts and flows into the nooks and crannies).

HEARTHS: the hearth is the heart of the home and the way they have been modified over the centuries tells much about the history of the property. When coal became widely available in the late 18th C, many of the earlier wood burning hearths were reduced in size to accommodate the requirements of the new fuel **(Figure 5.23)**. New styles of coal burning grates were introduced at regular intervals and earlier ones tended to be updated. In the latter part of the 20th C, the domestic use of coal declined and new central heating systems were installed. In many buildings, the hearth openings were blocked up completely **(Figure 5.24)**, to avoid heat losses via the old flue. In recent years these fireplaces have become regarded as an attractive feature of period properties and the tendency has been to re-open the hearth to its earliest form **(Figure 5.25, 26 and 27)**. This takes away evidence on the history of the house, so if this is being contemplated, always take copious photographs and make notes on what is found. If original coal burning hearths, with a period fireplace surround and grate are present, never remove them. Also, avoid the temptation to remove the grate and have a gas fire installed in the opening, as it takes away an important part of the character of the room. If there is a period coal burning grate surviving, which has been built into an earlier wood-burning hearth, consider the architectural merits of the grate, before making the decision on whether to recover the original wood burning hearth. If the building is listed, then permission must be sought before doing this sort of work, the coal-burning appliance may be covered by the listed building status. Restoration of a damaged coal burning grate and surround can be done by specialist companies, but can be expensive. Owners can also do much of the restoration work, although repairs to cast iron grates and surrounds are difficult. They can be welded, but this is a skilled job and should be left to a professional. The welding must be properly done if the grate is to be used again, otherwise it will tend to crack under thermal stress. Again, reclamation yards are a good source for replacement parts that may be needed. If a wood-burning hearth is being uncovered, go carefully as there are several things that need to be checked to ensure that it is structurally safe. It may have been blocked for several hundred years: age and other changes may have affected its integrity. Originally, it would have had either a stone or a wood lintel. It may have been removed or a section cut out when the hearth was modified. In either of these situations a new lintel will be required. It will be difficult to obtain a new stone lintel of suitable size, although if you are lucky, one may be located in a local reclamation yard. A new wood lintel can be prepared by one of the local timber companies, use oak if possible and ensure that it has the

Chapter 5

correct detail, including the flare on the inner side. It is unlikely that a hearth timber will be found in a reclamation yard, however, a section of floor support beam may be used **(Figure 5.28)**. In the latter situation it is worth considering cutting the flare on the inner side of the beam. This helps to ensure a smooth flow of air up the flue and avoid turbulence that can be induced in the lower part of the flue, with the consequence of smoke emission into the room. The state of the flue must also be inspected. It will be large, of a flattened bottle shape and constructed in stone rubble, which is bedded in soft earth mortar (17th C, perhaps lime mortar in the 18th C) **(Figure 5.29)**. Two aspects should be investigated during an inspection: whether the stones are tightly bedded, secure in their place, with the original profile of the flue intact and whether the mortar bedding is forming a good seal to the flue wall. Problems with the latter can enable smoke to leak into the house and more dangerously, sparks to get to the joist ends, which may be bedded in the hearth wall. The flue wall should be repaired with lime mortar or a soft mortar mixture, as necessary. With large flues, a ladder can be passed up the flue to facilitate basic repairs. Major repairs to a flue must be done by an experienced person, using the correct equipment to support unsafe stonework and to ensure that work can be done in safety. Also, beware of the wood and coal derived tars that have condensed on the stonework of the flue: they are carcinogenic.

INTERNAL PARTITION WALLS: There are several types of internal partition walls in the local vernacular buildings. If you are lucky, you may have stud and panel walls, either in oak or elm. They tended to be used in the higher status buildings. If they have survived they may need some specialist carpentry repairs, particularly if they are constructed in elm and if they rest on a stone floor. They should never be removed because of their rarity. The most common form of partition wall is the plastered stud wall. An early form of this is the timber-framed wall with wattle and daub infill panels. These can be repaired using daub, or may have to be replaced completely if the wattles have decayed. In the latter case, there are new materials available to infill panels and I would recommend consulting a builder with experience in working with timber framed buildings. The most common type of internal plastered wall in vernacular buildings is the lath and plaster wall and these can date from the late 17th C. They are comprised of vertical studs, with horizontal laths nailed between them. The whole is then covered with a coat of lime-based plaster. In the 18th C, the plaster was white, whereas from the early 19th c onwards, it was common to mix some coal ash in with the lime, which this gives the plaster a light grey colour. In simpler cottages and in attics, it is common to find the laths only fixed to one side of the studs. Both lath sides are then plastered to give a smooth face on one side and plaster between the studs on the other. Lath and plaster walls are remarkably durable. The main problem, with those on the ground floor, is rot caused by rising damp. This can take various forms including wet and dry rot and beetle infestation. They can be repaired by cutting out the affected lower parts of the stud and the lower timber plate, as necessary, and adding new treated timber. It is advisable to slide a damp proof course under the plate if there is a damp problem. If the wall is badly affected the simplest solution is to remove it completely and rebuild with new materials. However, think twice before doing this as original partition walls are an integral part of the history of the building and so many have been lost due to the attentions of over enthusiastic builders. Preserve them if you can. A very simple type of dividing wall found in some small 19th c cottages is the tongue and groove wall. It is comprised of pine boards locked together with a tongue and groove and fixed between the ceiling and floor. Sometimes they were covered in paper or sacking to improve their appearance, others were just painted.

Some 19th C houses have brick partition walls, sometimes with some horizontal timbers incorporated, presumably to spread loads and avoid cracking. Sometimes this type of wall can act as a transport route for dry rot from suspended ground floors and cellar ceilings to the upper floors. Also, the horizontal timbers can rot. They can be repaired, but if severe problems exist it may be better to remove and rebuild. But beware, these walls can be load bearing and also act to tie the building together.

CHAPTER 5

Figure 5.1. Stone tiled roof.
(Cottage at Waterlane, late 1990's)

Figure 5.2. Ribbon pointing.

Figure 5.3. Frost damaged stonework.
(Thrupp, 2006)

Figure 5.4. Wall pointed with lime based mortar.
(Cottage in Nelson St, Stroud, 2005)

Figure 5.5. Cement based pebbledash being removed from a stone wall.
(43 Middle St, Stroud, 1978)

Figure 5.6. Plastic window frames in a vernacular building.
(Post Office, Chalford Hill, 2003)

CARE AND REPAIR OF STONE VERNACULAR BUILDINGS

Figure 5.7. Modern window in a vernacular cottage.
(cottage at Oakridge Lynch, 1996)

Figure 5.8. Restored leaded light windows in new hardwood frame.
(Clematis Cottage, Chalford Hill, 1984)

Figure 5.9. Some scrapped iron opening lights.

Figure 5.10. New metal window frame in a stone mullion window.
(Old Duke of York Inn, Chalford Hill, 2000)

Figure 5.11. Cottage without chimneys.
(Cottage at Chalford Hill, 2006)

Figure 5.12. New stone chimney with a relaid stone tiled roof.
(cottage at Waterlane, late 1990's)

95

CHAPTER 5

Figure 5.13. Deathwatch beetle attack.

Figure 5.14. Some re-used joists (further pair) in an 18th C ceiling.
(Old Duke of York Inn, Chalford Hill, 1999)

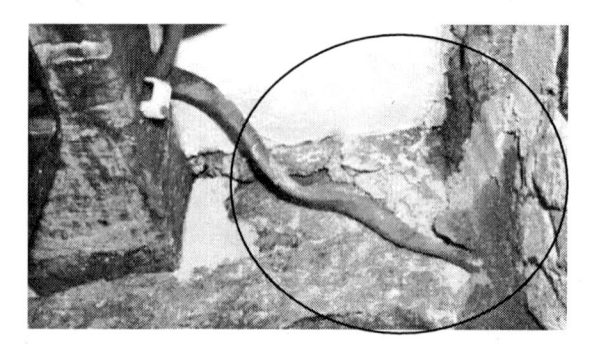

Figure 5.15. Remains of plaster between joists in an 18th C ceiling.
(Old Duke of York Inn, Chalford Hill, 1999)

Figure 5.16. Stone flagged floor.

Figure 5.17. Re-supported cellar beam.
(Stratford Park Mansion, 1995)

Figure 5.18. Coins (mainly late 18thC) found under floor boards.
(Old Duke of York Inn, Chalford Hill, 1996)

CARE AND REPAIR OF STONE VERNACULAR BUILDINGS

Figure 5.19. 18thC plank and ledge door, with frame in original position.
(Old Duke of York Inn, Chalford Hill, 2006)

Figure 5.20. Re-used 6-panel door stripped in a caustic bath.
(Old Duke of York Inn, Chalford Hill, 1999)

Figure 5.21. Reclamation yard.
(Reclamation Trading, Cirencester, 1995)

Figure 5.22. Ironwork recovered from a builder's bonfire.

Figure 5.23. Coal burning hearth infilling earlier hearth (late 17th C).
(Clematis Cottage, Chalford Hill, 1983)

Figure 5.24. Completely infilled hearth.
(Arundell Mill House, Stroud, 1990)

Chapter 5

Figure 5.25. Mid 20th C coal burning grate.
(Old Duke of York Inn, Chalford Hill, 1995)

Figure 5.26. Mid 20th C hearth partly removed, showing earlier form of fireplace.

Figure 5.27. Original early/mid 18th C fireplace fully uncovered.

Figure 5.28. Section of floor-support beam re-used as fireplace beam.
(The Ferns, Chalford Hill, 1990)

Figure 5.29. Large flue for wood burning hearth.
(Old Duke of York Inn, Chalford Hill, 1995)

CHAPTER 6

VERNACULAR BUILDINGS OF STROUD

Aerial view of Stroud, taken in the early 1930's. The vernacular core of the town is in the top left hand quarter of the photo.

CONTENTS OF CHAPTER

THE DEVELOPMENT of the town is described, starting with the early root in the 13th C. The early core of the town in the area of the Church, Shambles and High Street is described, with a description of the buildings/parts of buildings that survive in this area from the 16-19th C.

The following buildings are discussed in some detail.

Buildings with origins in the 16th C or perhaps earlier:

23 High St
26 High St
33 High St
27 High St
Market House

Buildings with origins in the 17th C:

57 High St
50 High St
Church Court
Webb's Alms Houses (demolished in the 1940's)
46 High St

Buildings with origins in the 18th C:

Corn Exchange (demolished in the 1960's)
25 Church St
15 High St
Bank House
55 High St
58 High St

Buildings with origins in the 19th C:

General discussion on 19th C development of the town and surviving buildings.

The chapter then goes on to describe the buildings that stood at the Cross. These were all demolished by the 1980's, so it is a retrospective look at this formerly important part of the town. The 17th C expansion of the early town into the Stroud fields is next described: an area that became known as the 'Top of the Town'. A general discussion on the area is given, which is followed by a description of specific buildings. Buildings in the following streets are described:

Parliament St
Nelson St
Castle St, Lower St and beyond
Middle St
Whitehall and Piccadilly
Chapel St
Acre St

THE STREETS OF STROUD

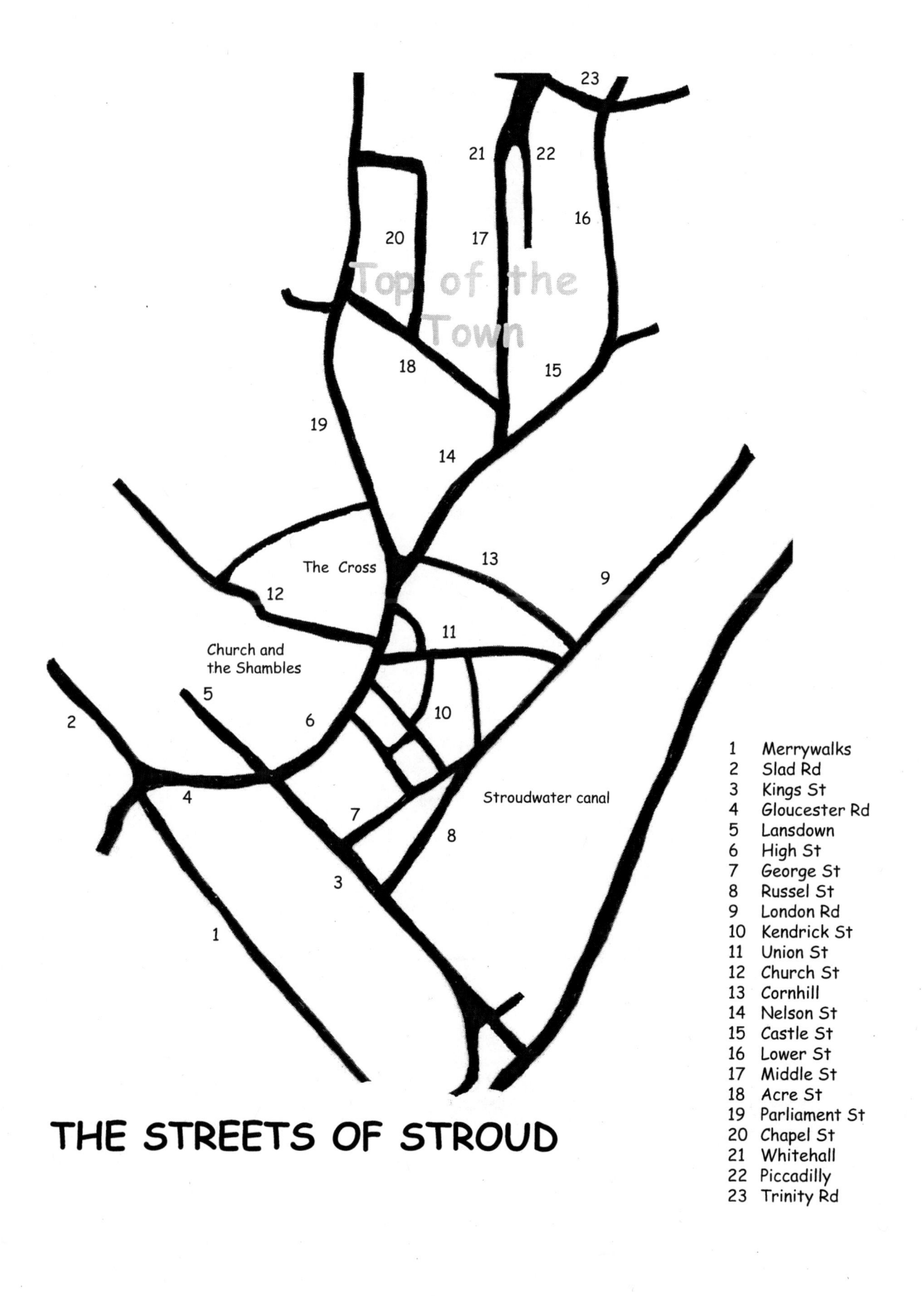

1. Merrywalks
2. Slad Rd
3. Kings St
4. Gloucester Rd
5. Lansdown
6. High St
7. George St
8. Russel St
9. London Rd
10. Kendrick St
11. Union St
12. Church St
13. Cornhill
14. Nelson St
15. Castle St
16. Lower St
17. Middle St
18. Acre St
19. Parliament St
20. Chapel St
21. Whitehall
22. Piccadilly
23. Trinity Rd

Chapter 6

6.1 Development of the Town

The origins of the settlement at Stroud are not known with certainty and it is not recorded in the Domesday Book (1087). It developed subsequently in the outer part of the parish of Bisley, within the manor of Lypiatt. Bisley is one of the earliest local settlements and has origins in the Saxon period, possibly earlier. The earliest documented reference is to 'La Strode' in 1221 and by 1248 it had been given the status of a vill. By 1279, it was of a sufficient size to justify the building of a 'Chapel of Ease'. This was built to enable baptisms to be done at Stroud rather than having to make the potentially hazardous journey to Bisley. At that time, babies were baptised soon after birth (as the mortality rate was high), and the journey to Bisley would be difficult in winter. Ten houses are recorded at Stroud in 1477, held from Over Lypiatt Manor. The Chapel was given parochial rights in 1304, but the church had no endowment of tithes and was regarded as a chapel of the Bisley Church, until the early 18th C. The tower was added to the church in the 14th C, which must mark increased local wealth and the growing importance of the settlement at Stroud. The church was rebuilt between 1866 and 1868, with the retention of the 14th C tower and this still stands today (**Figure 6-1**), which makes it the earliest standing structure in the town. The earlier church has been described in detail by Fisher. There would have been buildings around the chapel in early times, but they have not survived. Rudd (p. 162) provides some detail of the repair of the 'Vicarage House' at Bisley: in 1563 it was repaired using timber, daub and thatch, and adds that it is thought to have been replaced by one in stone between 1625 and 1635. In all probability, the earliest domestic buildings of Stroud would have been constructed out of the same materials, with thatch roofs. The original houses were probably built alongside the established highways in the area. A main route led from Gloucester, through Paganhill to Bath. At Paganhill, there was a route leading off to Bisley. This passed over the Slad stream at Badbrook and up the steep spur, formed by the junction of the Slad and Chalford valleys, to Bisley. The part leading up the spur eventually became the route of High Street. The early Chapel was built close to this thoroughfare. A market was soon established on a piece of land beside the church, this was originally known as Pridie's Acre. This was assigned as an endowment to the church in 1304. The market was well established by the 16th C and sufficient income must have been generated by the end of that century, to justify the construction of the Market House **(Figure 6.2)**. It was built in the early 1590's, by John Throckmorton (owner of the estate of Upper Lypiatt). It is also known that by the early 17th C, there were other properties built around the market place. One was on the corner of the Shambles and the High Street and was known as the Church House. However, these were removed during the 19th C and replaced by the buildings that stand today. The market place and the adjoining High Street leading up to the Cross is the early core of the town (**Figure 6.3**). The Cross marks the point where the early thoroughfare split to go to Bisley (up Parliament St) and to Bowbridge, Thrupp and Chalford (along Nelson St and Lower St). It is in the High Street leading up to the Cross **(Figure 6.4)**, that the remnants of the earliest surviving secular (non religious) buildings have been identified.

6.2 The High Street: the Early Core of Stroud

Earliest Buildings in the High Street

The frontages of the present High Street buildings suggest they were built mainly between the 18th and 20th C, with a few buildings surviving from the 17th C. However, this is a misleading impression. The High Street has been the main commercial street of the town, since the early growth of the settlement. As such it has been adapted and improved to meet the changing needs of an expanding, working town and to keep up with changing fashions in building. This change has not always involved the replacement of the earlier buildings, but rather re-fronting, with the retention of earlier parts behind a new façade. Three examples of this have been identified in the upper part of the High Street, all on the S side. These are Nos. 23, 25 and 33. They date from the 16th C, or earlier, and, as such, are the earliest standing secular buildings of Stroud. Each retains elements of their original form and the remains give a good impression of what the original buildings were like. It is possible that others remain to be identified, for instance No 27 contains an early beam to the rear of the shop, which could indicate remains of an early building behind the early 20th C front.

Each building stood on a fairly narrow, but deep, site that extended back from the High Street. The original buildings were rectangular in plan, with a gable end built directly onto the High Street (i.e. they were end on to the street). It is possible that each had an alley leading down to one side of the building to give access to the land to the rear. The street-facing gable ends of both Nos. 33 and 23 were timber framed, as substantial elements of these were retained in the later facades. In the case of No. 33, the first floor projected over the ground floor as a jetty. The first floor jetty timbers are still present embedded in the later façade. No. 23 had a similar form and there are still considerable remains of the original framing behind the rendering of the re-aligned façade and the former presence of a jetty can be read from the timbers in the current shop front. No. 25 has been completely re-fronted and no remains of the earlier form have been found, but it is likely that it was similar to No. 33 and No. 23. In all three cases the roof at the front end has been re-aligned parallel to the street (at different times). The evidence suggests that the original buildings were storied from their initial build, with 2 floors and attic in the case of Nos. 23 and 33, and one storey with undercroft and attic in the case of No. 25. No evidence has been found for the buildings originally being open halls. Although, this cannot be ruled out because the buildings have been subjected to so many changes and evidence has been lost. However, their former presence must be a matter of speculation.

No. 23 High Street

The group of buildings that comprise No.23 extend from the High St and S along the W side of Union St. This line of buildings, plus some of those now incorporated into the Swann Inn opposite, was The George Inn in the 18th and very early 19th C (it closed in about 1818) and was one of the most important coaching inns in Stroud. There were buildings linking the parts, now on opposite sides of Union Street, and these included an Assembly Room and a room over the entrance (from the High St) to the outer courtyard of the inn. There was access under the first floor Assembly Room to an inner stable yard. Union St was created in the mid 19th C, by demolishing the room over the entrance and the assembly rooms to provide a link down to the new London Road. This was part of an unsuccessful attempt on the part of the owner to maintain his coaching trade, once the new London Road was in use. The buildings that comprise No.23 are of 16-19th C origin, with the earliest part bordering the High St. The front façade, which is rendered and rather crudely realigned parallel to the street, retains significant parts of the original front timber frame gable end. The sidewalls are in stone, with that bordering Union St. being altered to include a gable end for the modified façade.

The building was investigated by Sheila Ely as part of her dissertation for an Architectural Conservation Diploma and these notes have in part been taken from this source. The front elevation retains much of the original timber framing at first floor level and above, but now contained within the squared off façade and behind a layer of render. The present façade, with its canted oriel window on the first floor and sash window at the attic level and the moulded cornice, date from some time after

Chapter 6

the George Inn was closed **(Figure 6.5)**. A postcard, from around 1840, shows an engraving of the upper part of the High St. It clearly shows No 23, before the front was altered and a steeply pitched roof of a gable end bordering the street can be seen **(Figure 6.6)**. In another postcard, dated around 1890, the present façade has been built. These two views of the street therefore show that the façade of No.23 was altered between about 1840 and 1890 and this is some time after the George Inn had closed. The timber framing of the original front-end truss could be seen within the front room of the attic at the time of the study. In the gable end there were vertical oak studs, closely spaced and pegged to the underside of the gable end truss. There were 4 other trusses (i.e. 5 trusses including the one in the front gable wall) forming the roof structure over the original building. The end of this building is shown by a change in the line of building in Union Street and a vertical building line in the opposite wall. Each truss is of the 'A' frame type **(Figure 6.7)**, with the feet anchored in a set of large tie beams. These tie beams were boxed in (with 19th C pine board) at the time of the study and were not inspected. However, wide chamfers, with draw or triangular stops set off the chamfer would be expected, provided the originals are still in place. The principals are halved at the apex of the trusses and joined with a diagonal, pegged joint. The ridge timber sits in a notch at the apex of the truss. The collars are morticed to the underside of the principals and there are 2 rows of trenched purlins on each roof slope. There are cut-outs on the back of the purlins and principals to indicate the former presence of windbraces: at the time of the survey, only one remained in place. The E side of this part of the building shows a blocked up arch, which was the entrance to the George Inn from the courtyard.

The building was extended to the S in the early 17th C **(Figure 6.8)**. The front (E) elevation of this part has a 2-light stone mullion window frame on the ground, and a 3-light window on the first floor and a chamfered stone surround to the doorway **(Figure 6.9)**. Inside on the ground and first floors were some good quality beams, with wide, flat, chamfers (about 125mm) and triangular stops (set off the chamfer) **(Figure 6.10)**. The length of this first extension is indicated by the straight joint with quoin stones that is visible in the rear (W) wall and the change in the roofline at this point **(Figure 6.11)**. No matching line is now present in the front wall, as it appears to have been modified in the 19th C. There were two roof trusses in the roof of this part, one was infilled with an oak stud partition **(Figure 6.12)**. Each principal was halved at the apex of the truss and joined with a diagonal joint. There were originally two trenched purlins per roof slope.

There was a second extension in the later 17th C and the limit of this was indicated by another vertical building line in the W elevation. The roof of this part had a single main truss **Figure 6.13)**, which had halved principals at the apex, the ridge placed in a notch, 2 rows of butt purlins (the upper placed at the level of the collar). It was thought that this extension linked to an existing single storey building, which was thought to be of early origin, possibly 16th C. The evidence for this was limited and included a 2-light wood mullion window (blocked with wattles in 1984) in the E elevation. This part contained a corner fireplace on the ground floor with a wood bolection moulding to the surround. This style of hearth is typical of the late 17th/early 18th C and shows that work was being done on the building at that time. By 1825, an 'L' shaped extension has been built off the S gable end of the 16th C part. This is shown on a map of the time, but was removed a long time ago, possibly when the street was created through the courtyard and stable yard of the George Inn. The 16th C part has been extensively remodelled to create the present building on the corner of Union St and Threadneedle St **(Figure 6.14)**. The façade of this part has large sash windows and an arch headed doorway, with slight shoulders, which are thought to date from the mid 19th C. However, the roof structure here contains some early timbers that may have been re-used from the single storey 16th C building. The façade of the late 17th C part, further N along Union St has also had a rebuilt façade, also of mid 19th C origin (although with different details to that of the end building). There were some good 19th/early 20thC coal burning hearths on the first floor of this group of buildings. Two are shown in **Figure 6.15.**

The buildings in this group have now been renovated and have found new commercial uses. The former Ball's fruit and vegetable store is now the Stroud Bookshop. The ceiling structure is exposed in the front part of the shop. The original joists (with some replacements) and some of the beams are still in situ. The joists are large, are laid flat and have narrow flat chamfers and stops all of which are consistent with a 16th C or earlier origin. The presence of stops, placed in from the street end of the joists shows the position of the former jetty beam. This is also shown by the lighter colouration of the joists, where their undersides have been protected by the deposed jetty beam. The present shop front beam could date from the 19th C. Some of the other ceiling beams within the shop area will be original.

This building shows how the earliest buildings of the town have been progressively developed. The original buildings bordered the street with undeveloped land behind. Over the centuries, the land behind has been progressively infilled, so that now it is completely developed. In addition, there have been regular changes to the existing buildings, perhaps to keep up with the changing fashions, to meet changing needs (e.g. when the group became the George Inn) or to keep the building in a structurally sound state.

No. 26 High Street

No. 26 (Baimbridge House) **(Figure 6.16)** is possibly the earliest of the group as it retains a stone vaulted undercroft. This was originally accessed from the street, down a set of steps to a sunken area, with a door and window to the undercroft (these are still visible from within the surviving cellar) **(Figures 6.17 and 6.18)**. It would have been used as a workshop/commercial premises and is a feature of urban medieval buildings. Inside the vault still exists with sub vaults to the rear, which terminate with single light stone window frames, which are now below ground level, but would formerly have provided some light to the rear of the undercroft. At the front end, the top of the vault has been removed and a wood floor inserted that is coincident with the current street level. However, the remains of the entrance and window of the undercroft are still present. In its earlier form there would have been several steps up from the street to the ground floor of the building. Not a bad idea and this would have helped to keep it dry. Inside on the ground floor, there was a large hearth, still present in 2003, as a much-altered wide recess in the sidewall. The heavily sooted stones beneath the modern plaster showed the former presence of the hearth. The chimneystack for this hearth still exists, but now encased in later first floor stonework **(Figure 6.19)**. This is the evidence that tells the height of the original building, since it is built on the top of the ground floor wall. The stack is built of finely dressed masonry blocks, hand dressed with fine joints and would have been built off the sidewall of the building. It possibly had a projecting chimneybreast. The stack is roughly square in section. Near the top there are two small arched openings into the stack, these sorts of openings are a feature of medieval chimneys. This feature, if correctly interpreted, is a rare survivor. Details of the stack were noted in 2003 during the renovation of the building, but it is probably now hidden under new plasterwork. No other remnants of the original building are thought to have survived within the present structure. The postcard of the 1840 view of the High St shows that No. 25 had been re-fronted by this date. The rear extent of the original building is indicated by a change in the detail of the building that projects to the rear of the remodelled front **(Figure 6.20)**. Although the early phase was almost entirely rebuilt in the 19th C, it seems to have used the early footprint. The original building has been extended backwards into its rear plot of land in the early part of the 17th C. The details of this part of the building survive, these include a four-light stone mullion window frame, rebated surround,

Chapter 6

with king mullion (part converted to a doorway) and an adjacent stone framed doorway (converted to a window) **(Figure 6.21)**. Internally, the early 17th C beams survive with 100mm chamfers and run out stops set off the chamfer **(Figure 6.22)**. There was a large blocked 17th C hearth (not uncovered) and a set of 'A' frame roof trusses with collars jointed to the underside of the principal rafters **(Figure 6.23)**. The side walls of both front and rear phases showed many 18th and 19th C modifications, with blocked door openings through to adjacent properties.

No. 33 High Street

No. 33 has been examined in most detail. It was restored in the early 1980's by the Stroud Preservation Trust. This trust was formed as a result of public opposition to the demolition of this and other buildings in the town, as they stood in the path of a proposed ring road. It was sold to the Trust for £1 and restored using labour funded by the Manpower Services Commission.

As it stands, it has an early 18th C front, which is aligned parallel to the High Street **(Figures 6.24 and 6.25)**. The detail of the window surrounds (bullnose architrave in stone with projecting keystones) **(Figure 6.26)** and the rusticated quoins indicate that the façade was built in the early 18th C. This façade is wider than the original timber frame gable end of the building. It seems that in the early 18th C part of an adjacent building was incorporated into the left side of the new front. This part now forms the entrance and stair to the first floor of the restored building. However, inside this entrance, there is a large 17th C hearth at approximate first floor level, but now sited in a narrow space. This must indicate that the early 18th C modification took in part of an adjacent, larger building. Documents of this period mention a room over an alley. It is speculated that the hearth was in the room over the alley and that the alley was subsequently converted to a shop. The shop was present in 1980, but was converted to the current entrance during the restoration of the building. The adjacent building, which had itself been modified in the 19th C, was demolished at this time (however, it is described in the part describing the buildings at the Cross).

To the right, and beyond the sideways limit of No. 33, is a building that was added in the late 17th C (now No. 32 High Street). The first floor oriel window is Edwardian and hides an early 18th C surround of the same form as those on No 33. This indicates common ownership at that time. Several internal linkages were found between Nos 32 and 33 during the restoration, which again shows common ownership at one stage. The front and side ground floor walls of No. 32 are in stone, but the side first floor wall is timber framed and rendered. The framing is not good quality and probably dates from the early 18th C (i.e. original build) and was a way of building the front part of the first floor out over the lane (where it forms a narrow jetty, which diminishes in depth along the lane).

The original form of the building (No. 33) can be seen in the wing projecting behind the realigned front part **(Figure 6.27)**. At the High Street end, the early building had a timber frame wall with a first floor jetty. Some of the original timbers remained embedded in the early 18th C mixed brick and stone of the front wall, but were mostly removed during the recent restoration. The form of this building is indicated in the photograph of a similar building that survived in Parliament Street until the 1970's demolitions **(Figure 6.28)**. The original building was extended backwards sometime in the early 17th C and this extension was subsequently modified again later in that century **(Figure 6.29)**. The current rear gable end is thought to have been rebuilt in the 19th C. The original form of the late 17th C rear addition was investigated prior to the demolition of the major part of it in the early 1980's. It is thought to have been built as domestic accommodation, as it was well served with hearths. It seems to have had twin gabled dormers in its rear facing elevation and was built off the end of the single rear gable of the original building, such that the line of the original gable was continued back to form one of the gables of the addition. The second gable was placed to the right hand side (viewed from rear) **(Figure 6.30)**. In the 18thC, this part of the building is recorded as the 'Tobacco Warehouse', which infers a commercial use at that time. However, it had large ground floor hearths with wood hearth beams, in each gable end wall. One had the remains of a winder stair to its side and a bread oven, which shows an original domestic use. There was a trimmer beam, with a wide chamfer (but narrower than in the original part of No. 33), across the hearth wall in the right hand gable end, which is consistent with an origin in the early/mid 17th C.

No. 33 was investigated by Trust Members to identify the early remaining elements of the building. Many features were discovered which seemed to remain from its original building phase. The depth of the original building was indicated by a former closed panel across the first floor of the building and the remains of a building line in the sidewall. The building line can still be seen in the sidewall of the rear wing that faces Cornhill **(Figure 6.31 and 6.32)**. It was 3 bays long, with roof trusses set in the front and rear timber framed walls (i.e. there are a total of 4 trusses, numbered 1-1111). The form of the roof structure is similar to that in No. 23. Each truss is comprised of a pair of principal rafters, joined at their apices by a vertical joint **(Figure 6.33)**. On truss 11, the ridge is clasped in this vertical joint. The bases of each principal pair are jointed into the ends of a large tie beam (which also supports the attic floor). The original collars were jointed (mortice and tenon joints) into the underside of each principal to further strengthen the truss. Only one decayed original collar remained and this was encased in the later front gable end wall. The others are replacements, but the redundant mortices show the earlier form. They were set fairly low and would have obstructed free passage along the attic. The timbers are oak and probably cut with a large pit saw and tidied up with an adze. There are 2 sets of butt purlins to each roof slope. The original roof had curved windbraces running between trenches in the back of the principals to trenches in the back of the upper purlins. Only one remained in situ **(Figure 6.34)**, but their former presence is indicated by the trenches.

There was a complete set of ground and first floor ceiling beams and joist sets. The width of the beam chamfers (100mm), the style of the beam stops (draw stops, set off the chamfer) and the dimensions and setting of the joists (large, laid flat and tenoned into the side of the beams on the ground floor) are all consistent with an origin in the 16th C **(Figure 6.35)**. The completeness of the joist set shows the building was storied from this time. The original floor levels were not altered when the building was refronted and consequently the floor levels and window heights in the early 18th C front wall are not consistent. At least one internal wattle and daub panel was left in a cross partition wall **(Figure 6.36)** on the first floor, which indicated the form of the original partitions. This type of partition is seen in 16th and early 17th C buildings. By the late 17th C lath and plaster partitions had replace wattle and daub. No evidence of original framing was found in the side walls, so it is inferred that they were constructed in stone at ground and first floor levels. There is a section of early frame wall, containing several redundant doorways, separating the first floors of Nos 32 and 33, however this seems to have been re-used as it has been so crudely installed **(Figure 6.37)**. Its length equalled the width of the building, so it may be a re-used cross partition. Remains of an early, unglazed window were found in the sidewall of the original building facing Swan Lane. This was placed close under the eaves and was wider than it was deep. Its detail suggested a 16th C origin. A replica, based upon the remains of the early window, was incorporated in the 1980 restoration **(Figure 6.38)**. The adjacent window is of a similar size, but no early remains were found. It is possible that this was of a similar form to the replica window. Below these windows on the ground floor are a late 17th C cross-window **(Figure 6.39)** and a sash window of the same style as added to the early 18th C façade. This detail shows the way buildings were being altered prior to the early 18th C: when the owner wanted a

Chapter 6

new window, a new one was positioned where it was required using the current style. The mis-match with existing windows or the lack of any symmetry in the revised arrangement did not matter.

There are no major early hearths on the ground floor of the original part of No. 33. The detail of the existing hearth on the ground floor shows that it was added in the late 18th C. This suggests an early commercial use for the ground floor. However, there is a large, but simple, hearth on the first floor, in the sidewall and near the front. This has a massive, deep stone lintel and stone jambs, all with a wide chamfer, but no stops showing **(Figure 6.40)**. Originally this would have had a projecting chimneybreast in the area now occupied by part of No. 32. This suggests a domestic or communal use for this floor. In the late 17th C, the original hearth was infilled with a hearth with a semi-circular back and smoke channel **(Figure 6.41)**, presumably the chimneybreast was also removed, as No. 32 dates from this time. The late 17th C hearth was itself infilled in the mid/late 19th C with a cast iron coal-burning hearth **(Figure 6.42)**. The remains of a stair turret that linked the ground and first floors of the original building were also identified. Initially this was thought to be a buttress supporting the side wall of No. 33 **(Figure 6.43)**. However, it was found to have a stone door frame, with rebates for a door and iron pin hinges, which led from the ground floor of No 33 into the turret. No remains of the original stair were present, but the semi circular shape showed that it was built for a stair. The existing stair was 19th C and associated with No. 32. The stone lintel of the door frame has a four centred arch head **(Figure 6.44)**. One of the jambs had been removed and the stones used to block the door opening and to form the splay of the late 17th C cross window (which was therefore proved to be an insertion) **(Figure 6.45)**. A single light stone window frame, with a round arch head and recessed spandrels **(Figure 6.46)**, was uncovered in the side wall. This would have originally looked down the High Street, but was blocked by the building of No. 32.

As already noted there were several hearths in the rear addition to No. 33. The remains of the original hearths were consistent with an early 17th C build date. The one in the part incorporated into the rear part of No. 33 was modified with a semi-circular back and channel and it is this form of the hearth that was reconstructed in the 1980's restoration **(Figure 6.47)**. A first floor hearth had been added in the late 17th C modifications **(Figure 6.48)**. No. 32 also contained hearths with the semi-circular back **(Figure 6.49)**.

There are cellars under the front (original part) and under the rear part of No.33. They are true cellars and not an undercroft, as has already been discussed for Baimbridge House. They are set in from the perimeter walls of the building and may therefore post date the original construction.

This building shows a succession of fairly regular changes throughout its life and the same is evident in other early buildings in Stroud. Buildings were modified and extended to meet the changing needs of the working population and changing fashions. Early on in the development of Stroud, there was space to expand and land was not at a premium. Consequently the original buildings grew by addition over the 16th-19th C and new buildings were placed between them as the High Street became progressively developed.

No. 27 High Street

This building has not been investigated, however, it is noted that in the 1840 and 1890 views of the High St and another of 1910, show that this building had a steeply pitched gable end facing the street **(Figure 6.50)**. A photograph thought to date from around 1908 shows that the gable end had two first floor sash windows and one for attic **(Figure 6.51)**. Until recently it was occupied by Wash Vac Services and in the rear of their retail space there is a large beam with wide chamfer and draw stops set off the chamfer. This is similar to the beams seen in the other 16th C buildings already described, so it seems that this is another early survivor. However, the extent of the rebuild that must have occurred after 1910 is not known. The present front elevation is Edwardian **(Figure 6.52)**. The building was extensively stripped out in 2004 after Wash Vac had closed and has been subjected to an unsympathetic conversion. It was not possible to gain access to gather details of the earlier form of the building.

The other 16th C building that survives in something like its original form is the Market House in the Shambles. It was built in the early 1590's for John Throckmorton, the Lord of the Manor of Over Lypiatt. It is sited on the old market place and until the mid 19th C, other early buildings also survived in this area. They were redeveloped by the Stroud Feoffes to form the current Shambles. The original Market House will have had an open area beneath the important first floor room. However, instability caused by the oriel window and the weight of the superstructure has required the ground floor to be re-supported at different times (starting as far back as the early/mid 17th C). The building has good Cotswold detail including the roof verge coping and rebated stone mullion window frames **(Figure 6.53)**.

If the current High Street is viewed from the Cross **(Figure 6.54)**, an impression can be gained of what the street looked like at the end of the 16th C. The line of the street remains unchanged, as it has been found that the gable ends of the 16th C buildings were built directly on the current roadside. On the S side of the street there was a procession of timber frame gable ends passing down the hill to just past the entrance to the Shambles. Four have been identified as survivors albeit in a much modified form, there are likely to have been others. There will have been spaces between the individual buildings for alleys to get to their rear ground and probably some undeveloped sites. No early survivors, apart from the Market House (and this is late 16th C) have been identified on the N side of the street. This side will have been dominated by the market place and we know from documentary records that there were other buildings around the market by this time. The Church House has been identified in the records as being on the corner of the Shambles and the High Street (until recently, New Look). From the viewpoint at the Cross, there may have been a view of the back of the Market House and the Church in the late 16th C. The upper part of the N side of the High St (above Church St) has some good 17th C buildings and may have been undeveloped before these were built, otherwise some earlier elements might have been found in these later buildings (but, no earlier detail has been found).

17TH C BUILDINGS IN THE HIGH STREET

The High Street developed significantly during the 17th century. There were additions to the rear of the existing buildings on the S side (so that their rear land became progressively infilled), and some good quality new buildings were added on the N side. The owners of these new buildings were those involved with the commercial life of the town. The quality and size of the buildings suggests they were successful tradesmen/merchants. There does not seem to have been much new build directly along the S side between the early buildings, except lower down, where No. 6 presents a gabled dormer to the street. The style of this is typical of the 17th C, with coursed rubble walls, a 3-light first floor window (the upper part of it is hidden behind the current shop sign) and a 2-light window in the dormer. Perhaps, the S side had more 16th C buildings than can be detected now, having been replaced completely by post 17th C infill buildings. However, new buildings were being added to the north side of the street, both above and below the entrance to the market place. Nos 46, 50 and 57 were built and originally presented a group of gabled dormers to the street.

No. 57 High Street

Chapter 6

No. 57 has a rendered elevation facing the High Street **(Figure 6.55 and 6.56)**, but the W gable end and the rear shows that the building is constructed in stone **(Figure 6.57)**. The detail of the façade suggests that it dates from the early 19th C. The building was inspected by members of the Stroud High Street Action Group, as part of their campaign to prevent the demolition of the adjacent buildings in the High Street. At that time it was occupied by Shire Training Workshops and operated as Starters Café. Prior to that, it had been a chemists shop for many years. The study showed that No. 57 had origins around the mid 17th C, as a substantial 'L shaped' building. The evidence showing the form of this original building was present in the attic of the present building. Here, the roof structure is formed by a group of slightly modified extended collar trusses, with principal rafters (i.e. the earlier form of truss, which means it predates the late 17th C). This roof structure had been modified with additional timbers at the S side to reduce the roof pitch and to enable the front wall to be raised to its current height **(Figure 6.58)**. There are two pairs of extended collar trusses and therefore the original front had two gabled dormers. At the rear of the current building there are 2 wings. The detail of the stonework and windows shows that the outer wing is original, such that one of the gabled dormers was continued backwards as the wing. The sash window and surround (and other internal detail) of the second (inner) wing show that this is an addition, dating from the phase when the façade was reconstructed in the 19th C. Within the roof space, there is a gabled dormer separating this later wing from the attic over the front part of the building. The evidence shows that the original building had a reversed 'L' plan. There are stone mullion window frames in the W sidewall and in the rear of the outer wing. These all have rebated surrounds with flat chamfers and have been noted in many 17th C buildings in Stroud. This style of window seems to have been used up to the latter part of the 17th C in the town.

Unfortunately, the ground floor of No. 57 has subsequently been ripped out and subjected to a most insensitive conversion to form the non-descript shop currently occupied by Boots. So, what follows is a description of the building as it survived until the early 1980's. It contained much detail from the 17th, 18th and 19th C. The ground floor was originally divided into three rooms, two in the front range and one in the rear wing. An axial corridor ran behind the rooms in the front range. The purpose of the corridor was not clear, as it was not in line with an original entrance doorway in the W gable end wall. It was thought to lead to the stairs that originally led down to the cellars under the front range. However, the access was closed off and the stairs had been adapted to give access to a cellar under the added wing (and this was reached via No. 56). The layout of the ground floor rooms was determined from the grooves for stud and panel partitions that were present in the undersides of the beams in the ceiling and from the actual remains of some of the original partition walls **(Figure 6.59 and 6.60)**. These remains had been overlaid by later plaster, in the remaining part of the wall separating the rear wing from the front part. Each room also had a main axial ceiling support beam, which had flat chamfers (75mm wide) and scroll stops. The original joists were laid flat (unusual for 17th C buildings) and were each jointed into the side of the ceiling beams with a mortice and tenon joint. The joint was held with a wood peg. The beam mortices and the tenons of the joists had matching Roman numbers. The joists and beams must have been cut in a timber yard and transported to the site, hence the need for the labelling. It was good quality work.

The gable end of the rear wing contained a large hearth with large jambs and a stone lintel **(Figure 6.61)**. The jambs were chamfered (90mm wide) and had scroll stops. The hearth had been partially infilled to accept a good sized cast iron range, which had subsequently had a 19th C bread oven built on top of it. In the attic above the front wall of the stack wall for this hearth was a hand-made wooden pulley wheel, which was thought to be a spit drive wheel. There would have been a rope attached to a drum on the spit and the rope would have been cast over the pulley **(Figure 6.62)**. A weight was tied to the end of the rope and the controlled downward movement of the weight drove the spit. There were the remains of a 3-light stone mullion window, with a rebated surround and flat chamfers, in the sidewall of the wing (facing W). All of the stone window frames in No. 57 were of this type. There was an original doorway in the W gable end of the front range, which had a chamfered surround (90 mm wide), without stops, and a dripmould, which continued over an adjacent blocked stone mullion window. This door entered the W room of the front part of the building. Originally this room was unheated, as the window openings in the W gable end wall had been blocked and converted to flues that served ground and first floor coal burning hearths **(Figure 6.63)**. This conversion has been noted in several local houses, the detail suggests it was done in the 19th C. The E front room would have been expected to contain a large original hearth (as two unheated rooms in the main (front) part of a building of this size would be unusual. However, the walls in this room did not contain an early hearth: the rear wall originally had a window and the E gable end wall had been rebuilt completely and contained a hearth with a brick arch lintel and of a size that suggested it was intended for coal burning **(Figure 6.64)**. Bricks bedded in white lime mortar had been used in the reconstruction of the E gable end wall. The type of mortar indicates an early 19th C date for the rebuild, as after this time it was common to add coal ash to the mortar mixture and this gave it a light grey colour. An early 19th stair was present in the rear wing in a hallway created beside the large hearth **(Figure 6.65)**. This was lit by a tall window with an arched head in the rear gable end wall.

The original plan of the first floor seemed to be the same as that on the ground floor. The original stair position was not located. It may have been a winder stair, next to the suggested hearth in the original E gable end wall of the street range, alternatively, it may have been in the area now occupied by the early 19th C stair. The rear wall of the E room of the front range of the building had a cupboard, with panelled doors (of a late 18th/early 19th C type) with H-L hinges **(Figure 6.66)**. This was created from a former window opening (the inside of the cupboard showed the internal splay of the window opening) and must have been closed up when second rear wing was constructed. The ceiling support beams had the same width of chamfer and stops as on the ground floor. One beam was cased in plaster, which was thought to be early in date **(Figure 6.67)**. All of the sash windows in the front wall of the first floor had their sets of early 19th C shutters. These are known to have been removed for 'restoration' during the work done in the early 1980's, but are not thought to have been replaced. An interesting feature was present in the floor of the W, first floor room. There was a set of 6 rollers **(Figure 6.68)**, which still rotated freely, set between adjacent joists in the floor space. These can only have been inserted when the floor was assembled and therefore must have been 17th C in origin. The rollers showed rope wear. The second floor had been created from the attics of the earlier house, by raising the front wall by filling in the area between the gabled dormers. It is also possible that the whole front wall was demolished and rebuilt when this modification was done, as no evidence of roof lines for the dormers was found in the stonework.

There were roof spaces above the second floor and these retain the original 17thC extended collar roof trusses. The attic over the rear wing contains the upper parts of two raised cruck trusses. These arise from the beam that also supports the floor of the second floor. This must mark the level of the original floor of the attics of the house in the 17th C and shows that the levels were not altered when the house was modified.

There are cellars beneath the rooms in the front of the building and another beneath the added wing. The front two cellars were entered through a door in the stonewall that separated the rear wings. There were stone stairs, which led under a brick arch into the cellars beneath the front range. The cellars

Chapter 6

were separated by a stone wall **(Figure 6.69)** and both had stone perimeter walls, which looked original build. The E cellar had a beam along its N wall, which was directly in line with the beam in the ground floor ceiling. This was thought to be the lower member of the ground floor stud and panel partition. The ends of the stone treads of the original cellar stair could be seen embedded in the later walling of the rear wall of this cellar, behind the beam. The W cellar had a semi circular profile to its SW corner **(Figure 6.70)**. A low stone bench followed the profile of the S and W walls of this room.

There was a detached 11/2 storey stone building behind the rear wing of the main house. This was very derelict in 1980 and had no remaining roof structure. However, it did have a 5-light stone mullion window in its front wall **(Figure 6.71)** of the same detail as in the main house and this looked to be in its original setting. Internally, it had a large ground floor hearth **(Figure 6.72)**, with stone jambs (built of stone blocks) and a stone lintel. There were no chamfers or stops around the hearth opening. There were 2 beams (of different dates), both fairly rough in nature, but without good chamfers. The wall thickness was only 18 inches, which was less than that of the main house. It had been extended to the N, as indicated by a change in the line of the front wall and there was a blocked doorway with a 19thC segmented stone lintel. The purpose of this building was not identified with certainty. The detail of the 5-light window suggests a similar date to that of the main house and it also suggests a good amount of light was required within. But the construction was poorer and the internal detail was rougher than in the main house. Suggestions for its original use include an external kitchen or lower status domestic accommodation. A weaving shed is also a possibility, but in this case the hearth would have to be a later addition.

No. 57 was a good quality house, with 3 rooms on each floor with good cellars and attics. It may have been built by a successful clothier or merchant. Its detail suggests it was constructed sometime around the mid/late 17th C. No detail of the original front wall was found and therefore it cannot be known whether it was built as a house alone or in combination with some commercial use. However, the original entrance in to the W gable end, may indicate a private entrance here, with perhaps any entrance in the street front required for commercial purposes. The front elevation was remodelled in the early 19th C to keep up with the latest fashions, the changes included sash windows with shutters and a proper second floor. The roof pitch was reduced by modifying the original one and a parapet with flanking urns was built. An extra wing was added at the back. The internal changes included the stair and more minor changes, but much of the original detail was left or hidden beneath new lath and plasterwork. In the 1980's the W end of the ground floor of the front elevation had a good 19th C stone shop front, whereas the E end contained the entrance to private accommodation. The shop front was lost during the conversion work, but it seems to have been used as the model for the new shop front added to the more sympathetic conversion of No. 58 High St. The whole of the detail of the ground floor was swept away during the 1980's conversion, so that none of the detail described here now remains. This is a pity as the detail was a rare survival and its retention would have enhanced the character of the High Street.

Fisher notes that in the early 19th C, No. 57 belonged to a Mr Thomas Hughes, medical practitioner. He notes that this and the adjoining building were rebuilt by Mr Hughes, sometime before his death in 1813. The recent evidence shows that it was only the front and party wall with the adjoining building that were rebuilt and the inner rear wing was added. Much of the earlier building was retained, but hidden under new plasterwork.

No. 50 High Street

No. 50 is another 17th C building and this has retained some of its original gabled dormers. It stands on the corner between the High Street and Church Street **(Figure 6.73)**. The building was inspected on two occasions. The first was before work had commenced on the refurbishment of the building in the mid 1980's. The second was during the building work and this provided the opportunity to see the structure of the building in more detail, although some of the early detail seen on the previous visit had been removed.

From the outside, an indication of its date of building is given by the presence of the 'owl' windows in the apices of the gabled dormers. These are not found in buildings before the late 17th C. It seems therefore that this house dates from the end of that century. The building has been altered, but indications remained of its original form. Originally, it had two gabled dormers facing Church St **(Figure 6.74)**. One remains as a gabled dormer and this has some good 17th stone window frames and an early blocked doorway **(Figure 6.75)**. The first floor and attic frames have recessed, plain chamfered surrounds (3-light on the first floor and 2-light in the attic gable). The ground floor window has a three mullion posts and a transom (in the upper part of the frame), giving a total of six lights. It has plain chamfered surround. It is an impressive looking window. This gabled dormer is matched by one at the rear of the building. There is a ragged building line separating this part from the more regular (and vertical) stonework of the chimney gable that is now seen immediately on entering Church St. This rebuilt section of wall must have replaced an original gabled dormer in this position. One gabled dormer remains facing the High St and this retains 17th C windows at the attic level, but the first floor windows are replaced by a pair of late 19th C sash windows. The ground floor walling is absent and there is a modern shop front. From 1854 until 1970, this building was the Bedford Arms Inn and a photograph of around 1910 **(Figure 6.76)** shows a typical Edwardian image with acid etched glass, showing the name of the Stroud Brewery Company, on the ground floor windows. The adjacent property, No. 49 High St, is a typical late 19th C building **(Figure 6.77)**. However, evidence within No. 50 shows that it originally extended further up the High St, onto the site of No. 49 and it is plausible that there was at least one more gabled dormer facing the High St. Originally, this must have been an important looking building with two gabled dormers on each of the High St and Church St frontages. Each of the arms of the building was one room deep.

Internally, the building has been altered on many occasions. No detail was visible on the ground floor apart from the location of the ceiling support beams and a large blocked hearth in the N gable end in Church St. Next to this hearth, there was a wood winder stair that ascended to the first and attic levels **(Figure 6.78)**. There was also a first floor hearth sharing the same chimneystack **(Figure 6.79)**. This had dressed stone jambs (with approx 50mm chamfers and scroll stops), a wood lintel (with an approx 50 mm chamfer and no stops) and a square hearth area. The beam structure was the same on both the ground and first floor ceilings. There was a cross beam set roughly between the two gables facing Church St: the beam on the first floor, at least, had a groove in the soffit, which shows the former presence of a stud and panel partition beneath it. The ground floor beam detail was not visible. There were two axial (i.e. parallel to the street) beams/floor passing to the N of the ground and first floor cross beams to terminate in the N gable end of the building. A single axial beam/floor passed to the S of the cross-beam. The axial beams on the first floor had chamfers that were 60mm wide with scroll stops. The beams over the former partition were narrower and had narrower chamfers than on the floor support beams. Where visible, the floor joists were jointed into the side of the beam and pegged in place. The joist ends and their accompanying mortice on the beam were numbered. The beam detail is consistent with a late 17th C origin. The first floor room of the N end of the building in Church St retained a good 6-panel door and a window seat with a panelled back and sides **(Figure 6.80)**.

When first visited, there was an early partition remaining in the attic **(Figure 6.81)**. It was sited

Chapter 6

under an extended collar truss and was of lath and plaster construction. The upright studs of the wall lodged in cutouts in the underside of the truss. The wall plaster was continuous on the inside of the room, whereas on the outside it was plastered between the studs. Some economy in the use of laths is evident in this, as only one side of the studs is covered by laths in this form of construction. The door through the partition was plank and ledge, with a wooden latch **(Figure 6.82)**. Its outside face had a recessed central plank. Both wall and door were removed during the refurbishment. The roof structure at the S end was of the extended collar type, without principal rafters: the structure was exposed during renovation work **(Figure 6.83)**. The collars had chamfers and draw stops set off the chamfer. The W end of the extended collars were bedded in the chimney dormer facing Church St **(Figure 6.84)**, however the E ends were jointed into an 'A' frame truss aligned N-S **(Figure 6.85)**. The form of the joint was a double mortice and tenon joint **(Figure 6.86)**. The 'A' frame truss provides a key piece of evidence on the history of the building. It is now part of the party wall between Nos 50 and 49 High St, but, it is an intermediate truss and would not be sited at the end of a building. Its presence shows that No. 50 used to extend further up the High St. It was fully exposed during the building work and its detail was recorded. The collar was morticed into the underside of the principals. The area above the collar was infilled with lath and plaster fixed to vertical studs (this looked original). The side of the collar that faced into No. 49 had cut-outs to accept floor joists. The principal rafters were jointed to a tie beam, beneath this, vertical studs were visible, which formed the first floor party wall between the two buildings **(Figure 6.87)**. The studs were of the same character as others seen in the attic of No. 50 and therefore were thought to be an early internal partition of the original building. There were trenches for purlins on the backs of the principal pair. The angles of the diagonal joint at the apex of the truss showed there was mortice and tenon joint in this position. The ridge lodged in a notch at the apex of the truss. The E face of the tie beam, i.e. that facing into the later building, had a near central lodging for an axial beam **(Figure 6.88)**. No beam remained and the level did not correspond with the ceiling level of the later building and therefore must indicate the heights of the earlier building on the site, i.e. they were at the same level as in No 50. Returning to the roof structure of No. 50, there was only one central extended collar that ran between front and rear gabled dormers at the N end of the building (in Church St) **(Figure 6.89)**. This was original. There were two rows of purlins on the roof slopes, some of these were thought to be re-used timbers.

There was a cellar beneath the High St end of the building. This was stone lined and had a wide arch in its rear (N facing) wall **(Figure 6.90)**. It is possible that there is a further blocked/filled in cellar behind this wall. There was a large ceiling beam, with an approx 50 mm chamfer and scroll stops. The joists were original and lodged in cutouts in the top of the beam. The beam and joist detail show that the cellar is original. There was a low shelf (in concrete) with angled semi-circular depressions to support barrels around two of the walls. This presumably remains from the time of the Bedford Arms Inn. Walls and ceiling timbers had been limewashed.

No. 50 is a good stone building in the 17th C vernacular style, although rather altered on the ground floor, it does retain some original period detail. The presence of owl windows, the style of the roof structure and the scroll stops on the beams all point to an origin fairly late in the century. There was no evidence of an earlier building on the site.

Church Court (formerly Rodney House) in Church Street

It seems that Church Street developed in the 17th C. Towards its N end is Church Court (formerly Rodney House, then the vicarage) **(Figure 6.91)**. The earliest part is thought to have been built in 1635, by the Webb family. This date is given on a datestone above the current entrance porch, in the angle between the main range and the S projecting wing. It is plausible that this is the original building date of the house. However, the datestone is not in its original position, as the porch dates from the 19th C. The house consists of a main range facing Church St and wings that pass S towards the street and backwards to the N. The wings are sited to the front and rear of the W end of the main range. There are gabled dormers to the front and rear of each elevation of each part. The windows are all stone mullions and are mostly of the same form, with recessed surrounds with plain chamfers. Many of the windows are in very good condition and must have been replaced during sympathetic building work. The evidence shows that the present house has developed in several phases, all in the 17th C. The S end of the wing (passing forwards towards Church St) has owl windows in the apices of the E and W facing gabled dormers, which show a late 17th C date for these parts. No owl windows are present in the front or rear gabled dormers of the main range, so this seems to be the earlier part (1635). Facing Church St, the main range has 4-, 3- and 2-light stone window frames on the ground, first and attic levels of the E gabled dormer. The stonework of this gabled dormer has some jumper stones, which are not usually seen in 17th C work, but are common in 18th C work and later. So, this wall may have been repaired fairly extensively in the 18th or 19th C. There is a centrally placed former front door between the gabled dormers. This has a hollow chamfer to the stone frame, but the stonework does not look original. The W gabled dormer (next to the S projecting wing) has 2-light stone frames at each level and the stonework has regular courses (without jumper stones) and there is no sign of any disturbance. There are chimneystacks, for gable end hearths, projecting through the ridge of the roof at the E and near the W end of the main range (at the junction with the wing). From Church St, this part seems to be of one build (although partly rebuilt). There is also a large stack projecting through the roof of the N projecting part of what appears to be the cross range from Church St. This stack is not in line with the ridge of the roof of the main range. The main range of the house has large 'A' frame roof trusses that are placed to each side of the gabled dormers (i.e. 4 trusses). They are not of the extended collar truss type (as might have been expected), but are of the conventional form and sit on tie beams in the first floor ceiling. They have normal collars, which are jointed to the underside of each principal.

The wings can also be viewed from the churchyard and this gives further evidence on the development of the house **(Figure 6.92)**. This elevation shows 3 gabled dormers. Both outer dormers have the owl windows, whereas the central dormer is blank. Importantly, a building line is showing between the N side of the part containing the central dormer and the N projecting wing. This clearly shows that the wing is an addition and the owl windows give a date for this in the late 17th C. The S projecting wing is also likely to be an addition, but the building line was not obvious from a distance. It can also be seen that the large chimney-stack, already noted, is structurally part of the central range and is in line with the back of the main range. In reality, the central gabled dormer is the modified gable end of the original house, which originally had 3 gabled dormers facing S onto Church St, with 2 gabled dormers and a chimney gable facing N. The W front gabled dormer was hidden when the S facing wing was built, and the chimney gable was hidden when the N wing was built. Both projecting wings have roof structures of the extended collar truss type, but without principal rafters. The central gabled dormer (modified or rebuilt from the original gable end) has a half extended collar: the collar extends to the gabled dormer, but the rear part of the truss is a part of a conventional 'A' frame. Internally, this part of the building has surviving square panel timber framed partition walls **(Figure 6.93)** and a good 18th C stair **(Figure 6.94)**. The redundant joist lodgings in the adjoining beam show that the stair is a later addition.

This is the only 17th C house which originally had three gabled dormers in the town and was

Chapter 6

therefore an important house.

Webb's Almshouses in Church Street (demolished)

There used to be a group of mid 17th C cottages on the edge of the Church St car park and built directly next to the street. These were known as Webb's Almshouses **(Figure 6.95)** and were demolished in the late 1940's. They consisted of a pair of single storey stone houses with gabled dormers. Each had been sub-divided over the years. There were four gabled dormers and each contained a 2-light stone mullion window, with a recessed plain chamfered surround and a dripmould. There were 3-light windows of the same form on the ground floor. There were two doorways, sited between each pair of dormers. Each had a stone doorframe with a flattened semi circular arch top and a flat chamfer to the surround (approx. 100mm wide). A continuous dripmould passed over the ground floor windows and doorways. The house existed by 1642, as in that year, the building was assigned as part of an endowment for a charity school, by Thomas Webb. It is thought that these houses are examples of what some of the earlier 17th C smaller houses of the town were like. Unfortunately, no examples remain, but there is evidence others: in some gable end walls of (now) 2-storey houses, the rooflines of single storey houses can be seen.

No. 46 High Street

Back in the High St, on the N side and near the Cross, is No. 46, which is another 17th C building (probably late) **(Figure 6.96)**. The ground floor has been divided into two shops for many years. The E shop is generally known as Mrs Barsby's, after the owner of a sweet shop, who occupied this shop for many years. It is a tall building, with 3 floors and attics. It retains what appears to be a late Georgian shopfront, but may be of more recent origin. The first floor windows of the front elevation have been changed and now have a 19th C character, although traces of an original stone frame, with rebated surrounds and a dripmould can be seen on the first floor above the oriel window. The second floor windows are 19th C in character and there is no evidence for early frames. The original windows (single light with rebated surround) remain at the apex of the gabled dormers. There is much machine cut stonework in the front elevation (which must be of 19th C origin or later). It is plausible that the gabled dormers have been rebuilt in the 19th C, to raise their height and generate a new second floor. The earlier single light windows were re-used to provide light for the new attic. Inside, there is a large hearth in the gable end wall of the E shop. This has a wood lintel and stone jambs. Upstairs, in the front room of the first floor, there is a cupboard with a ventilation grill in the upper part of the doorframe. These features must remain from the 17th C building.

There were other 17th C buildings in the High Street, which have either been demolished or completely disguised by later building changes. For instance, a photo taken around 1910 shows the building adjacent to No. 26 High St, has a first floor stone mullion window with dripmould.

At the end of this century, when looking down from the Cross, the High Street would have appeared as a street of many gables. On the S, there were timber framed gable ends of the 16th C buildings and on the N, a succession of houses with gabled dormers in the typical 17th C Cotswold style. This was the commercial heart of the town that served an expanding population of workers associated with the cloth industry. Some of these will have lived in courts of poor quality housing behind the street. However, it seems that in the 17th C the land in this part of the town became saturated with buildings, so that the town began to expand up the hill in the area of the Stroud fields. This 'new' area of development is now known as the 'Top of the Town' and the mainly domestic buildings of this part are described later on in this Chapter.

18TH C BUILDINGS IN THE HIGH STREET

The development of the street as the commercial hub of the town continued in the 18th C, with changes to some of the earlier buildings on the S side and new substantial buildings on the N side. This reflects the continuing development of the local cloth trade and the resulting population increase. The style of the 18th C buildings show some marked differences to those of the 17th C. These are reviewed at the end of Chapter 4. The changes to some of the earlier buildings have already been noted. It generally involved the realignment of the street end of the building, so that it appeared parallel to the street and only narrow (or no) alleys through to the rear buildings. These changes occurred from the early 18th C onwards and a guide to the date of the change can be indicated by the form of the windows in the upper part of the new front façades. Although, beware, these 'new' windows may have been subsequently replaced. In No. 33 High St, the stone architraves, with a bull-nose profile, that surround the sash windows of the front elevation are typical of very early 18th C work in Stroud. Several examples have been noted in other buildings in the area. Their date is consistent with documentary evidence for a change in ownership of No. 33 in the first years of the 18th C and it seems that the building was upgraded by the new owner. New building also occurred in the 18th C, with the main developments being on the N side of the street. Fisher notes that some of the buildings added to the N side of the street replaced earlier buildings that projected into the street.

Corn Exchange Building (demolished)

At the Cross, there was a fine early 18th C building **(Figure 6.97)** that filled the site now occupied by the modern building that was, until recently, Lewis's and Co, an electrical store, together with the space beside it, that was created to provide room for a proposed ring road in the 1970's. This rather ugly 1970's development replaced what would now be regarded as one of the most valued 18th C buildings in Stroud. It was built some time around the mid 18th C as 2 houses. Behind it stood the old White Hart Inn, which was redeveloped as houses and a corn exchange in the 1860's. The whole then became known as the Exchange Buildings **(Figure 6.98)**. As such it was an important part of the commercial activities of Stroud in the 19th C. By the early 20th C, the group of buildings were regarded as slums. Photos taken in the late 1960's show that the front façade had been reinforced with timber shoring. The building bordering the Cross was three storeys tall, with attics. The ground floor had a central entrance, which gave access to the upper floors. There was a shop on either side of the entrance door. The W shop was occupied by Lewis and Co. The façade was smooth rendered and the edges of the building had rusticated quoin stones, which were well dressed and regular, with chamfered edges. These could have been formed in the render. Similar ones can still be seen on No. 33 opposite. There were rows of six, multi pane sash windows on the first and second floors. These had stone architraves and projecting keystones of the same style as on No. 33. A projecting eaves cornice is noted across the front of the building. Another building with similar detail existed on the site of Nos. 47-48 High St, which must have been demolished early in the 20th C, to allow the present buildings to be constructed.

25/26 Church Street

Along Church St, there is a building **(Figure 6.99)** with a datestone, giving the year 1735, which although looking reset, is consistent with the style of the façade. The ground floor is the shop front for

Chapter 6

the Sunshine Health Food store. There are 4 multi pane sash windows on the first floor. These have dressed stone architraves that sit slightly proud of the stonework of the wall, with projecting keystones. The slightly proud setting of the architraves indicates that the wall was originally rendered. The profile of the window surrounds is different to those noted at the Cross. The surround has a square bead to its outer edge. The roof has an overhanging coved eaves cornice. There are no projecting quoin stones. However, these may have been originally formed in the render of the front façade.

15 High Street

No.15 High St (formerly Smith and Lee's, ironmongers, closed in 1994) **(Figure 6.100)** is another early/mid 18th C building. It is recorded as being an ironmonger's (in various ownerships), since the mid 19th C **(Figure 6.101)**. The internal detail shows it was built with the ground floor intended for commercial premises and living accommodation on the first and attic floors. There is also evidence that the cellar had formed part of the domestic accommodation. In 2004, it was in a sad state of repair, with no significant maintenance having been carried out for many years. Since its purchase by the present owner, it was being allowed to become derelict. Currently, the Stroud District Council is taking action to prevent further decay. Let's hope they are successful in saving this building.

It is thought to have been built in the early 1720's, as a deed of 1725 refers to it as being newly erected. It is built in brick, with stone dressings and is of a double pile construction, with an M shaped roof. The front and rear elevations have similar detail. The ground floor frontage has been removed to accommodate the shop front. The present shop front is thought to have originated in the 19th C. The ground floor rear wall has also been removed to create a long retail space that extends into what must have been the garden and orchard of the original house. The first floor elevations each have a row of 3 sash windows, with moulded stone architraves, with projecting keystones and bullnose cills. On the front, the design is more complex and the architraves are shouldered at the top and bottom. The sash windows are 19th C in origin and are without glazing bars. The rear windows also have architraves, which are without shoulders and are similar to those seen in the other buildings of this period. However, sash windows to the rear have been removed and odd frames are installed. The front and rear upper walls are smooth rendered and have projecting quoins, which are of the same style as on the demolished Corn Exchange. The building does not have an eaves cornice, but this seems to have been removed, when the roof was relaid. A photo taken in the early 20th C shows that a cornice was present then. Inside, there is a fine open well stair **(Figures 6.102 and 103)** leading from the ground floor to the first floor and then up to the attic. This has fluted balusters and a handrail that is ramped up to the newel posts. It is somewhat awkwardly fitted in places, but clearly intended to impress and is thought to have been installed, as a secondhand stair in the 19th C. The initial ground floor flight of this stair has been removed and replaced with a narrower stair that maximises the shop space. The remaining stair is intact, although somewhat distorted. It enters the attic floor in the central part, between the 2 parallel front and rear roofs. The joining section of roof is modified and this may be associated with the insertion of this stair. The internal ground floor walls are clad and have not been fully inspected, however, there is no evidence of a ground floor hearth. This suggests a commercial use here. The cellar has a blocked fireplace, which formerly contained a 19th C kitchen range, indicating that this was part of the domestic accommodation. The first floor landing contains 3 doorways with Georgian wood panels over the doorheads **(Figure 6.104)**. This is thought to be the main living area, but all fireplace surrounds and other detail have been removed and the hearths blocked. The upper floors of the building had been used as storage and offices for many years and the first floor rooms were sub divided. It is considered that originally, there were large rooms to the front and back of this floor. The attic floor was again used most recently for storage. However, two fireplaces remain **(Figures 6.105 and 106)**, one with a cast iron surround and the other with a marble effect surround. Both have a mid 19th C character. One retains a fabric apron across the front of the mantle shelf, showing the former domestic use of these rooms. There were also some two panel doors remaining on the 2nd floor **(Figure 6.107)**.

Bank House

This is the lowest house on the N side of the High Street **(Figure 6.108)**. It is constructed in brick, with stone dressings and dates from the early part of the 18th C. It is thought to have been built by Mr Adderley (a Baker), who also had No. 15 built. They share similar details, although Bank House is larger. In the 19th C, it belonged to the Gloucestershire Banking Company, hence the name, and they had their premises in the adjoining building. It has 5 ground floor and 6 first floor sash windows, all with stone architraves with a bull-nose profile and projecting keystones. The front entrance is offset and has a good porch in the Tuscan style. There is an intermediate plat band and a moulded eaves cornice. There is a tall parapet above the cornice and a mansard roof. These look out of balance with the façade and are probably a modification of the original roof. The brick of the façade is roughcast, but the brick construction is indicated by the thickness of the wall.

No. 55 High Street

No. 55 High Street is a good quality 18th C building, which is known to have been built in 1782, by William Knight (known as Banker Knight), who lived at Gannicox. It is also known that it replaced an earlier building, which projected further into the street, but nothing more is known about this. The first tenant was a Samuel Spencer, who was a grocer. After his death and several more tenants, it was leased to James Withey, who was a Chemist. He purchased the house in 1816. It stayed in the ownership of the Withey family until 1922 **(Figure 6.109)**, by this time it had become one of the more important Grocer's shops in the town. It was then sold to the International Tea Company Stores and it continued in use as a grocery shop until the 1970's. The building was purchased by The Stroud Preservation Trust for restoration in 1984 **(Figures 6.110 and 111)**. The upper floors had been unused for many years and the ground floor had an insensitive dominating shop front. The last tenant had been Robb's Electrical Shop. The ground floor was a large retail space, with a rear room, and partial infilled cellars beneath. There was no internal connection with the upper floors, which were reached via an external wood ladder and a fire exit. The upper floors had been leased to the adjoining drapers (Bell and Co.) in the 1930's. They had not used the second floor, and it had not been redecorated from the time of the Withey's. The association of the first floor with Bell and Co. ceased many years ago and the connection through to the adjoining shop was blocked. The second floor had been untouched for many years and retained its original access stair, doors and other fixtures **(Figures 112, 113 and 114)**. One room was full (to a depth of over 0.3m) with invoices and bills dating back to the late 19thC. This was an unexpected find, as the invoices were from many local companies and mills and the letterheads had steel plate engravings of their premises. The invoices were lent to the Stroud Local History Society for sorting and are still in their care. The Stroud Preservation Trust besides restoring the main building, also created Withey's Yard utilising some of the buildings that had filled the rear garden over the years. It was named after Withey's, the Chemists, who had occupied the whole site for many years.

The front elevation has much of the detail expected of a mid/late 18th C building. It is built of

Chapter 6

good quality ashlar stone, with a short return in stone to the side walls. The main part of the side walls is constructed in brick (now rendered). The W side return had a narrow sash window on the first floor, which looks down the High Street. There is a parapet and a central pediment, with a pair of brackets beneath it. The windows were fully developed wood sash windows with plain ashlar surrounds and stone cills. There are 2 upper floors, with the 3 second floor windows being modest in proportion compared with those of the first floor. It is a symmetrical façade. The sidewalls are party with the adjacent buildings and contain no further window openings. There is a projecting rear wing, in brick, that has been further extended to the N. The rear elevation was rather plain, but did retain some original wood window frames. One consisted of 3-lights, separated by wood mullions, with ovolo mouldings. The central light consisted of an opening light in iron, on pin hinges and closed by a turnbuckle handle and opened on a quadrant. The lights were leaded, with small square panes (18/light) and these were fixed to 6 horizontal iron bars/light.

Internally, the ground floor of the front part was one retail space in 1984, no hearths were found in this area during the restoration and hence, it seems to have been built as a commercial space. Evidence was also found for a former alley that passed from the High Street, through to the rear wing and garden. This was recreated during the restoration in the mid 1980's and now forms the entry to Withey's yard. The ground floor of the rear wing contained a wide hearth, with a stone lintel in three parts, jambs and a fireback that were mainly built of brick **(Figure 6.115)**. The presence of this hearth suggests a domestic use for the wing. The front part of the first floor was again one large redundant retail space in 1984, but marks in the ceiling plaster showed that it was formerly divided into 4 spaces, thought to be 3 rooms and a landing. This layout was also indicated by the presence of only 3 hearths. Two of the hearths retained rather plain stone surrounds and cast iron hob grates **(Figures 6.116, 117)**. Both surrounds had the same detail, but the hob grates were different and these were not thought to be of the same date. The earlier grate had two separate side plates, cast with an ogee outline to the side next to the hearth and a pierced apron joining the side plates across the front of the hearth. This style of hob grate is usually dated to the late 18th/early 19th C. The second grate had separate rectangular sidepieces, without decoration and straight grate bars and a plain apron. This style is usually dated to the early to mid 19th C. The rather plain detail of these hearths suggests they were in rooms that lacked any ostentation. The sash windows in the front elevation had window seats and plain architraves, which were very similar to those on the stone hearth surrounds **(Figure 6.118)**. The inside face of the exterior walls were lined in brick. There were two cased ceiling beams (subsequently shown to have no chamfers or stops), which were parallel to the High St. The stair to the second floor **(Figure 6.119)** was of the closed string type, had plain, square balusters, a simple turned newel post and a plain moulded handrail. This style of stair is seen in early 19th C houses. It is likely that the stair from the ground floor was sited beneath this stair. The second floor retained its original divisions and these were constructed of timber studs with lath and plaster. There was a flattened arch (in plaster) over the way through from the rear wing to the front part. This was divided into four rooms with a narrow central corridor. There were several original two panel doors with H-L hinges. The two front rooms had hearths with plain slab surrounds and narrow hob grates. These were fairly decorative, with apron detail in the Rococo style and this dates them to sometime near the mid 19th C. The ceiling beams (also the tie beams of the roof trusses) were plain and cased in plaster.

The roof space had never been used for accommodation. The roof was not steeply pitched and was 3 bays long **(Figure 6.120)**. It contained 2 main trusses, each consisted of a pair of principal rafters and tie beam, with a shouldered king post strengthened by a pair of struts, which ran from near the base of the king post to the underside of each principal. The top of the king post had a notch to retain the ridge piece, with the principals being jointed (mortice and tenon) to either side of the top of the post. There were 3 rows of butt purlins per roof slope. The purlins were joined by fish plates at the principal junction. The ceiling joists lodged in cut-outs in the top of the tie beam. The style of the roof with a king post goes back to medieval times, this one, with its regular cut timbers must date from the building of No. 55 in the late 18th C.

There were cellars under the whole of the building, entered from a stair in the rear wing. The rear section consisted of a brick vault on low stonewalls. A vaulted passage, with 2 small side rooms, led to the cellar under the front range, which had a stone flag floor and a modern ceiling.

No. 58 High Street

According to Fisher, No.58 was built around the year 1795, by the father of Mr Mills, the Grocer. He lived there until his death in 1827. It was built on the site of a blacksmith's workshop. The rear part of the 1795 building retains elements of an earlier structure, which may be part of the blacksmith's premises. In 1984, that section continued to the N as a row of what were formerly cottages, of different dates, to a brick built warehouse that borders Bank Gardens (this is now converted to accommodation). The cottages were demolished in the mid 1980's and are described separately. In the early 1980's Nos 58-62 High St belonged to Milwards (the shoe retailers) and attempts were made to get planning permission to demolish all of these buildings and re-develop the site. This caused much angst in Stroud and an action group physically prevented the progress of the demolition and fought a successful High Court action to ensure the retention of the buildings. The buildings were subsequently extensively refurbished.

The building is aligned roughly N-S and presents an ashlar façade to the High Street **(Figure 6.121)**. The present ground floor shop front was installed during the refurbishment and copies that formerly on No. 57. On the first floor there is a good Venetian window, the upper part of the window also provides light to the attic space. There is a near central pediment and flanking parapets that hide the roof, which is aligned at right angles to the front. The plan of the building is wedge shaped, with the E wall running back at an angle, whereas the W wall is at right angles to the front. Presumably, the E wall marks an existing property boundary or right of way and this could not be changed. The E wall is built of brick that merges into the stone of the rear walls of the earlier buildings. There were no windows in this side of the building. At the rear, the main range stepped down to the earlier buildings. The ground floor was one large retail space in the early 1980's. There were 4 ceiling beams, these were plastered, but an inspection showed that they were without chamfers and stops. No wall detail could be seen, as they were clad in timber shelves to hold the stock of shoes. The first floor was simple in its detail and only seemed to have one fireplace. This was in the front room, overlooking the street. The ceiling of this room had an acanthus leaf cornice and the ceiling beam (also tie beam of roof truss) was contained within the floor space. The floor joist ends were half dovetail shaped and were placed in similar shaped lodgings in the top of the beam **(Figure 6.122)**. The door had 6-panels and in a style typical of the late 18th/early 19th C. Perhaps this was the office of the owner? In the late 18th C, beams were generally hidden under a layer of plaster or in higher status rooms, contained within the floor space. There were 2 further tie beams and these were above the N and S partition walls that formed the second, first floor room. This did not have any windows, but there was a blocked way through to No. 59. The adjoining building was bought by Messrs Mills and Co, in 1854, to expand their grocery business. The tie beams were at right angles to the W wall. There was a corridor passing N along the first floor, past the second room to a plastered arch, there were then steps down to the lower, rear range. The attics were reached via a stair from the rear range. There were no signs of there ever hav-

CHAPTER 6

ing been stairs in the front part. The attic was 4 bays long (i.e.3 sets of trusses) **(Figures 6. 123 and 124)**. Each truss was comprised of a wide 'A' frame of moderate pitch, with tie beam and collar. The morticed collars were placed fairly high, under the upper row of purlins. The apex of the truss was formed by a diagonal, pegged mortice and tenon joint. There were ridge boards, supported on yolks nailed to the faces of the apices of the trusses. There were joists nailed to the top side of the upper purlins and the presence of nail holes in the soffit of these and in the rafters, showed that the whole roof space had been fitted with laths and plastered. There were no signs of any partition walls and the space is large. Presumably, this was storage and workspace for the shop.

The link between the earlier rear buildings and the front range of 1795 could be seen in the attic. The upper section of the N gable end wall of the 1795 building was constructed of timber studs with lath and plaster infill. This rose from a truss, which was part of the roof structure of the lower, rear range of buildings **(Figure 6.125)**. There was a brick wall, approximately 1.5 m in from the N wall, which had been raised on the gable end wall of the rear building. It was clear that the front range of No. 58 extended N over the end bay of the first building of the rear range.

Buildings to the rear of 58 High Street

These were demolished during the regeneration of the site. They consisted of a low, row of buildings of 2 storeys with attics **(Figure 6.126)**. The roofline and structures varied and a division into 3 separate cottages was evident (although this configuration had resulted by the modification of earlier cottages). Their rear walls bordered the alley between Nos 57 and 58. This alley stretched from the High St to the churchyard and seems to be an historic right of way. For ease of discussion, they are numbered buildings 1,2 and 3 moving N along the row. The row was terminated by the large late 19th C brick built warehouse (which was retained) **(Figure 6.127)**. Building No. 1 was 3 bays long with the first bay contained within the 1795 building and the second pair of bays projected to the N **(Figure 6.128)**. There were 2 roof trusses, with the first supporting the upper part of the gable end of the 1795 building. There was originally a single row of butt purlins on each roof slope, with those in the third bay resting on the collar (cut and re-supported) of the single truss, at the S end of the attic of the roof of building 2. The purlins were joined across the back of the principals using a fishplate joint. The joint at the apex of each truss was a diagonal, pegged, mortice and tenon. The trusses sat on low walls and there were no tie beams or collars. The timbers had sawn faces with rough edges. This building was incorporated into the High Street building and provided the stair access to the first and attic levels of both parts of the building. Building 1 was probably built some time in the last half of the 18th C. Building 2 was one bay long. The rear wall and N gable end wall were built of Cotswold stone. The north gable end contained a flue for a ground floor hearth. The side of the gable end wall showed in the front wall, where it was sandwiched between the brick front walls of Buildings 2 and 3. The gable end was structurally part of Building 2 and it was thought that the building had been refronted in brick, possibly when Building 1 was constructed. The brickwork may have replaced a timber framed front wall (there was one post left in the wall at the junction of the street and back range). The roof was slightly taller than that of Building 1, with the single truss forming the junction between the two buildings **(Figure 6.129)** . There were 2 rows of purlins on each roof slope: the upper set were butt purlins, the lower set were nailed in place and were therefore additions. There was a diagonal joint at the apex of the truss, the opposite face of each principal was halved and the two pegged together. The feet of the principals were jointed into a tie beam. The collar (nailed to the face of the principals had been cut to allow passage through the attics of the buildings. The nature of this junction suggested that part of Building 2 had been partly demolished to enable the construction of Building 1. Further confirmatory evidence for this was found in the stone lined cellar, which existed under both Building 2 and part of Building 1 **(Figure 6.130)**. The cellar must mark the footprint of the original Building 2. The detail of the roof joints could indicate that this was built some time in the 17th C, although further study was not possible to confirm this (it was demolished soon after this study was made). Building 3 was three bays long and had a rubble stone rear wall and a brick front wall. The building lines at either end of the rear wall showed that it had been built between the existing Building 2 and another building to the N. The latter had been deposed by the late 19th C warehouse. The stone gable end wall of Building 2 separated the attics of the two buildings and the good (external) stone was facing into the attic of Building 3, as would be expected for a former outside wall. There were two trusses within the roof space, which were more steeply pitched than the existing roof **(Figure 6.131)**. Their angle suggested they originally served a 1 or 11/2 storey building. However, the sections below the first floor ceiling had been removed, presumably when the wall plate was raised to create the existing form of the building, and the remaining trusses reinforced with much new timber. The truss apex joints were of the face halved type and the original purlins (removed and replaced by ones for the later roof) were trenched into the back of the principal. The trenches appeared low down in the existing form of the roof. However, in the original steeper and longer roof slope, there were probably 2 sets of purlins and it was the trenches of the upper set that survived. The detail of the roof was indicative of a 17th C origin or earlier. The relation with Building 2 was not resolved: either Building 3 had been added between 2 existing buildings or else it had been partly demolished when the flanking buildings were constructed. At the time of the inspection, Buildings 1-3 and the front range were linked internally at their ground floor levels, suggesting they had become storerooms for the shop. However, their detail suggests they were separate small dwellings in the 19th C (as indicated by the brickwork and simple sash windows of their front walls). It was also clear that this form of the row of cottages had been derived from earlier buildings (of different ages), which had survived since at least the 17th C. It seems that these buildings were the remains of some of the early small cottages of the town, built at a time when the population was increasing to meet the needs of an expanding cloth industry. Not many of these small cottages have survived to the present day.

19TH C BUILDINGS IN THE HIGH STREET

The vernacular period ended in this century. The end began in the previous century with the introduction of features, which can be regarded as 'national' in character and the changes continued over the next 100 years. Sash windows are the most obvious 'national' example and their use began early in the 18th C: by the early 19th C they had become the norm for any building of importance in the town and for houses of traders and merchants. The widespread use of pitch pine for internal fittings and fixtures, such as architraves and doors and the use of Welsh slate for roofs can also be regarded as other examples of the trend for using nationally available materials.

There was much building activity in the town during the 19th C, not only in the existing streets, but also in new areas of development. By an act of 1814, a new turnpike road was enabled, that linked Stroud and the villages along the valley bottom to Chalford with the Cirencester turnpike road. This was built by 1818. This stimulated much development on the good building land bordering the new road (now London Road) and on the land between the existing town and the new road. Union St, John St, George St, Bedford St, Russell St, Bath Terrace and Bath Place were all developed in this active period: the town became greatly enlarged.

There are some good 19th C buildings in the High Street, particularly in the Shambles and lower

Chapter 6

down on the N side of the street. The High Street frontage probably became fully developed by the 18th C, so the 19th C buildings stand on the sites of earlier buildings **(Figure 6.132)**. Fisher makes useful observations on the redevelopment of certain of the buildings and some of his comments are included in the following text. All of the 19th C buildings share some features in the national style, including the use of multi pane sash windows, without moulded stone architraves and the use of imported pitch pine for doors and other fixtures. The structural timbers are also likely to be machine-cut imported wood. They are all ashlar faced with the local Cotswold stone, but without pronounced quoins. There are a greater number of 19th C buildings on the N side of the High Street. These include Nos 52-53 (between Church St and the entrance to the Shambles), the buildings along the W side of the Shambles and Nos 59-62. No. 52 extends backwards for some distance and together with the rear of the Market House forms the W side of Church St. No. 52 seems to be an 18th C building that was refronted in the early 19th C. Fisher states that No. 53 was built in 1846 on the site of an earlier property. The earlier building and one on the W side of the Shambles were linked at first floor level, so that the Shambles was entered through a narrow entrance beneath. The entrance was widened when No.53 was built and the upper floor linking room demolished. In the Shambles, the Church Rooms, formerly the Corn Hall was commissioned by the Feoffees before the mid 19th C. The Corn Exchange moved here from the Cross at that time. The adjoining building was the Corn Hall Hotel, formerly called the Butchers Arms. Until the mid 19th C, meat and butter were sold at the regular markets in the Shambles (also then known as the Pitching). The stalls, which line the W side of the market place were erected in 1847 **(Figure 6.133)**.

Lower down on the N side of the High St are Nos 59-62 **(Figure 6.134)**. These were saved from demolition, by The Stroud High Street Action Group, in the early 1980's. They are thought to date from around 1836. They were much restored in the mid 1980's to create the present retail shops. The work involved the dismantling of substantial parts of Nos 60 and 61, so what exists today is really a rebuild. The Marlborough Head (subsequently called the Bedford Arms) inn formerly stood on the site of what is now No. 59. Prior to 1836, the front parlour projected into the street by 9 ft in front of No. 58. This caused problems with congestion and Fisher states that in 1836 the parlour was taken down and the whole 'face rebuilt'. The inn closed in 1854 and the building was used to extend the adjoining grocery business. When the buildings were inspected in the 1980's, the evidence suggested that they must have been completely rebuilt in 1836, rather than just refaced. Wood's map of 1835 shows properties in this part of the High Street with a different footprint to the present buildings **(Figure 6.135)**, which again suggests a complete rebuild here. All of the surviving group have good ashlar fronts, with brick used for the rear and party walls. The window lintels were dressed stone. However, their detail varied between the different properties, suggesting they were in separate ownership. No. 59 (the new Marlborough Head) was the most impressive of the group. It had a hipped roof and a brick chimneystack rising through the ridge near the centre of the building. The roof was slate, probably from its build date. There was an access into the rear yard under the W side of the building. This presumably gave access to the courtyard of the inn and also to the cottages behind No. 58. The rear windows of the whole group were multi pane sashes (mainly 12 pane). The window arrangement was rather random, as might be expected for the back of a building **(Figure 6.136)**.

On the S side of the street, just below the Cross, is a building dating from circa 1820 (Nos. 27 and 28) **(Figure 6.137)**. It has a simple façade with pilasters rising through the upper floors. Further down, Kendrick St was constructed in 1871-2 to link the High St with George St. Buildings were constructed along its E side in a style that is more national than vernacular **(Figure 6.138)**. At the N end, brick with terracotta dressings has been used, whereas at the S end ashlar was used. The lowest building was the

Cloth Hall, built for Libby and Pearce. This stands opposite the side of the Subscription Rooms, which was built in 1833, at the bottom of Bedford St **(Figure 6.139)**. It has some fine early 19th C detail in its main elevation, including a central pediment, semi circular headed windows on the first floor and a porch added in 1868. The Subscription Rooms are flanked to the W, by the Congregational Chapel, which was built in a classical style in 1837 **(Figure 6.140)**. The construction of these new civic buildings and the construction of the new roads moved the hub of the town away from the High Street, which although remaining an important shopping street for the next century, gradually declined with no great activity in new buildings.

This reaches the end of the vernacular period in the High Street. The street is the oldest in the town and has been the subject of regular, but gradual change. The appearance of the street has altered completely since its beginnings in the 16th and 17th C. The changes have mixed timber framed buildings of the 16th C, with gabled stone buildings of the 17th C and buildings with sash windows and pediments in the 18th and early 19th C. It is the survivors from these centuries that give the present street its character and the buildings that are most valued by the population. There have been some 20th C additions, but these are generally out of keeping with the majority of the street and seem to have been built to strictly commercial principles, rather than to enhance the street or impress the neighbours. To preserve the street for the future, all must recognise that the vernacular period of building ended over 150 years ago and that the surviving buildings must have regular and sympathetic maintenance and repair. Otherwise, the remaining character of the High Street will be further eroded and eventually lost forever.

6.3 THE CROSS

The Cross is the area at the top of the High Street, now terminated by a wall that separates the end of the High Street and Cornhill. Until the 1980's, the Cross marked the splitting of the highway to Bisley (up Parliament Street) and the old way to Chalford (along Nelson Street, Lower Street and Bowbridge Lane). In the 18th and 19th C it was an important commercial part of the town **(Figure 141)**. Since early times, it had been used for public meetings of all kinds. Fisher records that 'here sheep and oxen were roasted and eaten, and barrels of beer have been broached and drunk. Here multitudes have shouted for victories won, for peace restored, and other great and local causes of rejoicing…. Here too, wild beasts are exhibited in caravans and fairs and tamer animals are penned and sold'. There was a deep well, with a public pump sited near the centre of the Cross, however, this had ceased to be used by the early 19th C. By this time the building that covered the well was in use as a temporary lock-up for criminals (or blind house). Behind it stood the stocks, where drunkards were secured to sober-up and to serve as an example to others. Perhaps, they should be re-instated! Fisher states that the blind house was removed by 1811 and the materials used in the construction of a new lock-up in the Shambles, which in turn, was removed to Nelson Street. Attempts were made by the Improvement Commissioners to re-open the well for public use in 1839. It was deepened, but then found to be too deep for the pump to handle and, anyway, the water was polluted. As such, it remained in a useless state until 1866, when it was converted to a drinking fountain, following the introduction of a mains water supply to the town.

The character of the Cross was destroyed completely in the 20th C and all of the vernacular buildings that bounded the Cross were demolished. So now, it has a bland appearance, dominated by the link road that was built in the 1980's to improve access to the top of the town and avoid congestion

Chapter 6

in the High Street. Functional it may be, but pretty or social it is not **(Figure 6.142)**! The buildings, to the W side of the Cross, were investigated by the Stroud Preservation Trust, prior to their demolition in 1981 **(Figure 6.143 and 144)**. Numbers 32-33 stood in the High Street, they have already been described. No. 34, although a separate small shop, was integrated with the façade of No 33. In the restoration, it was fully incorporated into this building and now provides the access to the upper floors. However, evidence found during the renovation showed that it was the remnant of a longer building that formerly fronted the W side of the Cross. The large first floor hearth **(Figure 6.145)** (now in the entrance to the upper levels of No.33) and evidence for a steeply pitched roof over No 34 and 35 showed that they had originated in the 17th C, but had been split, probably in the early 18th C, so that one bay formed No 34 (with the shared façade with No 33) and 2 bays formed No. 35 High Street **(Figure 6.146)**. The evidence suggested that the 2 bays forming No. 35 had been extensively rebuilt, with a new front and a new wall between 34 and 35, in brick with lime mortar. The detail indicated that this had been done in the late 18/early 19th C (i.e. about 100 years after the modifications to 33/34). The brick of the party wall with No. 34 returned slightly to merge with the stone of the rear wall. The ground floor was split into two small shops by a 19th C style wood partition (tongue and groove). The shop fronts probably dated from the late 19th C. The first floor of the front elevation had two multi pane sash windows, which were 19th C in origin. When the rendering was removed from the front elevation (to salvage the bricks for the new gable end wall on No 34), evidence of an earlier pair of window openings was revealed. These had brick arched heads to their openings. There was a pair of dormer windows built off the front wall plate and these were hipped. Each had a 2-light wood window frame, with leaded lights (6 pane). One of the lights had an iron framed opening frame, on pin hinges. These dormer windows show on an early 19th C engraving of the Cross. The rear wall and S gable end were constructed in stone, with an opening at the W end of the rear wall to a small 2-storey wing. This contained a small wood stair to the first floor (so rotten, that a member of the Trust fell through it during the investigation) and a small hearth with a range. The rear wall also contained a hearth with a wide stone lintel and jambs constructed in regular shaped stone blocks, which projected inwards as a chimney-breast, by about 0.2 m **(Figure 6.147)**. The underside of the lintel was curved at the edges of the hearth opening, so that the lintel stone appeared to flow round to become the jamb. There were no chamfers or stops and the hearth was shallow. The detail suggests that the hearth probably dated from the late 18th/early 19th C. The ground floor ceiling joists were elm, fairly rough in their finish and irregular in profile. The floor boards were also elm and wide. The detail showed that there had formerly been a stair in the NW corner of the building **(Figure 6.148)**, but this had been removed a long time ago. There were two first floor rooms in the front part, separated by a wood partition. There were also two attic rooms, separated by a wood partition (sited under the roof truss) **(Figure 6.149)** and with the roof sitting on half height walls. The ceiling of the N room was barrel shaped, with the joists bent to the required shape: this was unique and no similar style of ceiling has been seen in the area. The lower part of the principals were cruck shaped, such that they rose vertically from the tie beam against the half height walls and then turned at the top of the half walls to follow the roof slope. No joint is remembered at this position, but should not be ruled out. A similar roof design has been seen in several local buildings (all 18th C) and they had a vertical post jointed between the underside of straight principals (whose bases rested on the top of the half walls) and the tie beam in the floor. There was a morticed collar at the level of the attic room ceiling. The principals did not meet at the apex of the roof (as is normal) in the roof space above the attic rooms. Instead, they were joined by a heavy yolk approximately 0.6 m below the ridge **(Figure 6.150)**. The yolk was fixed with a wood pegged, mortice and tenon joint to the top of each principal and a short post rose to support the ridge.

VERNACULAR BUILDINGS OF STROUD

This type of arrangement has been seen in other, generally earlier buildings. It has been suggested that this design of truss was used if the principals were too short. There were two rows of through purlins/roof slope.

The Crown Inn **(Figure 6.151)** was sited next to No. 35 High Street. This was a red brick building with some nice Edwardian detail. It had been built as a public house and remained so until a couple of years before its demolition. Internally, it was plain and no detail was recorded. An engraving made in the early 19th C of the Cross, shows an earlier building on the site. This was also called the Crown Inn. It had a continuous dripmould over the first floor windows, which indicates that the façade, at least, originated in the late 17th C. A large, rendered brick building stood adjacent to the Crown Inn. There was a pet shop on the ground floor in its latter years, with domestic accommodation above. The first and second floors of the front elevation had sash windows, with the central, first floor window also functioning as a loading door. At the rear of the building there was a courtyard with flight of good stone stairs, giving access to the first floor. There were good, dry cellars under the building. There was some nice pitch pine detail inside and a ground floor hearth with stone jambs and a wood lintel on the ground floor. The detail indicated that this building originated in the late 18th/early 19thC. The gable end wall, with its ground floor hearth is all that remains from this building and this can be seen behind the scaffolding that is shoring –up the side-wall of the former Marshall Rooms, on the W side of Cornhill (this evidence was removed during building work in 2005). Both No. 35, the Crown and the Pet Shop stood in the area now cleared for Cornhill. They formed a continuous street frontage that merged into Nelson Street. Opposite these buildings is the junction with Parliament Street (formerly called Hill Street (lower part) and Silver Street (upper part)). The buildings on the N side of the High Street were formerly continuous with those on the N side of Parliament Street. The Exchange Buildings (already mentioned) stood at the point where the two streets merged. The side of the Cross, formed by the junction of Parliament Street with Nelson Street, was redeveloped in the 1930's to become the Co-Op building. This still survives, although not connected with the Co-Op anymore **(Figure 6.152)**. Prior to the redevelopment, there was a pretty group of vernacular buildings on the site. Just up Parliament Street, there was a wide flight of stone steps, which ascended to about the level of the current car park. Here, there was a stone building, with pairs of ground and first floor 3-light stone mullion window frames, without dripmoulds. It faced Parliament Street and the W gable end had a half hipped roof. It probably dated from the early/mid 18th C. There were two buildings facing the Cross itself. Next to the junction with Parliament Street, there were what appears to be a 17th C house, with a steeply pitched roof, with a modified front elevation that had a central pediment and parapets. The ground floor was a shop front (for Guest, the Draper), with a pair of sash windows with large panes on the first floor **(Figure 6.153)**. These windows had moulded architraves with projecting keystones. There was a central sash window on the second floor (same detail as first floor windows) and flanking half circular blind lunettes (with projecting keystones). There was a circular blind lunette beneath the apex of the pediment. The façade appears to have been rendered and there were regular formed quoins marking the edge of the building. The façade had a rather 'country' appearance and possibly originated in the mid/late 18th C. The adjoining building was lower and two-storeys in height **(Figure 6.154)**. There was a ground floor shop front, partly constructed at an angle, at the corner, where the Cross merged into Nelson Street. There was one small ground floor sash window, with external shutters, facing onto the Cross. There were two first floor sash windows (two panes tall, three panes wide) facing the Cross, and a further similar window above the angled shop entrance. The style of the windows suggests a late 18th/early 19th C date for this building.

Chapter 6

6.4 The Top of the Town: The first expansion of the town in the 17th C

The area bounded by Parliament Street, Nelson Street, Lower Street and Hollow Lane represents the area of the first extension of Stroud, from its early core in the High Street/Cross area. The basic layout of roads is shown on Wood's map of 1835 **(Figure 6.155)**. It is known locally as the 'top of the town' and the expansion was needed to accommodate the increasing population that was employed in the local cloth and related industries. Prior to this expansion, the land was divided into fields (such as the Seven Acre field and the Square Acre). The historic routes passed by the fields to Bisley (now Parliament Street) and Chalford (now Nelson, Castle and Lower Streets). Ian Mackintosh has done extensive documentary research on the early history of Stroud and the early estates and through his work much information on the development of this part of the town has been discovered. As well as the main routes, there were also tracks and paths running between the fields: one of these became Middle Street and another Acre Street (formerly Acre Edge). It is apparent therefore that the upper town developed into the existing unplanned, network of routes and paths of the area, which explains some of the unexpected kinks and dislocations in the line of the houses along the present built up streets. The evidence in the buildings suggests that the expansion began in the mid 17th C and continued through to the late 19th C. The early houses were of reasonable size and set in generous plots of land. As time progressed, and undeveloped land became more scarce, the areas between and behind the early houses became developed. In Middle Street and Chapel Street, several courtyards (churs) of small houses developed behind the original buildings (e.g. behind 43/44 Middle street and in Queens Square, behind Chapel Street). Here the houses were bunched together, without much garden space, and this must reflect the 'industrial conditions' existing in Stroud in the 18th and 19th C. Apart from The Castle (origins in the 17th C and Corbett House (19th C), both in Castle Street), the houses are generally small and are the homes of a working population. Many of the houses must have been provided for those associated with the cloth industry, but mixed in with these were the homes of those involved in all of the trades needed by a vibrant expanding, working settlement. Within this developing mass of buildings there were also demolitions/redevelopment at different times and regular changes/additions to the earlier buildings. The result is an apparently complex development with buildings of all ages mixed in together. In addition, the external appearance of a building may be misleading, as what may appears to be 19th C on the outside, may retain substantial parts of an earlier building inside. In many instances there have been several phases of major change to individual buildings and it can be quite a challenge to work out what changes have occurred and what the original building was like. The area was fully developed and classed as overcrowded by the early 19th C. There was no mains supply of water and no effective sewage disposal system. Groundwater, which supplied the local wells, became contaminated at times and this was the source of disease.

Prior to the 19th C, the water for the town was supplied by a group of wells. The main well was Gainey's well to the NE of the town, with Hemlock well to the S and the well at the Cross (already noted). There were also many subsidiary wells associated with individual properties. They are often located during building work, some of these were exposed during the work in the Chapel Street area in the 1970's and also to the rear No. 32 and 33 High Street. Lead pipes were connected to Gainey's well in the mid 18th C, and these supplied a reservoir near the Cross. This supplied water to houses in the lower part of the town, on payment of an annual fee. This was owned by the Stroud Water Company. In the early part of the 19th C a second system was laid to convey water from springs at Kilminster Farm to the upper part of the town. This system was purchased by The Stroud Water Company in 1834, who sold the company to the Stroud Board of Health in 1864. The Board continued to supply water from Gainey's well, but also built the (new) reservoirs at the top of Bisley Road. In 1825, the Stroud Improvement Act was passed and commissioners made contracts to further improve the town. Streets were paved and sewers were laid in the mid 1820's. A sewage works was built at Fromehall in 1863, by the Stroud Board of Health. Between 1830 and 1870, gas lighting was extended throughout the parish. Initially, the gas was supplied to the main town and W part of the parish, by a company formed by a group of local businessmen. In 1858, their company was incorporated as the Stroud Gas, Light and Coke Company. The gas to the E end of the parish was supplied by the Brimscombe Gas, Light and Coke Co, which was formed in 1822. The Stroud Company took over the Brimscombe Company in 1936. Electricity was not laid on to the town until 1916, again by a private company, with the agreement of the Urban District Council.

There were some substantial demolitions in this part of the town in the 1960's and early 1970's. At one time there was the attitude amongst some councillors that all of the old buildings here should be demolished. Luckily, the scale of the demolition was limited, however the loss of some good buildings is now regretted. The redevelopments that have resulted are not aging well and they add nothing to the character of the town. In the early 1970's, there was an influx of new people to the town and they appreciated and sensed the importance of the historic buildings and heritage of Stroud. Over a number of years, they successfully opposed various applications to demolish more buildings. This was achieved through both direct and indirect action. Since this time, there have been no demolitions of the vernacular buildings in the 'top of the town', apart from those at the Cross to enable the construction of the link road and a row of derelict cottages at the top of Parliament Street (on the site of the old scrapyard that has recently ceased operations). There has been an on-going redevelopment on sites that were cleared by the mid 1970's, however, the new buildings lack any distinctive character. This reinforces the need to maintain and preserve the earlier buildings that have survived, so that future generations are given the opportunity to enjoy historic Stroud as we do.

The earliest houses in the 'Top of the Town' were well spaced and in fairly generous plots of land (in contrast to the narrow plots present in the High Street). However, over the centuries, the land between and behind the earliest buildings became progressively infilled, so that eventually the area became crowded with a conglomerate of houses and cottages ranging in dates from the mid 17th to late 19th C. Because of the lack of services it came to be regarded as a slum area by the mid 20th C. It is a pity that the importance of the cottages and houses to the local historic environment was not recognised earlier by the planners and buildings were upgraded and restored, rather than demolished. However, although much has been lost, much still remains and it is vital that these survivors are protected and preserved. It is one of the purposes of this book to promote the remaining historic vernacular buildings in this part of the town to ensure that they can be appreciated and enjoyed by future generations. Even though the buildings remain, it is easy to lose their character by inserting inappropriate windows and doors, and by using inappropriate pointing and render, which can damage the fabric of the building. If you are lucky enough to own one of these buildings, take advice when considering repairs to ensure that the character of the building is maintained. Remember a light touch is more sympathetic to a building (and cheaper) than a heavy handed 'renovation' (but some builders prefer more drastic work, as they can charge you more for it!).

The following sections discuss some of the surviving and demolished vernacular buildings in

CHAPTER 6

this area.

PARLIAMENT STREET

Tower Hill and Silver Street were the former names for the lower and upper parts of what is now Parliament Street. It is the steepest street in the town and ran from the junction with the High Street to Town's End and beyond. Town End was at the junction of Silver/Parliament Street with Acre Street (formerly Chapel Street), which, in turn, ran down to meet the upper part of Nelson Street and presumably marked the limit of the town at some stage. The vernacular buildings of this street have all been demolished and nothing of character remains, apart from the cottages/houses on the S side of the upper part (above the Nelson Street car park). Prior to the demolitions, the street was lined by small buildings of various dates, built directly adjacent to the street. In the lower part of the street, there were generally shops on the ground floor, with living accommodation above, whereas in the upper part of the street there were mainly cottages and houses. Progressing up from the Exchange Buildings on the N side, there was:

- a brick building with multi pane sash windows (19th C) **(Figure 6.156)**,

- a low building, with its gable end facing the street, occupied by Hobbs Ltd in the late 1960's. This may have been an early building, but disguised with modern windows and render.

- A stone building aligned parallel to the street, with 2 multi pane sash windows on the first floor. DD Flooring occupied the shop on the ground floor in the late 1960's. The building appears to be of early 19th C origin **(Figure 6.157)**.

- A building that was 3 storeys tall and of approximately the same width as the adjacent uphill gabled building. The ground floor façade was exposed stone, but the upper floors were rendered. It is possible that this building originated in the 16th C and had a timber frame gable end bordering the street.

- A building with a tall gable end facing the street, that appears to have been timber framed with a jetty **(Figure 6.158)**. This must have originated in the 16th C. A Georgian shop front had been added under the jetty and this was very similar to the one on No. 46 High Street. A photograph shows the building in the 1960's and this gives a good impression of what No's 33 and 15 High Street must have been like, prior to the re-alignment of their facades.

- A symmetrical rendered building parallel to the street, with 3 first floor large pane sash windows and a central ground floor entrance, with flanking sash windows. This appears to be of 19th C origin **(Figure 6.159)**.

- A small building with a pair of 2-light stone mullion windows on the first floor, with an arched entrance and a sash window on the ground floor. This appears to be a 17th C building.

- A tall brick building, with contrasting brick surrounds to the sash windows. A ground floor shop window and separate entrance. This must have been built in the late 19th/early 20th C.

- Further up the street the buildings seem to have dated from the 19th C.

All these buildings were on the site, now occupied by the Magistrate's Court and the Police station.

VERNACULAR BUILDINGS OF STROUD

The facing buildings on the S side of the street had been demolished by the 1960's **(Figure 6.160)** and the Nelson Street car park had been formed. However, a 1950's photograph suggests that the buildings here were mainly of a 19th C date. Behind, these buildings, in the area of the car park were some earlier cottages, which were regarded as slums in the post war period. Some undoubtedly remained from the 17th C. The only remnant of the houses on the lower part of the S side of the street is the gable end wall with hearth and a short section of front wall (with string course) at the top end of the car park. Beyond this, a group of retained cottages (with sympathetic modern infill building) gives a good impression of how the majority of the street must have appeared prior to the demolitions. This is a mixed group of mainly 19thC houses and cottages of stone and brick construction **(Figure 6.161)**. Details that are noted in this group are:

- Use of arched lintels for the windows of both stone and brick cottages

- Predominantly stone in the lowest cottages of the group and brick in the upper part. Although one of the upper cottages has stone incorporated in the lower part of the front wall, which shows it has been formed by modifying an earlier structure.

- Apart from No. 6, they are all small cottages. No 6 has detail which suggests a mid 19th C origin. It has a symmetrical façade with sash windows and parapet, but no stringcourse.

- The lowest cottages in the group are built at right angles to the street and have a stone front wall, with some stone mullion windows, without dripmoulds. This detail suggests an origin in the 18th C. The gable end wall is brick, which seems to have a 19th C character. It seems that the stone part represents the remnant of some 18th C cottages, which were modified in the 19th C, possibly to improve the road conditions.

- The uppermost house, in brick is dated 1893.

Beyond Town End on the N side of the street is the first workhouse of the town. This was built in 1724 and consisted of a stone built row of cottages, 16 bays long and of two-storeys, with attics **(Figure 6.162)**. This was replaced by the new workhouse (now renamed Stone Manor), built in 1837, on the N side of Bisley Road. Two of the cottages of the old workhouse survive (Nos 21 and 23 Parliament Street). These were in a poor state in 1960 and attempts were made to have them demolished. However, this was stopped by a Council Officer, who showed a greater degree of care for the buildings of Stroud than many council members. He showed that a viable renovation was feasible and his recommendations were followed. They now give an impression of how part of the old workhouse would have appeared. The red brick fronted houses further up the street are also part of the workhouse (but re-fronted or rebuilt) and each probably correspond with a unit of the workhouse. Further parts have been incorporated into St Albans Church (built 1914-1916). In the side wall of the church some blocked stone window frames and a doorway can be seen **(Figure 6.163)**. Opposite the workhouse, there was a group of good early 19th C houses **(Figure 6.164)**

NELSON STREET

In the 18th C, what is now called Nelson Street was a rather sunken, narrow track. It formed the first part of the road to Chalford, but also served as a way for carts to avoid the steep incline of Silver Street (by going along Nelson Street and up the less steep Chapel Street (now Acre Street)). Fisher notes that it was in need of constant repair. The first 'improvement' of the town was the widening of this street.

Chapter 6

This was done by cutting back the bank and constructing retaining walls to support the foundations of the 2 or 3 properties that stood close to the edge of the bank on the E side. This retaining wall can still be seen towards the top of the street, on the E side. Some of the surviving buildings on both sides of the street, predate this improvement and the evidence given here shows that there were at least several buildings alongside the early track in the 17th C. Those on the W side, were directly adjacent to the track, whereas those on the E side were set a little back, on top of the bank that dropped down to the track.

There is a near complete line of buildings on the W side of the street. Towards the Cross, there are shops, some formerly with living accommodation above **(Figure 6.165)**, others are single storey lock-up shops, with rooms above in the roof spaces only. The single storey shops (Trading Post and Barnes and O'Hara (Dentists) probably date from the 19th C **(Figure 6.166)**. Although the latter was probably formed by conversion of an earlier single storey building (the lower roof line showed in the gable end wall when the building was being converted in the early 1990's). Some have been investigated in some detail and some notes on these are given below.

26 Nelson Street: This has rendered façade, with rusticated quoins and an overhanging eaves cornice. There are two, 18 pane sash windows on the first floor, which have plain architraves and projecting keystones. The detail suggests it was built in the first half of the 18th C **(Figure 6.167)**.

22 Nelson Street (The Duke of York Public House): The Duke of York has a early/mid 19th C, rebuilt front **(Figure 6.168)**. This is constructed in brick and has wide, multi pane sash windows characteristic of that period. However, the S gable end and rear walls are rubble stone. The gable end wall contains a large hearth with wood lintel and modified rear hearth wall. There is a winder stair to the side of the hearth. During recent building work on the adjacent building (21 Nelson Street), the outer stonework of the gable end was exposed and this enabled the development of the Duke of York to be clarified. It was apparent that the adjacent building (which was constructed in the late 17th C) used the existing gable end wall of the Duke of York as its side wall i.e. the Duke predates the late 17th C. It was also apparent that the height of the gable end wall was raised to accommodate the needs of the adjacent building and that the roof pitch of the Duke of York was reduced at this stage. The former, more steeply pitched roofline of the Duke of York could be seen in the walling stone. The area of the rear hearth wall was seen to have been modified, possibly by the removal of an external chimney-breast. Also, there was a blocked ground floor window, without a stone frame, that formerly would have provided light for the stairs. This evidence shows that the Duke of York was built in the 17th C.

21 Nelson Street (Tradewinds closed in 2002): At the time of writing, the building was being converted to a private dwelling. It is an interesting building. It has a narrow frontage, with a tall gabled dormer and does not have quoin stones to the sides of its front wall **(Figure 6.169)**. This shows it was originally constructed as an infill building between existing buildings on each side. However, the adjoining buildings have subsequently been modified, which makes this building now seem to be the older of the group, when in reality it is the younger! This has been proved on the side adjacent to the Duke of York (see above). However, on the other (S) side, the building was demolished and redeveloped in the late 18th C. The replacement building survives, set back from the road. However, as the gable end of the earlier building also served as the side wall of Tradewinds, the front section had to be left in place. This explains the rather odd section of wall, which forms the front part of the side wall of Tradewinds, which stands forward from the 'newer' building. Inside, it was seen that the side of the new building was constructed to form a new side wall to the rear part of Tradewinds **(Figure 6.170)**. There is a straight junction between the ragged stonework of the old (front part of the wall) and the ashlar stonework of the return of the replacement building. The majority of this newer section of side wall is in brick (apart from the ashlar return), however, the lower section retains what might be the original, late 17th C, hearth for the infill building **(Figure 6.171)**. This has stone block jambs and a wood lintel, without chamfers or stops. It is not particularly large, but it is in scale with the building. The front façade has 3 and 2-light stone window frames at the first and attic levels respectively, these have flat chamfered surrounds without rebates. There is a similar 2-light window in the rear gabled dormer, the first floor rear window has been modified. There are owl windows at the apex of the front and rear gabled dormers **(Figure 6.172)**. The roof structure is of the extended collar truss type, without principal rafters **(Figure 6.173)**. All the detail described here is consistent with an origin in the late 17th C. The building retains its original floor structures. The first floor is supported by a near central axial beam (parallel to the front wall) **(Figure 6.174)**. This has approx 50-75mm flat chamfers and elongated scroll stops. The attic floor is supported on a similar beam, but this is a cross beam (at right angles to the front wall) **(Figure 6.175)**. The attic floor also has a similarly detailed half beam against the party wall with the Duke of York **(Figure 6.176)**. The joists are jointed into mortices in the side of each beam on one side and on the other they sit in lodgings in the top of the beam **(Figure 6.177)**. The opposite ends of the first floor ceiling joists that are lodged in the side of the beam, sit in lodgings on the top of the half beam against the side wall. Where the joists are lodged on top of the beam, the opposite ends are embedded in the walls. This is the most convenient way for joists to be installed in a building that had the walls constructed and the beams in place.

19/20 Nelson Street: Set slightly back from the street and on the site of a property that was structurally the side of No. 21. The building was constructed as a pair of properties with a shared early 19th C ashlar façade, with brick side walls **(Figure 6.178)**. The central section breaks forward slightly and is surmounted by a pediment. There are matching entrances, with fanlights, all set within a rounded arch recess. There are matching bullseye windows above the recessed arch. The shop fronts are not original and the building was probably originally a pair of good quality houses. The detail of this building is similar to the demolished building at the Cross (Guests, Draper).

16 Nelson Street, Godolphin House (demolished circa 1960): This stood on the site now occupied by the Church of the Latter-day Saints. All that remains of the earlier building is the column of rusticated quoin stones in the wall adjoining No. 17 Nelson Street. Godolphin house was a quirky looking building **(Figures 179 and 180)**. Its dominant character was 18th C (early/mid), but it may have incorporated an earlier structure. There were two unequal width wings projecting back to the street from the ends of the main range. This seems to have been the rear of the building. The main range between the wings had ground and first floor sash windows (8 pane) and a ground floor entrance (this had a 6 panel door and a good 18th C wood surround). The roof at the end of each wing was hipped. The end wall of the ground floor of each wing had a double 8 pane sash window (i.e. 16 panes total), whereas each first floor had a 12 pane sash. The walls were roughcast, with exposed rusticated quoins stones (one section survives). The front elevation had a break front (projecting central part), surmounted by fairly low and wide gabled dormer, with a sash window. The elevation was rubblestone (not roughcast) and there were no rusticated quoins, infact the quoins were rather modest in size. It was probably rendered, when first built. The breakfront had a good entrance door to one side, with a classical architrave with flat columns, frieze and pediment. The windows were all sashes, mainly 8 pane and

Chapter 6

surrounded by a moulded architrave with a projecting keystone. The N gable end wall had a pitched roof on either side and incorporated a flue and stack, whereas the S gable end wall was hipped and continuous with the S roof slope of the wing.

14-15 Nelson Street: These two properties **(Figure 6.181)** are rendered, but seem to be constructed in brick and present their gable ends to the street. No. 15 probably originated as a shop/workshop with accommodation on the first floor, in the late 18th/early 19th C. It has a simple moulded stone detail outlining the roof shape in the upper part of the gable end. No.14 seems to infill the space between No's 13 and 15. It has sash windows and probably dates from the early/mid 19th C.

13-15 Nelson Street: These form a group of what appear to be early 18th C buildings near the junction with Castle Street and Middle Street **(Figure 6.182)**. All are stone built. No. 13 has a good stone façade, with an entrance to the side of the front facade. The stonework is comprised of well-formed stone blocks and there are no pronounced quoins. The windows are currently sashes, but the detail of the stonework shows that the windows have been changed and one first floor window has been blocked. The first floor windows have wood lintels. There is a moulded eaves coving supporting a parapet. The parapet may be a later addition. The N end of the building (adjacent to No. 14) is hipped, which is consistent with this being the end of the building when No. 13 was built. Walcourt House (No. 12) was named by Wallace Court, the owner in the mid 20th C. This stands forward from the other houses and may be the earliest house in the group. It has a symmetrical front elevation, with a central front door (directly entered from the street), flanking ground floor windows and 3 first floor windows. The first floor windows are of the cross type and retain some early timber frames. This type of window seems to immediately predate the introduction of sash windows and, in Stroud, this dates the building to the very early 18th C. The ground floor windows are sashes (the large pane sashes (19th C) were replaced with the multi pane sashes in the 1990's). There is a timber overhang at the eaves and this is consistent with an early 18th C origin. The ground and first floors were constructed with hearths and therefore the origins of the building are domestic. There are several good 'cellar' rooms underneath the building, which, because of the steepness of the hillside, have external access to the rear garden. No. 11 has similar detail to No. 13, i.e. a moulded eaves coving (without a parapet), hipped roof (S end) and openings for sash windows with wood lintels. Nos 11 and 13 were probably built as symmetrical additions to the original house.

Laurel Villa: The sits close to the top of the retaining wall that was constructed when the road was widened in the 19th C. The front range of the building has internal and external detail that shows it was built in the early 18th C **(Figure 6.183)**. The rear wing is earlier and seems to be the remains of a house that formerly came forward at right angles to the lane **(Figure 6.184)**. It was partially demolished when the present front range was built. The wing has rubblestone walls and a large hearth in the gable end wall. This has an inwardly projecting, stepped, chimney-breast **(Figure 6.185)**. The hearth opening was not exposed in the late 1980's when the building was inspected. A pair of original roof trusses remained in situ, one at the junction with the front range and the other approximately mid-way along the wing **(Figure 6.186)**. They were steeply pitched. The central one had a mortice and tenon joint at the apex of the principal rafters, a collar fixed to the underside of the principals with a mortice and tenon joint. There were 2 rows of trenched purlins per roof slope and these overlapped across the back of the principal. The timbers were very irregular. The first floor window openings on the S side of the wing were rectangular and sited directly under the eaves and were intended for wood frames when originally constructed. These may be the original window openings. The ground floor window opening on the S side had been enlarged and had a 3-light wood mullion window **(Figure 6.187)**, possibly late 18th/early 19th C in origin. The other side of the wing had an addition with segmented stone arched lintels above wood window frames **(Figure 6.188)**. This indicates the addition was built in the early/mid 19th C. There was a large floor support beam with approx 100mm chamfers (and without stops) in the rear wing **(Figure 6.189)**. This is a typical 17th C beam, although the absence of stops may indicate that it has been re-located. The detail of the wing gave the impression that it was built in the early rather than late 17th C. The main range has a good façade in well dressed stone and is 4 bays wide. There are four cross windows on the first floor and three ground floor windows of the same type. All of the windows have a fairly light moulded stone architrave and there is a single iron opening light per window. The shape of the windows is consistent with the range being built just prior to the introduction of wood sash windows, i.e. very early 18th C. The front entrance is off centre and has a segmented arch head with an architrave that is the same as that of the windows. There is a deep, coved eaves cornice and there are rusticated quoin stones on either side of the front façade. This detail is also seen in other early 18th C buildings in the High Street. Each gable end has a flue with the base of a stone chimney-stack showing beneath a later brick top. There are ground and first floor hearths in each gable wall. There are two roof trusses and a near central wall (with a blocked doorway) that divide the roof into 4 bays. The structural timbers were hand cut and fairly regular. The collars were lodged in cut-outs in a side face of each principal **(Figure 6.190 and 191)**. They were cut so that the front face of the collar lapped over the faces of the principals where there was a threaded fixing bolt. A similar collar/principal form was seen in the front roof of No.33 High Street, which was modified in the early 18th C. This date is consistent with the outside detail on the façade of Laurel Villa. Bolts did not come into widespread use until the late 18th/early 19th C, so the bolts seem to have been added. There were 2 rows of purlins, which were rather small and very regular: these were almost certainly replacement timbers. The upper purlin of one of the trusses sat on a block fixed to the back of the principal, which again suggests the original purlin timbers had been replaced. There was an open stone hearth exposed in each ground floor room **(Figure 6.192 and 193)**. These seemed to have been recently uncovered. They had timber lintels (which looked original) and rough stone jambs. One of the lintels had a wide, slightly arched cut-out, presumably to accommodate a fireplace that had been added to the original hearth, but was now removed. This lintel had neither chamfer, nor stops. The lintel of the other hearth had a very minor, irregular chamfer (10mm) and small triangular stops. This hearth also had a good cupboard with a curved back and shaped shelves to the right side. It had a semi circular arched top and a simple moulded architrave. Beneath these shelves there was a low cupboard with double doors (each with a single panel). There was a high and a low level cupboard in the wall to the left side of the hearth. Each has a single panel door. All cupboard hinges were of the modern type. The cupboards were thought to date from the late 18th/early 19th C. The room was clearly a parlour. The upstairs rooms retained at least one panelled window seat **(Figure 6.194)**. These have been seen in several 18th C houses in the area. Neither of the front rooms had evidence of it being a kitchen. This must have been sited in the remains of the earlier building in the rear wing.

4-6 Nelson Street: These formerly stood on the E side of the street in what is now the car park. They were demolished in circa 1970 as part of the widespread clearance of buildings that occurred around this time. They formed a nice group of 17th C gabled dormer houses **(Figure 6.195)**. Their detail as gleaned from photographs shows they developed in several phases. Overall, the front elevation had 4 gabled dormers (1-4). The N pair (1-2) was built as a 2-storey house with attics. There were ground and

CHAPTER 6

first floor 3-light stone mullion window frames, with rebated surrounds and separate dripmoulds over each window. There were matching 2-light windows in each gabled dormer, with owl windows above them. There were chimneys in each gable end wall, suggesting each room was heated. The presence of the owl windows indicates that this part originated in the late 17th C. The S pair of gabled dormers (3-4) were lower and formed the part of the building that was 1 1/2 storeys tall. The stonework of each of these gabled dormers was different, showing they were built in phases. The part with dormer 4 had very similar detail (windows, stonework and owl window) to the house containing dormers 1-2. The entrance to this part had a stone lintel, with a slightly cambered door head and a dripmould. The lintel was carved with the date 1676, which seems consistent with the presence of the owl window. The part with dormer 3 was constructed of smaller rubble stone, there was a 3-light wood mullion window in the dormer and no owl window. There was a 3-light ground floor window, but this was taller than in the other parts of the building and the plain chamfers were not recessed. This may have been the earliest part of the building, but further work would need to be done to help clarify the chronology.

Castle Street, Lower Street and Beyond

The former Methodist Chapel (now converted to flats), at the entrance to Castle St, was built in 1875.

Two of the larger houses of the town are in Castle Street: these are The Castle and Corbett House. The Castle **(Figure 6.196)** was the former home of P H Fisher, who wrote 'Notes and Recollections of Stroud'. The building has origins in the 17th C, however, the original house was substantially rebuilt in the late 18th C. It has an ashlar façade of three storeys and a Tuscan porch with a pediment. The 'castle' wall to the front with a round and a square tower was added in the early 19th C. This does contain a datestone showing the year 1656, but this has been re-sited. Corbett House was built in approximately 1830. It is of ashlar construction, with large sash windows and a wide roof overhang at the eaves. Wood's map, of 1835, shows that both of these properties were sited on large plots of land, which bordered fields/orchards. Nos 9-11 Castle St are a group of town houses, all with sash windows, dating from the mid/late 19th C. No. 9 has an ashlar front, whereas Nos 10 and 11 are rendered and may be brick built.

Castle St merges with Lower St at the junction with Spring Lane. Nearly opposite, No. 4 is built at right angles to the street. It has a steeply pitched roof and large stone mullion window frames **(Figure 6.197)**. It must date from the 17th C. Opposite, No.5 Lower St has detail that dates from the 19th C **(Figure 6.198)**. This detail includes the style of the windows, the nature of the stone work in the gable end wall and the shallow pitch of the roof. These two cottages seem to be built on a lane running N from Lower St. It is possible that there have been some other cottages demolished here.

Houses in the main part of Lower Street are built directly onto the pavement on the N side (although the line of the properties is uneven) **(Figure 6.199)** and directly onto the road on the S side (in a near straight line) **(Figure 6.200)**. The upper side (N side) of Lower Street contains two pairs of gabled dormer houses **(Figure 6.201 and 6.202)**. No. 8 has had its rendering removed and this shows the coursed rubble stone construction that is typical of these houses. As with some of the houses in Middle Street, the ground floor windows are taller than those on the first floor. If this is original, then they may have formerly had the taller form of stone mullion frame, however, the surrounding stonework has been modified, so nothing can be said with certainty. The first floor and attic windows have stone frames with dripmoulds and plain chamfer surrounds. There are quoin stones at the junction with No. 9, which shows that they were built at different dates, with No. 8 being the earliest.

No. 9 is rendered and the random positioning of the window frames suggests there have been some modifications. All window frames are 2-light stone mullions with plain chamfer surrounds and all but one have dripmoulds. This latter frame may be an addition. There is also an owl window on the first floor, these may also be an addition to provide light for a closet. These windows are normally sited in the apex of the gabled dormer (and only in late 17th C houses). The ground floor windows have taller 2-light stone window frames and this may be the original type. Nos 15-18 is another pair of gabled dormer houses (with one being split in two, which explains the three house numbers) **(Figure 6.203)**. These are rendered and each has a near symmetrical arrangement of windows: the first and attic levels retain the original stone mullion frames, which have plain chamfers and dripmoulds. The ground floors have central doorways, with flanking windows (with later window frames). No. 16 has a pretty, little, early 19th C shop window (much altered by 2006). The gabled houses seem to be the earliest houses on this side of the street, with the intervening space infilled with one early 20th C pub building (No 10) **(Figure 6.204)** and a short row of what may be 17th C cottages (Nos 11, 12, the early origin is suggested by the steep roof pitch) **(Figure 6.205)**. No. 14 is built in brick and seems to be 19th C in origin. Some of these show on Wood's map, so were in existence by 1835. Further along on the N side of the street are some more good houses, but these date from the mid-late 19th C and are built to a more national style and are therefore outside the scope of this book. The houses on the S side of the street are mainly comprised of a row of terrace houses of different dates. They begin next to Hemlock Well House (late 18th C house) **(Figure 6.206)** with several groups of brick built houses (19th C). These are succeeded by a group of 3 stone cottages with well coursed rubblestone walls and stone arch heads over the wood casement windows (early 19th C) **(Figure 6.207)**. The first double fronted cottage was formerly the New Inn, which closed around 1974 **Figure 6.208)**. These are followed by another group of stone built cottages which are rendered (Nos 44-47). These are thought to be stone built and have tall ground and first floor windows **(Figure 6.209)**. The windows are unusual (or perhaps they are a rare survival), they have an 18th C character. No. 40 has an origin in the latter part of the 17th C. It was derelict in the early 1970's and the subsequent rebuild involved the replacement of the timber floors and roof structure, and the construction of the new wing facing the street . It does retain some parts of a wide, open stone fireplace with a bread oven in the side-wall, and an adjacent winder stair. The adjoining cottage has a hearth with a semi circular back with a smoke channel, which indicates a late 17th C origin. Further along on this side of the street, No. 43 seems to date from the early 19th C, this is indicated by the stone arched heads over the windows. No. 37, a fairly tall building, with rebated stone mullion window frames, is possibly early 18th C. The building at right angles, which partly obscures the front of No. 37 is later, with the style of the windows suggesting an origin in the early 19th C **(Figure 6.210)**. Nos. 32-33 are set back from and at roughly right angles to the street **(Figure 6.211)**. The steep pitch of the roof suggests it dates from the 17th C and is therefore the earliest building on the S side of Lower Street. It does not have gabled dormers and was possibly built as one larger and one smaller cottage. The orientation indicates it was built before the time when the street was properly established. At the end of the street, Nos. 26-28 are rendered **(Figure 6.212)**, but the presence of 3-light stone mullion window frames without dripmoulds, the half height attic walls and the height of the building suggests an 18th C origin.

Lower Street ends at the junction with Trinity Road. Just to the N of the junction, Nos 1-4 Trinity Road are a pretty group of attached cottages, all constructed in coursed rubble stone, and they retain their stone tiled roofs (one of the few surviving examples in the town) **(Figure 6.213)**. No. 1 has a single gabled dormer, a central entrance and flanking ground and first floor windows. The windows are 2-light stone mullions, with dripmoulds and plain chamfer surrounds. This is the earliest house

Chapter 6

in the group and dates from the mid/late 17th C. The adjoining cottages are of 18th and 19th C origin, becoming younger down the row.

Bowbridge Lane represents the continuation of the original road to Chalford. It progressed to Bowbridge itself and then along Thrupp Lane to Chalford. There are several early houses along this lane and when originally built, these would have been out of the town and sited by the lane to Chalford amongst fields and orchards.

The Field: This is a 17th C house, which had a classical (W facing) front added in the early/mid 18th C **(Figure 6.214)**. The later front has a parapet, rusticated quoins and a row of 5 sash windows on the first floor with shouldered architraves. There were further changes in the 19th C, when the bay windows were added. Some of the original 17th C stone mullion windows can be seen in the rear gable end wall facing Bowbridge Lane. These have rebate surrounds, hollow chamfers and dripmoulds.

Daneway, 6 Bowbridge Lane: This was sold at auction in the mid 1970's and these notes were made at that time. It is a gabled dormer house **(Figure 6.215)**, which has the earlier form of extended collar truss roof. This dates the building to the mid 17th C or earlier. The façade facing the lane (originally the rear of the building) has two wood framed windows on the first floor (plus a blocked window indicated by the wood lintel in the walling) and a 2-light stone mullion frame, with rebated plain chamfer surround and dripmould in the gabled dormer. The opposite side has stone window frames. There are ground and first floor 3-light stone mullion window frames, placed centrally under the 2-light window of the gabled dormer. These windows are of the same form as the gabled dormer window in the other elevation. The first floor also has a pair of 2-light stone mullion windows flanking the 3-light frame. The presence of the stone framed windows on this elevation, shows that this was the more important side of the building. All the detail noted so far, is consistent with an early/mid 17th C origin. However, the lower stone work (up to the top of the ground floor) of the approx E facing gable end wall and the short returns of the front and rear walls are comprised of earlier well-dressed stone blocks (hand chiselled), in contrast to the rubble stone of the rest of the house. The chiselling on the stone is fine and this is indicative of early work. This is confirmed by the presence of two single-light, arch headed windows in this section of walling (one in the wall facing the lane and the other in the gable end wall). Each frame was approximately 700mm wide and 900mm tall, with an iron grill in each light. There were recessed spandrels on either side of the arched top of the window frames. The detail of the walling and frames suggests that this part of the house must date from the 16th C or earlier. Internally, there are 2 extended collar roof trusses (with principal rafters) providing the main roof support on either side of the gabled dormers (the extended collar was approx 9in wide and 11in deep). The roof structure towards the E gable end wall (i.e. above the early stonework) has been modified and there is mixed brick and stone in the inner side of the gable wall at attic level. It is possible that a large early hearth has been removed from this area, probably in the 19th C (when the surviving brick fireplaces were constructed). The W gable end (party with the adjoining 18th C house) has a large Cotswold stone chimney-stack. This serves a large chimney-breast (comprised of well dressed stones), which is large for the current size of the property. It possibly contains back to back hearths (one facing Daneway and the other facing Mulberry Tree Cottage). The hearth facing Daneway has a stone lintel. The structural beams within the house have draw stops and approx 50mm chamfers. The date 1674 and the initials RW, HW and SW are carved on the sill of the S facing attic window.

At the time of the sale, the agent noted that the house was built around 1620 and was owned by the Calne family. They extended it in the 18th C, to the right of the existing house and the old part was used as domestic offices . The new part is now Mulberry Tree Cottage. In the 1920's, the house was considered to be too large and the old part was separated from the 18th C part.

Ivy Cottage: This has a small cusped 2-light window set in the central part of the rear wall **(Figure 6.216)**. This window is early and is thought to date from the 14th C. There are changes in the nature of the stone-work of the rear wall, with the central section (containing the window), being different to that on either end. The front wall has a central, large, externally projecting chimney-breast **(Figure 6.217)**. The windows on either side look to be of an 18th C origin. This house has not been examined in any detail, but the limited information suggests it is of medieval origin.

Field House: The rear part has two gabled dormers, with owl windows in the apices of the dormer and some surviving stone mullion window frames (these have rebated surrounds with plain chamfers) **(Figure 6.218)**. Inside this part of the house has an open well staircase (in oak). The detail here suggests an origin in the late 17th C. A new range was added in the early 19th C to the SW to provide a new entrance and living rooms and parts of the older walls seem to have been rebuilt. Up to about 2000, it was the headquarters of the Gloucestershire wing of the Air Training Corps. In 2004, after lying empty for 4 years, it was being renovated and converted.

MIDDLE STREET

There is one surviving 17th C house at the entrance to Middle St **(Figure 219)**. This is built with its gable end directly onto the street. There are two first floor cross windows with a continuous dripmold over them. The transoms are in the upper part of the window frame. The continuous drip and the position of the transom indicate a late 17th C origin. There is a similar window within the attic gable.

There are deeds in the Gloucestershire Records Office, which relate to the sale of plots of land along the lower edge of the Seven Acre Field. These bordered a footpath that ran along the edge of the field. The documents date from the mid to late 17th C and one of the requirements of the leases was that houses, surrounded by a stout wall or hedge must be built on each plot within a couple of years. Middle Street developed along the path and the gabled dormer houses along the N side of the street must be the houses that were built on the plots of land sold off in the latter part of the 17th C. Four groups of gabled dormer houses survive today and these are spaced between the junction with Nelson Street and Whitehall (top of Middle Street). These are Nos 24-25, 26-27, 43-44 (Devonshire Villas) and 55-57 (Trinity Cottages) Middle Street. Each group is set slightly back from the current pavement. Nos 24-25 are roughcast with 2 gabled dormers (one with an owl window at the apex of the gable) **(Figure 6.220)**. Built as a pair of houses, each with a central doorway and symmetrically arranged windows. There are stone mullion window frames on each floor, with rebated chamfered surrounds and dripmoulds. The presence of an owl window is consistent with a late 17th C origin. No. 24 is partly obscured by a cottage built directly onto the pavement. This must post date the construction of No. 24. It is built directly onto the pavement and has a first floor stone mullion window frame in the front elevation and also similar frames in the gable end wall. These windows are of a similar character to those of the main house. The detail suggests it was built not long after Nos 24/25. Perhaps it was added by the owner of No. 22 as a workshop/shop in the late 17th C. The alternative possibility is that the building was added at a later date and the window frames were re-used. An investigation of the building would reveal which is the more plausible explanation. Nos 26 and 27 are partly rendered and appear to be semi detached **(Figure 6.221)**. However, in reality they are detached by a couple of

Chapter 6

centimetres with the space filled with render in the front elevation. No. 26 does not have a gabled dormer, but has stone mullion window frames, which appear to have rebated surrounds on ground and first floors. There is a central ground floor entrance. No. 27 has a gabled dormer and ground and first floor stone window frames and an entrance door to the side of the ground floor elevation. The position of the door gives an indication of the internal layout. When there is a central door, there are generally 2 rooms on the ground floor separated by a central through passage. When the door is positioned at the side, there is a single ground floor room and a passage. The passage links front and rear doors. The hard render was removed from the front of No. 27 several years ago to reveal the Cotswold stone detail. This shows that there was formerly a continuous dripmould over the pair of ground floor windows. This is a feature that appears in late 17th C stone buildings of the area. The windows have plain surrounds, i.e. not rebated, which suggests a different builder/date to the adjacent house. Nos 43 and 44 were built at the same time as there is no building line between them **(Figure 6.222)**. No. 43 has a central front door and was formerly of the 2 room plan (although the divisions were removed as part of the improvement grant work in the early 1970's), whereas No. 44 with the side entrance is of the one room plan.

No. 43 Middle Street. This was owned by the author between 1974 and 1982. In the preceding years, the building had been the subject of 'renovation' work funded by a Council 'improvement' grant and prior to that it had been vacant for more than a decade. This was the time when many of the buildings to the rear and in Chapel Street were demolished, so it is lucky that these good buildings have survived. The rendering was removed from the front elevation in 1978 **(Figure 6.223)**. The render was not original and was badly cracked and this was allowing water penetration behind the render. The underlying stone retained many patches of limewash, which showed how the building must have looked in earlier times. There were many layers of limewash, in a range of tones, mainly white or ochre, but with variations between the two extremes. The rubble stone work is well coursed and is without jumper stones. It has a single gabled dormer, with a 2-light stone window frame with a plain chamfered surround. The original ground and first floor windows must have been removed many years ago. They should have been stone frames, but there are no photographs or remains of the frames left in situ. A photograph taken before the improvement grant renovation, showed 19th C wood windows in place. The first floor reconstituted stone frames were added in 1978, to replace some ugly wood frames added in the early 1970's. The ground floor sashes were added in the mid 1980's. In the side gable end wall, there is a blocked original stone mullion window **(Figure 6.224)**. This is taller than the normal late 17th C stone mullion and probably shows the form of the windows that were formerly on the ground floor of the front elevation. It is worth noting that some of the gabled dormer houses in Lower Street also have fairly tall ground floor windows, so this may have been a more common style used around this date. This window was blocked and the internal opening was incorporated into new flues for ground and first floor coal burning hearths sometime in the 19th C. The wall plates to either side and between the gabled dormers of Nos 43 and 44 have been raised to construct parapets, with lead valley gutters. This modification has slightly diminished the impact of the gabled dormers. However, the original form of the wall can be read from the stonework of the front wall. The modification of the front wall was probably around the mid 19th C. There is a good stamped lead hopper and lead downpipe fitted to the gutter draining the area between the gabled dormers, which is consistent with a date before the late 19th C. This is the period when some of the terraces of town houses were built in the street and attempts were being made to upgrade some of the older properties. The rear wall also has a gabled dormer, but with a wood mullion window (original), rather than a stone frame.

Presumably this was a cheaper option for the rear of the house. The rear wall is now mainly obscured by later additions, however there were formerly ground and first floor windows at the E end of the rear wall in the original form of the house. Internally, the house was built with a central through passage to a rear door. There was a room on either side of the passage, one heated (E room) and the other (W room) unheated. The latter had windows looking S and W (this one, now blocked). There is a large open stone hearth in the E room **(Figure 6.225)**, which was unblocked in 1975. This retains its original wood beam, which has an approx 30mm chamfer and geometric stops. The jambs are comprised of large stone slabs, again with an approx 30mm chamfer and remains of stops. The hearth is fairly shallow and formerly had a bread oven in the side wall. The room above has a smaller hearth with original jambs and part of its original lintel. This has a semi-circular back with a smoke channel and is a style not seen before the late 17th C **(Figure 6.226)**. When this hearth was uncovered, a coin dated 1805 was found lying on the hearth. It is not uncommon to find some sort of token in a filled-in hearth. The coin was worn, and suggests that the hearth was filled in the early part of the 19th C. This was the time when coal was being imported into the area using the canal. The ground floor has a cross beam, which was originally over the partition (now removed) separating the passage from the unheated room. This is only chamfered on one side and was narrower than a typical unsupported beam of the period. There was a large mortice at its mid point for an axial beam that formerly passed to the front wall of the hearth in the E room. The beam had been cut out many years ago, but the tenon of the axial beam was left lodged in the mortice of the cross beam. The ceiling over the W room retained its original joists. These were approx 100mm deep by 75mm wide and were of irregular shape, the best wood from the tree having been used as beam timber. There were 2 upstairs rooms each with a cross ceiling beam (tie beams of the roof trusses). These had approx 30mm chamfers and scroll stops **(Figure 6.227)**. There were some irregularities in the shape of the beams and some bark was left in place. They had been hacked at some stage to provide a key for plaster (removed by 1974). The first floor also retains some two panel doors **(also Figure 6.227)**, fairly lightly constructed, with slab locks and brass turnbuckle handles. The height of the door openings was slightly less than 6 foot. These doors were thought to be early/mid 18th C. The original stair from ground floor to first floor and to the attic had been removed many generations ago, but was thought to be next to the chimney-breast in the E gable wall. The roof structure was not of the extended collar type, as might have been expected for a house with front and rear gabled dormers. Instead there was a pair of 'A' frame trusses, with tie beams and collars pegged to the face of each principal rafter **(Figure 6.228)**. There is a diagonal joint at the apex of the principals. There are two rows of through purlins per roof slope, these sit in shallow trenches on the backs of the principals. There are three sections to the upper purlins, which are linked across the back of the principals. The central section is continuous across the gabled dormer. The lower purlins are in two sections, with a break between the trusses, i.e. across the space formed by the roof over the gabled dormer. The rafters of the gabled dormer roofs are supported on purlins, which run from the gabled dormer wall to the upper purlin. The trusses are not symmetrically placed with respect to the gabled dormers. The roof structure is original, with all the parts numbered. It would have been made in a timber yard and assembled on site from the numbered parts. The underside of the roof is lath and plastered. This probably dates from the 18th C. There is an internally projecting, curved chimney-breast showing in the E gable end wall in the attic. The stair was originally to the S side of this wall, where there is the remnant of the newel post showing in the floor. A 1795 Thames and Severn Canal Co. truck coin was found under the floor of the attic in the 1970's, which suggests the floor had been untouched for many years. There was also an 1860 copy of the Bristol Mercury behind some timber shuttering, this was given to the Stroud Museum.

Chapter 6

44 Middle Street: The front wall retains its pebble dash cement rendering. The façade has its original stone mullion windows at the first and attic levels. These have plain chamfer surrounds, with drip-moulds. The ground floor windows are fairly tall and have modern timber frames. They were possibly originally of the same form, as the blocked gable end window on No. 43. There is an entrance door to the side of the front elevation, which indicates that there was a through passage and one room on ground and first floors in the original form. The ground floor room has a hearth with stone jambs and a wood lintel constructed across the corner of the room. Hearths in this position are not found before the late 17th C.

Chur behind 43 and 44 Middle Street: A chur is a courtyard of fairly densely packed workers houses reached by an alley from the street. It is probable that the alley itself was called a chur. They developed during periods when the cloth industry was expanding and there was a growing need for houses for the industrial workers. They developed by the progressive infilling of the original garden land behind existing properties. Fisher notes that, in the mid 19th C, they were generally 'ill kept'. There was formerly a group of workers houses behind 43 and 44 Middle Street, but all evidence has now been removed. It was reached via the path (now private) to the side of No. 43 and some details of it can be seen on an aerial photograph of Stroud taken in 1932 **(Figure 6.229)**. There was a terrace of stone cottages running along the garden of No 44 and facing into the garden of No. 43. There was a cottage in the garden of No. 43 in the area of its garage, with its rear wall forming the boundary with No. 42. There was a further one or two cottages built onto the rear of No 43 and facing onto the alley running in from Middle Street. They all shared a courtyard, now under the garden of No. 43. They were all demolished prior to 1970, but the ground had not been tidied and some remnants of the walls still remained in 1974. The garden wall between 44 and 45 Middle Street is the rear wall of the terrace of houses. These do not show on Wood's Map of 1835 and were probably built around the mid 19th C. The gable end wall and the rear wall of the cottage on the site of the garage remained in 1974 **(Figure 6.230)**. It was of two-storeys and there was a the curved section of wall for a wood winder stair in the gable end wall, next to ground and first floor hearths. Both of these hearths were built for coal burning and this would date them to the late 18th C or later. They do show on Wood's Map, so they must have been built by 1835. The walling was rubble stone in an earth matrix and there were 2 openings for wood windows in the remaining ground floor of the rear wall. One retained the timber window frame and this had an iron opening light, hung on pin hinges. The iron frame was re-used on a workshop constructed using the remains of the cottage immediately behind No. 43. The ground floor of buildings directly behind No. 43, were left buried, under the new garden level, when the upper parts were demolished. They were excavated in the late 1970's. There seemed to be 2 parts, the inner building was linked through to the rear extension to No. 43. There was a blocked doorway with a plank and ledge door still in situ (although somewhat rotten, having been buried for over 10 years) **(Figure 6.231)**. It had a good pair of strap hinges with decorated ends, and a thumb latch, which were of a late 17th C style. The latch and hinges were marked with a X, between 2 uprights. These are marks to deter evil spirits from entering through the doorway. The hinges are re-used at the Old Duke of York Inn at Chalford Hill. The outer part of the building seemed to be a separate property **(Figure 6.232)**. It was entered via several steps up, from a sunken area behind No. 43 and may have been a workshop of some form. It was stone built and had a stone flagged floor. The excavated stone was reused to build up the remaining walls to form a new workshop. The ceiling of this, used joists from a house that was being demolished in Chapel Street. These are chamfered and possibly date from the early part of the

17th C. A new extension was built on the site of the inner building in 1980. This extended an existing addition (19th C) to the rear of No. 43.

Nos 55-57 Middle Street is a group of three houses, each with a gabled dormer **(Figure 6.233)**. The front elevation is rendered, however as with 43/44, the apparent height of the dormers has been reduced, by building up the walls between the dormers to form a parapet and valley gutter. The dormers are not equally spaced, which may suggest they are not all of the same build date. There do not appear to be any stone window frames remaining in the upper floors. These houses are taller than those further down the street. No. 58 Middle Street has modern render and replacement windows, however, the steep roof pitch does hint that this is also a late 17th/early 18th C house.

The houses so far described on the N side of Middle Street are all well built and of a reasonable size, they are not small cottages. This shows that the initial developments in the Seven Acre Field in the late 17th C were intended for those with a reasonable income. Each stood in a good sized plot of land. Wood's map of 1835 shows that these plots and the early houses along the N side of Middle Street were still well defined and there was only limited further development behind the houses and in the upper part of the street at this time. There does seem to be some pre 1835 development (i.e. showing on Wood's map) in the lower part of the street, above the junction with Acre Street and before No. 24. Here there is a stretch of predominantly stone cottages **(Figure 6.234 and 235)**, built directly onto the pavement (No. 23 has already been mentioned). Presumably something was demolished to enable the construction of the 1960's house belonging to Middle Street Garage. The lower ones were raised, in brick, and the roof pitches reduced (done in the 19th C) to generate the terraced houses with two full storeys. They have been much altered, but do retain some parts of the original cottages (the stonework of the original houses has been partly exposed). The upper ones have been subjected to less radical alteration, there are a couple of stone mullion window frames, one with (23) and one without (22) rebated surrounds (probably late 17th C). No. 21 has a wood casement window with a stone arched head (late 18th/early 19th C), however, the section of wall containing this window has clearly been rebuilt. The gable end wall also shows signs of roof modifications, which suggests that this is also an early cottage. Beyond these cottages and between the original houses, the line of the street has been infilled completely. Fern Royal dates from the late 19th C **(Figure 6.236)**. This does not seem to have a street number, which shows it was built after the date when the street numbers were allocated. Next there are two terraces of brick built town houses. Fort View, the first terrace, is dated 1872 **(Figure 6.237)**.

The S side of Middle Street does not retain any 17th C cottages. It consists mainly of blocks of brick built terraced houses. The exceptions are Nos 70 and 71 Middle St, which are stone built **(Figure 6.238)**. The stone arched heads to the windows suggest they date from the early 19th C. Wood's Map shows a reasonably long footprint of building, directly onto the street line, in this part of the street. It is logical that the pair of stone cottages are the remnant of this building. It seems that this side of the street was redeveloped in the 1870's and the dates of 1872 and 1873 are given on the plaques for Lancashire and Westbourne buildings **(Figure 6.239)**. These later developments are in the national style.

Reference to Wood's map of 1835 shows that the 17th C houses on the N side of the street are identifiable, together with their plots of land. The rear side of these plots is now marked by the access road that was built to the rear of these properties in the late 1970's as part of the 'Chapel Street redevelopment'. In 1835, there had only been a limited amount of infilling, so following the initial development along the side of the Seven Acre Field, the development remained fairly static for approaching 150 years. The map also shows buildings along the S side of the street. There are four or five main footprints of buildings shown, each widely spaced from its neighbours. Apart from Nos. 70 and

Chapter 6

71 none of these buildings have survived, however it is worth copying some notes made by Fisher. He says that (in the 1850-1870's, when Fisher was writing)'…on the S side of the street, is an old house, an example of the original irregularity of the front lines and levels of the streets. It stands 11 feet back from the adjoining houses; and its lower floor was once 5 foot below the present roadway. It still bears, as the date of its erection, '1686' in large figures, with some quaint devices, which were wrought into the plastered front nearly 200 years ago. Both the adjoining houses were on the same level…' These houses must have been demolished when the brick terraces were built and within 20 years of Fisher writing his notes. Wood's map does show several footprints of buildings on the S side that are set back from the road and these must be the ones referred to by Fisher.

WHITEHALL AND PICCADILLY

This is the of section road connecting Middle Street with Bisley Old Road. Some larger town houses were built here in the early 18th and mid 19th C. These stand on the N side of Whitehall. Opposite is Piccadilly, which is a separate track leading down to Piccadilly Mill. It may be an early track, which became partially developed in the late 17th/early 18th C, but was never converted into a proper street. There are some late 17th/early 18th C gabled dormer houses, facing N, on the S side of the track.

Nos 1 and 2 Whitehall: This impressive block was originally built as a row of 3 houses in the early 18th C **(Figure 6.240)**. They have subsequently been altered so that there are currently two houses. The roof pitch is fairly steep, there is an overhanging coved eaves cornice and there are rows of sash windows (some blocked) on each floor. The stonework is dressed stone blocks, rather than coursed rubblestone. This detail is typical of early 18th C houses in Stroud and their proportions show that they are houses of the 18th C middle class.

Nos 4-6 Whitehall: A mid/late 19th C terrace of large town houses. There is sufficient detail to indicate they may have been designed by Benjamin Bucknall (who also designed the Imperial Hotel in Stroud). This detail includes the ground floor windows each with flanking shafts, which have a foliage pattern on their capitals, the first floor shoulder headed windows, stone gutters and the banded roof tiles.
Nos. 9-11 Whitehall: This is a row of three cottages each with a front facing gabled dormer **(Figure 6.241 and 242)**. Their detail varies and there are vertical building lines between them, which shows they were built at different times. No. 9 is the earliest of the group (shown by the direction of the building line between 9 and 10). It has stone mullion window frames with plain chamfer surrounds and dripmoulds. The front is symmetrical with a central ground floor entrance. The detail suggests a late 17th C origin. No. 10 has wood window frames and a near symmetrical front, with a central door. There is no evidence to suggest that the wood frames have replaced stone frames. Evidence from other buildings indicates that that stone mullions were falling out of use for new buildings by the early 18th C, so this building must date from around 1700. No. 11 also has wood framed windows, but these are not arranged symmetrically. The late Claire Toy lived there in the 1970's and 1980's. She found evidence, which showed that it had been built around 1704. All of these houses have coursed rubblestone walls.

No. 12 Whitehall: This is a good example of how houses can be substantially remodelled to meet the changing fashions in building. The house has recently been restored by a new owner **(Figure 6.243)**. From the exterior it appears as a scaled down version of a gentleman's residence of the mid 19th C, with a hipped roof in Welsh slate and overhanging eaves. However, the new rendering hides the story of the building, which shows that an earlier house was re-modelled to create the current form. The stone of the front wall only had quoin stones on the W side of the building, this shows that this side is the end of the original building **(Figure 6.244)**. The absence of the quoins on the E side shows that it was formerly continuous with another building, which must have been removed many years ago. This must have been a separate property, as there is an original stone dividing wall here. The quoins on the W side did not ascend to the roof level, but stop about 1 m below the eaves. This shows that the wall height has been raised. There is also a higher density of jumper stones in the raised section of wall. The walling around the window openings has not been altered, which shows these are the original window openings.

Inside, a large open fireplace was discovered on the ground floor **(Figure 6.245)**. This retained its original timber fireplace beam and stone jambs. The beam had a narrow chamfer (about 25mm). The hearth opening was wide, but not deep and was similar to the hearth in 43 Middle Street. The ceiling beam arrangement was also the same as in 43 Middle Street, with a cross beam to the side of the entrance door and a central axial beam passing from the cross beam to the front hearth wall **(Figure 6.246)**. The beams had narrow chamfers and scroll stops. The ground floor was formerly divided into two rooms, one heated and one unheated. The unheated room had a cellar beneath it and a shallow curved profile to the corner, front wall. This shows that the stairs to cellar and first floor were in this room and not next to the hearth, as is usually seen in 17th C cottages and small houses. The evidence given here suggests that the original house was built in the very early 1700's. The first floor had been remodelled, but the plasterwork clearly showed the extent of the changes that were made in the mid 19th C. Below the line of the raised walls, there was white lime plaster, the raised section had the grey form of plaster **(Figure 6.247)**. The grey colour is due to the presence of coal ash in the plaster mixture. The junction between the two types of plaster passed around the building at the same level, including across the window openings. This latter observation confirmed that the window openings had not been altered when the roof was raised **(Figure 6.248)**. No evidence remained to show whether the original building had a gabled dormer, but it seems likely as all the other surrounding houses are of that type.

No. 13 Whitehall: This is detached, but immediately adjacent to the side of No.12 **(Figure 6.249)**. It is orientated at right angles to the lane and has a gabled dormer at the N end of the front elevation. It has a mixture of stone mullion window frames, all with plain chamfered surrounds. Those under the gabled dormer have dripmoulds, those to the S end under the eaves of the roof do not. This must predate No. 12 and was probably built towards the end of the 17th C.

Chapel Street

Until the mid 19th C, this was known as Meeting Street, after the Presbyterian meeting-house that was established there in the early 18th C. The meeting adopted the Congregational system in the early 19th C and at that time was known as the Old Meeting, to differentiate it with the new Congregational Chapel being built in Bedford Street. The old chapel was remodelled, with a new front in 1844, in a Romanesque style. This was sponsored mainly by Samuel Marling, a prominent Chapel member. There were Sunday school rooms beneath the Chapel. In 1970, the congregations of the two chapels were merged and the chapel in the now re-named Chapel Street ceased to be used

CHAPTER 6

and it became derelict. The area was the subject of much demolition in the late 1960's and again in the late 1970's, when the area underwent substantial redevelopment. Some of the early houses and cottages were retained on the N side of the street, but all buildings on the S side were removed, prior to the redevelopment. The notes given below are partly a retrospective look at the buildings that were demolished, together with some information about the retained buildings.

The street was developed along the N part of the Seven Acre field. The development along the N side of the street is rather uneven, as has also been seen in Middle and Lower Streets, which suggests that the development started before the present line of the street had been established. In contrast, the S side, which is now completely removed, but can be seen in surviving photographs, was built closely against and in line with the street. This suggests most of the S side was developed later, when the street was more established. However, it is noted that there was at least one 17th C cottage on the S side, near the E end, remodelled in the early 19th C.

The S side was demolished in 2 stages, in the late 1960's, when most of the houses in the central section were removed, and in the late 1970's when the cottages at the upper end and lower end were removed, but leaving the uppermost house adjacent to the 'Tween walls Chur' (No. 37). The properties in the central section belonged to the Co-Op, prior to their demolition. Some general views looking down the street give the impression that those in the central part of the S side were built in the 19th C, as several blocks of cottages **(Figures 6.250, 251 and 252)**. At the upper end, next to the one remaining house on this side (No. 37), were a group of 3 stone buildings, which had earlier origins **(Figure 6.253)**. The middle cottage had been largely demolished by 1970, but it had been a single storey cottage with a steeply pitched roof. This is thought to be the style of some of the earlier workers houses of the area. Indications of several examples have been seen in different parts of the town. They have not survived, as presumably they were seen as low status houses and have either been demolished or substantially altered. They also required a greater land area, than the equivalent floor space 2-storey cottage. So, as the land became more fully developed, additional accommodation was provided, by converting earlier single storey cottages to several 2-storey cottages. An example of this change could be seen in the building at the W end of this group. This was formerly of the single storey type, but its walls had been raised to generate a 2-storey building with attics **(Figure 6.254 and 255)**. At the same time, the modified building was split vertically to form a pair of semi-detached cottages, each with one room on each floor. The modification seems to have been done in the late 18th/early 19th C. There was a row of outside toilets against the gable end wall of the cottages. There were no internal services, apart from a cold water tap and Belfast sink in one of the cottages. They were partly constructed below the road surface at the rear, so their back walls were damp. They gave a good impression of the style of the early 19th C workers houses in Stroud. They had rooms with low ceiling heights and modest floor areas, a narrow, steep stair to the upper floors and a small hearth for cooking. Under these conditions, large families were raised to provide the workforce for the local industries. The form of the original single storey cottage could also be detected in the modified structure. It had two rooms on the ground floor, beneath a steeply pitched roof. There were attic rooms, presumably used for sleeping and storage. There was a large hearth in the gable end wall, with a stone winder stair built in the recess next to the hearth. There was a closet in the recess on the other side of the hearth. The ground floor ceiling joists were chamfered and stopped and must have been exposed in the ceiling of the original cottage. No joists were straight and reflected the profile of the branches and trunk from which they had been cut. Some of the joists were removed and used in the ceiling of an outbuilding behind No 43 Middle Street. There was a large centrally placed, cross ceiling beam, with approx 50mm chamfers. The size of the chamfer suggests a later, rather than earlier date in the 17th C. A third, 2-storey cottage, with one room per floor had been added between the two originally single storey cottages. This had sash windows and probably dated from the early 19th C as an infill building. The last house in the group (at the E end) was 2 storeys tall, with attic under a fairly shallow pitched roof. There was one room on each floor. The windows on each floor, at both front and rear, were 3-light, multi pane wood casements, under a segmented stone arch lintel **(Figure 6.256)**. There were no signs of modifications to the outside walls and only coal burning hearths in each of the ground and first floor rooms. The joists spanned from wall to wall with no intermediate ceiling beams. The detail suggests an origin in the early 19th C. These cottages together with the Chapel were demolished in circa 1978.

Most of the houses were retained on the N side of the street and refurbished as part of the Chapel Street redevelopment **(Figure 6.257)**. Wood's Map (1835) shows that most of the retained buildings had been built by the time the map was drawn. There were several smaller cottages demolished, which were either sited between the larger houses or as additions to them. At one stage there were plans to demolish all of the properties here, but there was growing opposition to further losses of the older buildings of the town and a pressure group was formed, Chapscorp, to lobby against their demolition. It published a booklet called 'Jerusalem on Chapel Street' to raise the profile of the plight of the remaining buildings. Eventually, the SDC decided to retain and refurbish rather than demolish and rebuild. The redevelopment went ahead and the older buildings enhance the character of the regenerated Chapel Street. The detail of what was done to the old buildings, as part of the refurbishment, can certainly be criticised by standards of today. But they undoubtedly continue to provide nice homes to live in. New flats were built along the S side of the street and this required much excavation of the remaining cellars and footings of the previously demolished street. In this process wells and lisomes were exposed, some about 5m deep. Lisomes are natural fissures in the rock strata and were formed by a process known as cambering. This can occur where rigid rock strata sit on more flexible clays. Towards the side of the valley the rigid strata can shear and sink slightly into the clay, thereby creating a vertical fissure. The lisomes were used as an early form of sewage disposal, with the drains from some of the nearby houses simply piped into them. These must have functioned adequately for more than 100 years. However, this practice must have led to the contamination of some of the wells, which were not too far away. It must also have caused a level of pollution in the water at the lower spring line: used as the water supply by those living lower down the valley side.

No. 3 Chapel Street: This cottage was given a thick overcoat of hard render during the refurbishment **(Figure 6.258)**, so much of its identity is now hidden. In appearance, it formerly looked **(Figure 6.259)** quite similar to the adjacent cottage (No. 1). The walls are constructed of well coursed rubblestone, with quoin stones to the E end of the front wall and a more ragged line of stones at the W end. This showed that a directly adjacent building had been removed at this end. The form of the removed building was indicated by some features remaining in the W gable end wall of No. 3. There was the roof line for a more steeply pitched roof and with lower front and rear walls. There was also a blocked window with a wood lintel. The evidence showed that the removed building was earlier than No 3, which had been built onto its gable end wall. No. 3 had stone arched heads to the windows (two on the first floor and one on the ground floor). There was a near central front door, with a blocked-up door immediately to the left (the current front door). There was a large 3-light attic dormer window, built off the wall plate. Internally there was stone fireplace on the ground floor of the E gable end wall, with a stone lintel in 3 parts (the central stone acting as a key stone) **(Figure 6.260)**. The hearth was

Chapter 6

similar in size to that expected for a coal burning range. There was rear addition in brick, containing a small coal burning cast iron grate. The detail of the cottage suggested that the stone part dated from the early 19th C, with the brick addition being added later in the century. Despite there being two doors in the front wall (one blocked) it was felt to have retained its original internal form (i.e. as a single dwelling). The front stone work was rather perished in places and it was more economic to render it during the refurbishment than to replace the stone. The layout of the ground floor windows and doors was changed during the refurbishment, with the blocked doorway being opened up, and the central doorway being converted to a window. The dormer was also removed and presumably, the attic taken out of use.

No. 5 and 7 Chapel Street: This has coursed rubblestone walls with two doorways, each with adjacent ground and first floor windows in the front elevation. This suggests it was built as a pair of cottages **(Figure 6.261)**. The windows have stone lintels with some ashlar stonework lining the openings. The ashlar stonework around the windows does not look quite correct and suggests that the windows have been modified. There were multi pane sash windows in-situ in 1980 and these were retained during the refurbishment **(Figure 6.262)**. The height of walling above the first floor windows suggests that there are half height walls within the roof space, i.e. each cottage was 2 1/2 storeys tall. The hearths were relatively small and intended for coal use. There were coping stones topping the gable end walls. The details suggest that the building originated in the early/mid 19th C. There is a brick built wing at the rear, which probably dates from later on in the 19th C.

No. 9 Chapel Street: This detached house has a stone front wall and red brick gable end and rear walls **(Figure 6.263)**. It seems to date from the early 20th C and does not appear to have been altered much. The front façade has multi pane sash windows, with the central first floor window surmounted by a small gable. A small, stone built, cottage stood between this house and No. 11, until 1980. This was demolished as part of the redevelopment. It stood back from the street, such that the apex of its roof was in line with the rear wall of No 11. It was an earlier building, as the lower part of its gable end wall had been incorporated into the gable end wall of No 11. Its roof had a moderate pitch and the windows were 2-light wood casements. It probably dated from the mid 18th C.

No. 11-13 Chapel Street: This is a tall stone building, with three floors and attics, built originally as three houses, but split into two during the recent redevelopment. These notes describe the building prior to this work **(Figure 6.264, 265 and 266)**. It has an ashlar front, with rubble-stone gable end and rear walls. The front elevation has a parapet with a central pediment containing a blind lunette (these have also been seen in Nelson Street and in a house formerly at the Cross). The area beneath the pediment is built slightly forward from the adjacent walling. There is a stringcourse between the ground and first floors. The end sections of the front wall had subsided, causing deflection of the lintels and stringcourse: this was rectified during the renovation. The first and second floor windows were wood casements with stone lintels. The ground floor windows had been boarded up for many years, but were larger than the upper windows and may have been sashes. Each house had an entrance in the front wall. The central house (beneath the pediment) was larger than the pair of outer houses. Each house had a large ground floor hearth. One survived in a fairly intact form **(Figure 6.267)**. It had a timber beam and jambs built of large stone blocks. There were no chamfers or stops and the hearth was not deep. This was a wood burning hearth, probably also used for cooking. One of the other houses had a similar hearth, but of slightly smaller proportions and with the timber beam replaced with a brick arch (2 rows bricks) **(Figure 6.268)**. There was a curved recess to the right hand side of this hearth with a wood winder stair to the upper floors. The detail of this building suggests it was constructed in the latter part of the 18th C. There was a 2-storey rear wing, at the W end of the building, which was linked through to the main part of the building on each floor. The wing was demolished in 1979 **(Figure 6.269)**.

No. 17 Chapel Street: This is built gable end on to the street. It is constructed in coursed rubblestone and the main elevation, facing W, has sash windows. There are quoin stones at each end of the elevation, which shows that the current building has maintained its original size. There are no signs of any changes to the wall heights. However, the sash windows are not original. Large pane sashes, with slightly arched stone lintels, were replaced by the current multi pane sashes, with cement architraves, during renovation work in the early 1980's **(Figure 6.270)**. The N gable end retains first and attic level, 2-light stone mullion frames (with flat chamfer surrounds) **(Figure 6.271)**. These give an indication that the house has origins in the 17th C (probably late). Prior to 1980, the rear roof slope had a wide chimney gable, which suggests the house may retain its early fireplace. The chimney gable was removed during the renovation. A late 19th C, rendered brick cottage was demolished next to this building in 1980. This was in line with the rear gable end wall of No. 17. A chur leads up hill between Nos 13 and 17 to Parliament St. There is a 2 storey 18th C stone cottage (No. 15) set back from this alley, which was renovated during the redevelopment. This has a roof of moderate pitch and wood casement windows. There is another chur behind No. 17, which leads to a courtyard of cottages **(Figure 6.272)**. One is thought to date from the 17th C, the others are late 18th/early 19th C in origin. This is known as Queen's Square. In 1855, fourteen cottages are recorded in this area and in 1914 it was called the poorest part of the town. Further up Chapel Street, there is a low stone building, which has had the walls raised further in brick. The gable end wall shows the line of a steeply pitched roof and this could be another fairly early single storey cottage, although it was a commercial/industrial premises for many years. It has now been converted for domestic use.

No. 25 Chapel Street (Rowbotham Cottages): This is a house with a gabled dormer at the front and is aligned parallel to the street **(Figure 6.273)**. There was presumably a dormer at the rear as well, but this was rebuilt in brick with lime mortar, when some rear additions were built **(Figure 6.274)**. There is a central ground floor entrance, with flanking 2 and 3-light stone mullion windows with plain, flat chamfer surrounds. The first floor has a pair of 2-light frames and there is another similar window in the gabled dormer. There is another ground floor window (with a wood frame) to the left of the 2-light stone mullion. This was formerly an entrance and was a later addition to the house. Its construction may have been associated with the former use of part of the ground floor as a bakery. The whole of this and the adjoining building is covered with a rather hard looking pebble-dash rendering. It was extensively and rather roughly stripped out during refurbishment in the late 1980's and these notes were made at that time. The ground floor of the original house would have been originally divided into 2 rooms, with a dividing front to back corridor, although all partitions had been destroyed by the time the building was inspected. The length of the whole ground floor was 26 feet, the width was 15.5 feet and the height to the base of the beams was 6.5 feet. There was a large hearth in the E gable end wall, with its original wood beam (which was rather degraded) and jambs constructed of stone blocks **(Figure 6.275)**. There were no chamfers or stops to the hearth opening. There were the remains of a stone winder stair to the left **(Figure 6.276)** of the hearth and a recess to the right (possibly for a closet). The stair continued from the first floor to the attic as a wood winder **(Figure 6.277 and 278)**. There was another large hearth in the rear wall at the other end of the ground floor **(Figure 6.279)**. This was

Chapter 6

not original as the wall plaster continued behind the side wall of the hearth and the scroll stop of the ceiling beam was embedded in the side hearth wall. It had stone block jambs and a wood lintel. The width was 86 inches, the depth was 29 inches and the height of the opening was 58 inches, which were similar dimensions to the original gable end hearth. It must have been added soon after the house was built. The rear of the hearth had been modified by the construction of a large bread oven, which projected beyond the rear wall of the house **(Figure 6.280)**. The entrance to the oven was in the rear hearth wall and this had a brick arch. There was a fire chamber beneath the oven, but this had largely been removed by the time the building was inspected. There was probably a rear flue to ensure that the oven was evenly heated. A second, smaller oven was sited to the right of the hearth and this had an entrance in the rear wall of the room. It also had a brick arch and the two ovens looked contemporary with each other. The presence of these ovens suggests that at some stage the house was a bakery. The rear wall of the house above this hearth and the whole of the remaining rear wall had been rebuilt in brick with lime mortar (with no coal ash added). This rebuild must have been associated with the construction of rear additions, which project at right angles to the rear of the original house. There were two cross floor support beams (each nearly 8 inches square) in the ceiling with joists that were lodged in notches in the top of the beam **(Figure 6.281)**. The joists were elm and were each nominally 90mm deep by 75mm wide. The beams were not of the best quality and had approx 50mm chamfers and scroll stops. The first floor was also completely stripped out. The brick of the rebuilt rear wall was exposed and there was a doorway through to the rear addition **(Figure 6.282)**. A rather crude hearth had been added in stone in front of the rebuilt brick chimney-breast of the ground floor hearth (the hearth with the ovens) **(Figure 6.283)**. Another hearth had been added above the original ground floor hearth (in the E gable end wall) **(Figure 6.284)**. The chimney-breast for the ground floor hearth was semi circular in section and the first floor hearth had been constructed, in stone, in the space between the chimney-breast and the front wall. It did not completely fill the space and there was a narrow gap (several inches) between the side of this hearth and the front wall. The opposite side of the chimney-breast was occupied by the wood winder stair to the attic. The added hearth had a stone lintel and thin (100mm) slab jambs with a bead moulding. The hearth was semi circular in section and had a smoke channel to the rear. The width was 31 inches, the height was 34.5 inches and the depth was 16.5 inches. The attics contained a roof structure of the extended collar truss type, but without principal rafters. The pair of extended collars ran from side to side, rather than front to back **Figure 6.285)**. A timber stud partition with lath and plaster infill between the studs separated the attic of the original house from the attic over the rear addition **(Figure 6.286)**. The original rear wall in this area must have been removed when the addition was built.

The evidence suggests that this house was built in the later part of the 17th C. It had extra hearths added within a couple of decades of its construction and a rear wing added in the 18th C.

No. 23 is a separate property, but attached to No. 25. It does not have gabled dormers, but does have a 3-light stone mullion window frame on the ground floor (same details as the windows on No. 25). The roof line is slightly lower than that of No. 25, which indicates a different build date. It has not been inspected internally, but a slightly later build date is suspected.

The garden behind No. 23/25 had been partly infilled over the years. There is a pair of semi-detached one up, one down cottages in the NE corner of the garden, which face directly onto the chur, which runs along the side of the property boundary **(Figure 6.287 and 288)**. They have rubblestone walls under a stone tiled roof and there are entrances in both front and rear elevations. They each have a ground floor hearth with wood lintel and a tight winder stair to one side. The window openings have wooden frames. Prior to the 1980's renovation they were used as a pigeon loft. They were made wind and weather tight as part of the renovation, but are now deteriorating again. They must date from the early 18th C and are a unique survival of the type of workers accommodation that was being built in Stroud in that century. In the NW corner of the garden, there is a rubble stone built workshop. It consists of a ground floor and a first floor with half height walls and a steeply pitched roof. There is a large window in the gable end wall that provides light to the upper floor **(Figure 6.289)**. The roof structure appears to be of a 19th C origin, the timbers are well cut and the whole upper room has been limewashed at some stage. It currently has a corrugated asbestos roof, but may have been originally stone tiled. There is no evidence for a domestic origin and this is possibly an example of a 19th C weaving shed. There is also a wing behind each of Nos 23 and 25 Chapel Street. Each is stone built, with a pitched roof, a gable end chimney-stack and a door from the first floor to the garden **(Figures 6.290 and 291)**. The ground floors of both wings are well below ground level. The first floor of the addition behind No. 25 had a plain, regular cut ceiling beam without chamfers or stops **(Figure 6.292)**. The floor joists were also regular in profile and lodged on top of the beam. There was access through to the first floor of No. 25. The stone work of the original rear wall had been modified in brick to form the opening and this seemed to be later work than that of the addition itself. The large bread oven noted in the rear wall of the hearth in No. 25 projected out into the space between these two additions and the detail of the brick appeared similar to that used to modify the rear wall of No.25. There appeared to have been a further addition built out over the oven and between the additions, but this had largely been removed when the building was inspected. It seems that the stone built additions were constructed in the late 18th C and that the oven was added in the early 19th C. It was also at this stage that the addition behind No.25 was linked through to the main house. The original function of the additions was not obvious, they were most likely built as workrooms, but a domestic use cannot be ruled out. The developments in this property do illustrate how the land of the early houses in the area became progressively developed in the 18th and early 19th C, with a mixture of workers houses and industrial/commercial premises.

The old chapel stood next to No.25 on the other side of the chur. **Figure 6.293** shows the remodelled front in Romanesque style (1844), but it was demolished as part of the redevelopment.

Acre Street

This has developed from a track that led along the W end of the Seven Acre field. The area at the top of the street was formerly known as 'Townend' and this presumably marked the end of the settlement, prior to the expansion in the late 17th C. The upper part of the E side was subject to complete demolition in the late 1960's and 1970's. The lower section of this side of the street was retained, together with most of the buildings on the W side. Buildings that were demolished on the E side in the late 1970's included an early 19th C cottage (one room per floor), built in well dressed stone with arched stone lintels over wood casement windows and a large stone/brick building known as Hillside flats, which may have had origins in the 19th C, as a factory **(Figure 6.294)**. The retained houses at the lower end of this side of the street are mainly 19th C terrace houses in ashlar stone. Acre Street Stores, on the corner with Middle Street, may have earlier origins. The houses on the W side of the junction with Middle Street may also have early origins, but the fronts have been remodelled in a 19th C style. Further up, on the W side of Acre Street, there is a pair of mid 19th C semi detached houses with one stone and one brick gable end and rendered fronts. These are followed by Acre House, dated 1862 and constructed in brick. Behind this are the Plymouth Brethren Rooms, dating from 1852 and constructed in ashlar stone. The Salvation Army Chapel, dating from 1763, is higher up the street. This was built as

Chapter 6

an octagonal Methodist chapel and was extended in 1796.

42 Acre Street: This house was formerly the Butchers Arms **(Figure 6.295)**, which closed many years ago. At that time the building was rendered, however, the presence of stone mullion windows may have suggested that the building had origins in the 17th C. It has subsequently been updated and the rendering has been removed and this has enabled the development of the house to be interpreted **(Figure 6.296)**. The detail in the stonework shows that the house originated as a single storey house with a pair of gabled dormers facing onto Acre Street (rather similar to the Alms Houses that were formerly in Church Street). This house was one room deep, had a centrally placed entrance and was probably built during the earlier part of the 17th C. The walls of the original house have been raised to form a house with two full storeys and a rear wing was added (that is parallel to the original house). This is the house that survives today. There are some detailed differences in the stone mullion window frames of the front elevation. Most of the frames have plain chamfer surrounds and those of the first floor are too large to fit into the original gabled dormers. The frames are rather heavy looking, are relatively large, with side members comprised of several stones. These must have been added when the walls were modified, and the window detail suggests this was done in the 19th C. One frame is smaller, with a rebated surround and this may be the original style. More rebated surrounds have been seen in buildings that are thought to be of an earlier date in the 17th C in Stroud. The plain chamfer surround is more common in the late 17th C buildings and again in a 19th C revival. However, a photo of the Butchers Arms, taken in the mid 20th C, shows a doorway in the position of the recessed chamfer window frame. Clearly, when the building was refurbished, an early window frame was re-used, when the doorway was modified. No. 44 is one of the two remaining 1½ storey houses in Stroud **(Figure 6.297)**. It has not been studied and its identity is hidden by render and modern window frames. However, it may be an example of a cottage type that was fairly widespread in Stroud in the 17th and 18th C. There is a further example along Bowbridge Lane, below the junction with Spider Lane **(Figure 6.298)**.

The top end of this side of the street was redeveloped in the early 1980's. A mid 19th C stone building, with an ashlar front and rubble stone gable ends was demolished on this site in the late 1960's **(Figure 6.299)**. It had 3 storeys, sash windows, with stone cills and a string course between the ground and first floors. It was built as a pair of houses. The roof pitch was shallow and was probably constructed with a slate roof. A lock up shop had been added against the N gable end wall. There were more houses of this type in the upper part of Parliament Street, opposite St Alban's Church. Some of these did not have the string-course, one had a set of string courses between both ground and first and first and second floors.

VERNACULAR BUILDINGS OF STROUD

Figure 6.1. 14th C spire of church.

Figure 6.2. The Market House.

Figure 6.3. The early development of High Street *(2005)*.

Figure 6.4. Mid 19th C view of the Cross, looking down High Street.

Figure 6.5. Front elevation of 23 High Street *(1985- all photos of 23 High St)*.

Figure 6.6. Print showing 23 High Street in the mid 19th C.

CHAPTER 6

Figure 6.7. 23 High St: Truss 4 (16th C)
(1985- all photos of 23 High S).

Figure 6.8. 23 High St: early 17th C Phase 2.

Figure 6.9. 23 High St: detail of phase 2 facing Swan Lane.

Figure 6.10. 23 High St: ground floor phase 2.

Figure 6.11. 23 High St: rear side of phase 2 addition.

Figure 6.12. 23 High St: truss 6 (early 17th) in roof of phase 2.

VERNACULAR BUILDINGS OF STROUD

Figure 6.13. 23 High St: roof over phase 3, Truss 8 (mid/late 17th C).

Figure 6.14. 23 High St: early 19th on site of 16th C building.

Figure 6.15. 23 High St: some coal burning hearths (present in mid 1980's).

Figure 6.16. 26 High St: front elevation (early 19th C). *(August 2001)*

Figure 6.17. 26 High St: undercroft looking towards rear end. *(August 2001)*

Figure 6.18. 26 High St: undercroft showing steps down from street. *(August 2001)*

157

Chapter 6

Figure 6.19. 26 High St: early chimney stack, encased in later walling. *(August 2001)*

Figure 6.20. 26 High St: rear extent of phase 1 building (rebuilt 19th C). *(August 2001)*

Figure 6.21. 26 High St: phase 2, early 17th C, 4-light window with king mullion. *(August 2001)*

Figure 6.22. 26 High St: phase 2, floor support beam, early 17th C. *(August 2001)*

Figure 6.23. 26 High St: roof structure over early17th C addition. *(August 2001)*

Figure 6.24. 33 High St: front elevation during early stages of restoration. *(1984))*

VERNACULAR BUILDINGS OF STROUD

Figure 6.25. 33 High St: restored front elevation. *(1987)*

Figure 6.26. Early 18th C window with architrave with bullnose surround and projecting keystone. *(1982)*

Figure 6.27. 33 High St: from rear showing original form of building. *(1982)*

Figure 6.28. 33 High St: as it would have looked before the front was altered in the early 18th C. *(shop in Parliament St mid 1960's)*

Figure 6.29. 33 High St: rearwards extension of original building in 17th C, with gable end rebuilt in 19th C. *(1982)*

Figure 6.30. 33 High St: 'Tobacco' warehouse, demolished to make space for the link road. *(1950's)*

Chapter 6

Figure 6.31. 33 High St: end of original building, as uncovered during renovation.

Figure 6.32. 33 High St: building line, showing end of original building retained in restored walling.

Figure 6.33. 33 High St: original roof truss (No 2), with early 18th C collar (associated with modifications to realigned roof).

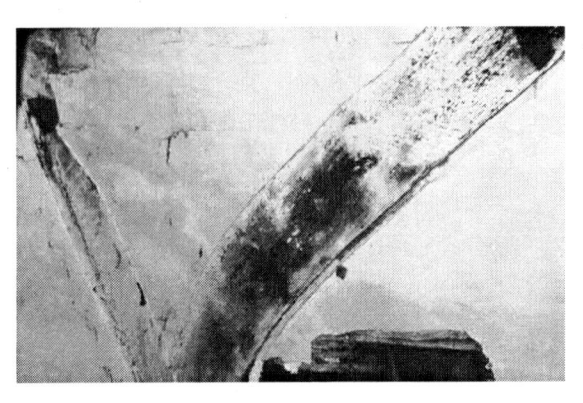

Figure 6.34. 33 High St: last surviving windbrace.

Figure 6.35. 33 High St: showing original joists exposed during restoration.

Figure 6.36. 33 High St: wattle and daub panel.

Figure 6.37. 33 High St: timber frame panel separating Nos 32 and 33.

Figure 6.38. 33 High St: replica early window frame.

Figure 6.39. 33 High St: late 17th cross window.

Figure 6.40. 33 High St: large first floor hearth in restored building.

Figure 6.41. 33 High St: late 17th C hearth constructed in earlier opening.

Figure 6.42. 33 High St: coal burning heath (mid 19th C) infilling earlier hearths.

Chapter 6

Figure 6.43. 33 High St: stair turret (16th C), partly removed by rear addition to No 32.

Figure 6.44. 33 High St: four centred arch head to door of stair turret, blocked by reused stones of one door jamb.

Figure 6.45. 33 High St: lower part of rebated door frame into stair turret, showing pin hinge and blocking stones.

Figure 6.46. 33 High St: 16th C window frame with round arched head and recessed spandrels.

Figure 6.47. 33 High St: reconstructed late 17th C hearth, originally built in earlier hearth opening.

Figure 6.48. 33 High St: late 17th C fireplace on first floor of extension to original building.

Figure 6.49. 32 High St: late 17th C hearth at earlier floor level.

Figure 6.50. 27 High St in the mid 19th C.

Figure 6.51. 27 High St in the late 19th C.

Figure 6.52. 27 High St: rebuilt in early 20th C.

Figure 6.53. The Market House in the 1860's.

Figure 6.54. Looking down the High St from the Cross in 2005.

CHAPTER 6

Figure 6.55. 57 High St: renovated façade with modern shopfront. *(1995)*

Figure 6.56. 57 High St: early 20th C postcard showing No. 57 with 19th C shopfront (removed during renovation).

Figure 6.57. 57 High St: rear gables, right hand gable is original, left hand is 19th C.

Figure 6.58. 57 High St: upper part of extrended collar truss roof structure. *(1990)*

Figure 6.59. 57 High St: remains of stud and panel partition walls. *(1990)*

Figure 6.60. 57 High St: groove in soffit of beam for partition wall. *(1990)*

Vernacular Buildings of Stroud

Figure 6.61. 57 High St: original fireplace with 19thC range in rear wing.

Figure 6.62. 57 High St: spit drive wheel in attic over rear wing.

Figure 6.63. 57 High St: window opening converted to fireplace in early 19thC.

Figure 6.64. 57 High St: coal burning hearth in rebuilt gable end wall

Figure 6.65. 57 High St: late18th/early 19th C stair.

Figure 6.66. 57 High St: cupboard installed in redundant window opening.

Chapter 6

Figure 6.67. 57 High St: beam cased in early plaster.

Figure 6.68. 57 High St: rollers forming part of floor structure.

Figure 6.69. 57 High St: cellar wall.

Figure 6.70. 57 High St: W cellar room.

Figure 6.71. 57 High St: 17th C stone window frame in outbuilding.

Figure 6.72. 57 High St: fireplace in outbuilding.

VERNACULAR BUILDINGS OF STROUD

Figure 6.73. 50 High St from High St.

Figure 6.74. 50 High St: in Church St.

Figure 6.75. 50 High St: 17th C window frame and blocked door in Church St.

Figure 6.76. 50 High St: from High St in about 1910.

Figure 6.77. 50 High St: No 49, built in late 19th C on site of part of No 50.

Figure 6.78. 50 High St: stair to attic.

CHAPTER 6

Figure 6.79. 50 High St: first floor hearth in N gable end wall.

Figure 6.80. 50 High St: window seat in part facing Church St.

Figure 6.81. 50 High St: early partition wall and door in attic (S room).

Figure 6.82. 50 High St: early wood latch on attic door.

Figure 6.83. 50 High St: S attic room stripped out, showing extended collar trusses.

Figure 6.84. 50 High St: extended collar trusses embedded in rebuilt chimney gable.

Figure 6.85. 50 High St: intermediate truss now separating 50 and 49 High St.

Figure 6.86. 50 High St: double mortice for extended collar to principal joint.

Figure 6.87. 50 High St: intermediate truss seen from No 49, showing studs and beam lodging.

Figure 6.88. 50 High St: beam lodging in collar of intermediate truss, facing into No 49.

Figure 6.89. 50 High St: N attic room before being stripped out, showing extended collar truss.

Figure 6.90. 50 High St: cellar looking at N end wall.

Chapter 6

Figure 6.91. Church Court, formerly Rodney House.

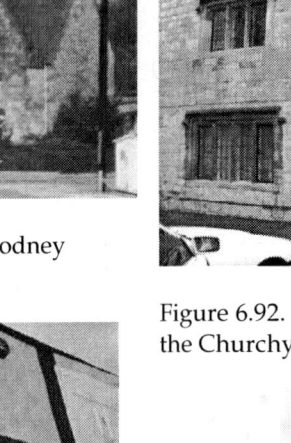

Figure 6.92. Church Court showing part facing the Churchyard.

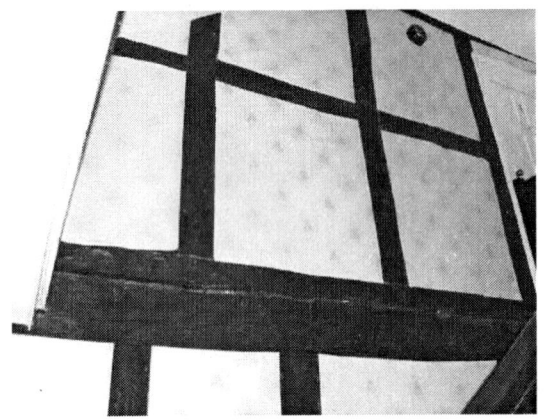

Figure 6.93. Church Court showing late 17th C timber frame walls associated with the added wings.

Figure 6.94. Church Court: 18th C stair.

Figure 6.95. Webbs Alms Houses in the 1930's, Church Court is at the end of the street.

Figure 6.96. 46 High Street in the late 1960's.

VERNACULAR BUILDINGS OF STROUD

Figure 6.97. View of the Corn Exchange from Nelson St in the early 20th C.

Figure 6.98. The Corn Exchange Hotel in the early 20th C, demolished 1960's.

Figure 6.99. Sunshine Health Stores in Church St.

Figure 6.100. 15 High St: in the mid 1990's.

Figure 6.101. 15 High St: in the early 20th C.

Figure 6.102. 15 High St: open well stair (early 19th C).

CHAPTER 6

Figure 6.103. 15 High St: open well stair.

Figure 6.104. 15 High St: wood panel above door (early 18th C).

Figure 6.105. 15 High St: hearth on 2nd floor (mid/late 19th C).

Figure 6.106. 15 High St: hearth on 2nd floor (mid/late 19th C).

Figure 6.107. 15 High St: two panel door with H hinges.

Figure 6.108. Bank House. (2006)

VERNACULAR BUILDINGS OF STROUD

Figure 6.109. 55 High St: in the early 20th C.

Figure 6.110. 55 High St: just prior to purchase by the Stroud Preservation Trust.

Figure 6.111. 55 High St: during restoration.

Figure 6.112. 55 High St: room on 2nd floor.

Figure 6.113. 55 High St: 2nd floor landing.

Figure 6.114. 55 High St: early 19th C hob grate on 2nd floor.

Chapter 6

Figure 6.115. 55 High St: ground floor hearth in rear wing, late 18th C.

Figure 6.116. 55 High St: late 18th C hob grate on first floor.

Figure 6.117. 55 High St: mid 19th C hob grate on first floor.

Figure 6.118. 55 High St: sash windows and architraves on first floor.

Figure 6.119. 55 High St: late 18th C closed string stair.

Figure 6.120. 55 High St: roof structure.

VERNACULAR BUILDINGS OF STROUD

Figure 6.121. 58 High St: front façade (1795), with new shopfront (early 1990's).

Figure 6.122. 58 High St: joist to beam lodgings in ground floor ceiling.

Figure 6.123. 58 High St: roof structure, looking towards High St.

Figure 6.124. 58 High St: roof structure, looking towards rear, showing entry from rear buildings.

Figure 6.125. 58 High St: during demolition, showing rear of building built over end bay of rear cottage.

Figure 6.126. 58 High St: cottages to rear, just prior to demolition.

175

CHAPTER 6

Figure 6.127. 58 High St: warehouse (early 20th C).

Figure 6.128. 58 High St: roof structure of cottage 1, looking towards entry to attic of No.58.

Figure 6.129. 58 High St: roof structure of cottage 2, looking towards cottage 1.

Figure 6.130. 58 High St: cellar (spooky, rats, yuch) under cottage 1.

Figure 6.131. 58 High St: roof structure over cottage 3, showing the extent of reinforcement of the early timbers.

Figure 6.132. Upper part of High St highlighting 19th C buildings.

176

VERNACULAR BUILDINGS OF STROUD

Figure 6.133. Stalls in the Shambles.

Figure 6.134. 58-62 High St in about 1940.

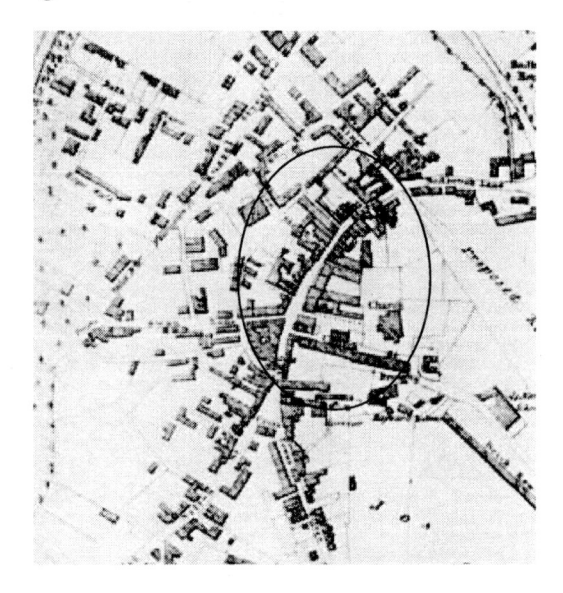

Figure 6.135. Wood's map of Stroud (1835).

Figure 6.136. Rear of 58-62 High St, after partial demolition in 1984.

Figure 6.137. 27 and 28 High St.

Figure 6.138. Kendrick St showing buildings with a 'national style'.

177

Chapter 6

Figure 6.139. The Subscription Rooms.

Figure 6.140. Congregational Church showing classical detail.

Figure 6.141. The Cross during the mid 19th C.

Figure 6.142. The new road and junction with Nelson St.

Figure 6.143. The buildings at the Cross prior to demolition in 1982 (same view as 142).

Figure 6.144. 35, 36 High St during demolition.

VERNACULAR BUILDINGS OF STROUD

Figure 6.145. Fireplace now in entrance to first floor of 33 High St.

Figure 6.146. 35 High St in the late 1970's.

Figure 6.147. 35 High St: late 18/early 19th C hearth.

Figure 6.148. 35 High St: site of earlier stair.

Figure 6.149. 35 High St: attic room partition and truss detail.

Figure 6.150. 35 High St: roof structure.

179

Chapter 6

Figure 6.151. The Crown Inn and Pet shop (late 1970's).

Figure 6.152. Co-Op building on N side of Cross.

Figure 6.153. The Cross- N side next to Parliament St, circa 1900.

Figure 6.154. The Cross: N side next to Nelson St, circa 1900.

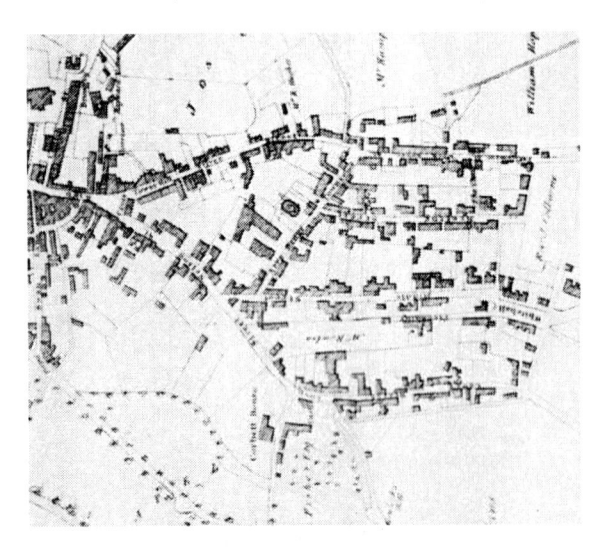

Figure 6.155. Wood's Map showing top of the town.

Figure 6.156. Parliament St in the 1960's.

VERNACULAR BUILDINGS OF STROUD

Figure 6.157. Parliament St in the early 1960's.

Figure 6.158. Parliament St in the early 1960's.

Figure 6.159. Parliament St in the early 1960's.

Figure 6.160. S side of Parliament St in the early 1960's.

Figure 6.161. Looking down Parliament St in the early 1960's.

Figure 6.162. The Old Workhouse at the top of Parliament St *(2006)*.

181

Chapter 6

Figure 6.163. St Albans Church.

Figure 6.164. Houses opposite St Albans Church in the early 1960's.

Figure 6.165. Nelson St: shops with accommodation above.

Figure 6.166. Nelson St: 19th C lock-up shops. (*1985*)

Figure 6.167. Nelson St: Early 18th C house/shop.

Figure 6.168. Nelson St: The Duke of York.

VERNACULAR BUILDINGS OF STROUD

Figure 6.169. 21 Nelson St: front elevation. *(in 1987)*

Figure 6.170. 23 Nelson St: side wall showing junction of 'new' building (brick side, ashlar front wall) with remains of earlier rubblestone wall. *(2005)*

Figure 6.171. 23 Nelson St: late 17th C hearth overlain by later brick wall. *(2005)*

Figure 6.172. 23 Nelson St: late 17th C owl window from inside. *(2005)*

Figure 6.173. 23 Nelson St: extended collar truss roof. *(2005)*

Figure 6.174. 23 Nelson St: ground floor ceiling structure.

CHAPTER 6

Figure 6.175. 21 Nelson St: first floor ceiling structure.

Figure 6.176. 23 Nelson St: half beam against side wall of Duke of York. *(2005)*

Figure 6.177. 23 Nelson St: detail of joist:beam lodging. *(2005)*

Figure 6.178. 19-20 Nelson St (early 19th C origin. *(1987)*

Figure 6.179. Nelson St: Godolphin House, demolished in the early 1960's.

Figure 6.180. Nelson St: Godolphin House, rear view.

VERNACULAR BUILDINGS OF STROUD

Figure 6.181. 14-15 Nelson St *(2006)*

Figure 6.182. 13-15 Nelson St. *(1990)*

Figure 6.183. Laurel Villa, 23 Nelson St: detail of front façade. *(1990)*

Figure 6.184. Laurel Villa, Nelson St: rear wing. *(1990)*

Figure 6.185. Laurel Villa, Nelson St: stepped chimney breast in attic.

Figure 6.186. Laurel Villa, Nelson St: roof truss in rear wing.

CHAPTER 6

Figure 6.187. Laurel Villa, Nelson St: ground floor wood window in rear wing. *(1990)*

Figure 6.188. Laurel Villa, Nelson St: segmented arch lintel in addition to rear wing. *(1990)*

Figure 6.189. Laurel Villa, 23 Nelson St: floor support beam in rear wing. *(1990)*

Figure 6.190. Laurel Villa, Nelson St: roof truss front part of building. *(1990)*

Figure 6.191. Laurel Villa, Nelson St: roof truss front part of building, showing opposite side to 6.190. *(1990)*

Figure 6.192. Laurel Villa, Nelson St: ground floor hearth. *(1990)*

Figure 6.193. Laurel Villa, Nelson St: ground floor hearth. *(1990)*

Figure 6.194. Laurel Villa, Nelson St: window seat on first floor. *(1990)*

Figure 6.195. Nelson St: houses formerly on E side (now the car park). *(1960's)*

Figure 6.196. The Castle, Castle St. *(2006)*

Figure 6.197. 4 Lower St. *(2005)*

Figure 6.198. 5 Lower St. *(2006)*

Chapter 6

Figure 6.199. N side of Lower St. *(early 1980's)*

Figure 6.200. S side of Lower St. *(early 1980's)*

Figure 6.201. 8 Lower St *(early 1980's)*

Figure 6.202. 9 Lower St. *(early 1980's)*

Figure 6.203. 15-18 Lower St. *(early 1980's)*

Figure 6.204. 10 Lower St. *(2006)*

188

Vernacular Buildings of Stroud

Figure 6.205. 11-12 Lower St. *(2006)*

Figure 6.206. Hemlock Well House, Lower St. *(2006)*

Figure 6.207. 8 Lower St *(early 1980's)*

Figure 6.208. New Inn, Lower St in about 1910

Figure 6.209. 44-47 Lower St. *(2006)*

Figure 6.210. 37 Lower St and 19th C building gable end to street. *(early 1980's)*

189

CHAPTER 6

Figure 6.211. 32-33 Lower St. *(2006)*

Figure 6.212. 26-28 Lower St. *(2006)*

Figure 6.213. Cottages in Trinity Rd. *(early 1990's)*

Figure 6.214. The Field. *(2006)*

Figure 6.215. Daneway, 6 Bowbridge Lane. *(mid 1970's)*

Figure 6.216. Ivy Cottage, Bowbridge Lane, early window frame. *(2006)*

Figure 6.217. Ivy Cottage Bowbridge Lane, chimney breast in front wall. *(2006)*

Figure 6.218. Field House, Bowbridge lane. *(2006)*

Figure 6.219. Late 17th C building at start of Middle St. *(2005)*

Figure 6.220. 24-25 Middle St. *(2005)*

Figure 6.221. 27-28 Middle St. *(2006)*

Figure 6.222. 43-44 Middle St. *(1978)*

VERNACULAR BUILDINGS OF STROUD

191

Chapter 6

Figure 6.223. 43-44 Middle St. *(1974)*

Figure 6.224. 43 Middle St: blocked window in gable end. *(1980)*

Figure 6.225. 43 Middle St: ground floor hearth. *(1978)*

Figure 6.226. 43 Middle St: first floor hearth. *(1978)*

Figure 6.227. 43 Middle St: late 17th C beam and 2-panel door. *(1982)*

Figure 6.228. 43 Middle St. roof structure. *(1978)*

VERNACULAR BUILDINGS OF STROUD

Figure 6.229. 43-44 Middle St. aerial view of cottages to rear in early 1930's.

Figure 6.230. 43 Middle St: remains of cottage to rear of garden. *(1974)*

Figure 6.231. 43 Middle St: excavated remains behind house. *(1978)*

Figure 6.232. 43 Middle St: excavated cottage to rear of house. *(1977)*

Figure 6.233. 55-57 Middle St. *(2005)*

Figure 6.234. 6-8 Middle St. *(2006)*

Chapter 6

Figure 6.235. 23 Middle St. *(2006)*

Figure 6.236. Middle St: Fern Royal. *(2006)*

Figure 6.237. Middle St: Terrace, including Fort View. *(2006)*

Figure 6.238. 70-71 Middle St *(2006)*

Figure 6.239. Middle St: Lancashire and Westbourne Buildings. *(2006)*

Figure 6.240. 1-2 Whitehall. *(2006)*

Figure 6.241. 9-11 Whitehall. *(2006)*

Figure 6.242. 9-11 Whitehall. *(2006)*

Figure 6.243. 12 Whitehall with new render. *(2005)*

Figure 6.244. 12 Whitehall without render. *(2004)*

Figure 6.245. 12 Whitehall: late 17th C hearth. *(2004)*

Figure 6.246. 12 Whitehall: original ground floor ceiling beams. *(2004)*

Chapter 6

Figure 6.247. 12 Whitehall: showing different colour plasters. *(2004)*

Figure 6.248. 12 Whitehall: showing original window widths. *(2004)*

Figure 6.249. 13 Whitehall. *(2006)*

Figure 6.250. S side of Chapel Street looking E. *(early 1960's)*

Figure 6.251. Chapel St looking W. *(early 1960's)*

Figure 6.252. Chapel St: cottage on S side at W end. *(demolished 1978)*

VERNACULAR BUILDINGS OF STROUD

Figure 6.253. Chapel St: S side, E end, three remaining cottages in the mid 1970's. *(demolished 1978)*

Figure 6.254. Chapel St: originally a single storey cottage in the 17th C, raised to 2-stories in the early 19th C and split into two. *(demolished 1978)*

Figure 6.255. Chapel St: the day before demolition. *(1978)*

Figure 6.256. Chapel St: cottage at E end of group shown in Fig 253. *(demolished 1978)*

Figure 6.257. Chapel St: N side in the mid 1970's.

Figure 6.258. 3 Chapel St: after refurbishment. *(1980)*.

CHAPTER 6

Figure 6.259. 3 Chapel St: before renovation. *(1978)*

Figure 6.260. 3 Chapel St: ground floor hearth opening *(1980)*

Figure 6.261. 3, 5 and 7 Chapel St in the early 1960's

Figure 6.262. 5 and 7 Chapel St during renovation. *(1980)*

Figure 6.263. 9 Chapel St. *(1978)*

Figure 6.264. 11-13 Chapel St in the early 20thC.

Figure 6.265 11-13 Chapel St: before renovation. *(1978)*

Figure 6.266. 5-13 Chapel St: after renovation. *(1983)*

Figure 6.267. 11 Chapel St: original hearth. *(1979)*

Figure 6.268. 13 Chapel St: fireplace and winder stair. *(1979)*

Figure 6.269. 11-13 Chapel St after demolition of rear wing. *(1980)*

Figure 6.270. 17 Chapel St just after renovation. *(1983)*

CHAPTER 6

Figure 6.271. 17 Chapel St: before renovation. *(1979)*

Figure 6.272. Chapel St: Queens Square. *(2005)*

Figure 6.273. 25 Chapel St: front. *(1995)*

Figure 6.274. 25 Chapel St: rear. *(1995)*

Figure 6.275. 25 Chapel St: original hearth on ground floor. *(1995)*

Figure 6.276. 25 Chapel St: remains of original stair. *(1995)*

Figure 6.277. 25 Chapel St: original winder stair to attic. *(1995)*

Figure 6.278. 25 Chapel St: original winder stair to attic. *(1995)*

Figure 6.279. 25 Chapel St: hearth added on ground floor with later ovens. *(1995)*

Figure 6.280. 25 Chapel St: detail of partially demolished ovens added to 6.279, viewed from rear. *(1995)*

Figure 6.281. 25 Chapel St: ceiling structure on ground floor. *(1995)*

Figure 6.282. 25 Chapel St: rebuilt rear wall in brick with lime mortar. *(1995)*

Figure 6.283. 25 Chapel St: hearth added on first floor. *(1995)*

Figure 6.284. 25 Chapel St: hearth added next to original chimney breast on first floor. *(1995)*

Figure 6.285. 25 Chapel St: extended collar, without principal rafters. *(1995)*

Figure 6.286. 25 Chapel St: stud wall in attic, through to rear addition. *(1995)*

Figure 6.287. 25 Chapel St: cottages in rear garden. *(1995)*

Figure 6.288. 25 Chapel St: cottages as seen from the chur. *(1976)*

Figure 6.289. 25 Chapel St: first floor of workshop. *(1995)*

Figure 6.290. 25 Chapel St: addition behind No. 25. *(1995)*

Figure 6.291. 25 Chapel St: rear addition behind No. 23. *(1995)*

Figure 6.292. 25 Chapel St: beam in rear addition. *(1995)*

Figure 6.293. Chapel St: the old Congregational Chapel. *(1995)*

Figure 6.294. Acre St: E side showing Hillside Flats and early 19th C cottage. *(1976)*

CHAPTER 6

Figure 6.295. 42 Acre St: Butchers Arms. *(mid 1960's)*

Figure 6.296. 42 Acre St: with rendering removed. *(2005)*

Figure 6.297. 44 Acre St. *(2005)*

Figure 6.298. Single storey cottage in Bowbridge Lane. *(2005)*

Figure 6.299. 19th C houses demolished at the top of Acre St (W side). *(mid 1960's)*

Chapter 7

What Happened to Stroud between 1960 and 2003

Cottage about to be demolished in Chapel Street: it originated as a single storey home in the 17th C, much of the original structure remained inside.

CONTENTS OF CHAPTER

There was much demolition of vernacular buildings in Stroud in the period up to the late 1970's: many good buildings were removed and some are described in the previous chapter. Further demolitions were planned, but, the attitude of many people who mainly moved into Stroud from the early 1970's was at variance with the plans laid down by the local council. There was opposition, which involved public campaigns and legal action, to stop further demolitions. These actions were successful and resulted in the saving of important buildings in the town, which in new uses are appreciated by many. The following 'areas of activities' are reviewed in this chapter:

> Further demolitions in Chapel St
> The Ring Road
> The Stroud Preservation Trust
> 58-62 High St
> Hill Paul

WHAT HAPPENED TO STROUD BETWEEN 1960 AND 2003

IN THE preceding chapter, the development of Stroud has been described according to the evidence left in the surviving historic buildings and from evidence found in old photographs and maps. It is clear that the town has evolved over many centuries and that part of the attraction of the place is that it contains a wide range of building styles. A high proportion of the buildings in the town itself and in the 'top of the town' can be described as vernacular. They are built using local stone and in a local style and they are in harmony with the landscape. The town expanded outside these areas in the second half of the 19th C to provide homes for the expanding industrial population. These buildings were constructed using nationally available materials and to a more national style. They are part of the history of Stroud and they do not look out of place along the sides of the Stroud valleys. The pace of development of Stroud was relatively slow until the mid 20th C. When extra houses were required, it just expanded outwards a little more or space around existing buildings in the older parts of the town was developed. However, matters changed dramatically in the post Second World War period. After the war, the desire was to look forward and a view developed that the old buildings of the town were time expired. Certainly, by this time the houses and cottages were regarded as poor quality housing and the shops were no longer considered able to meet the needs of post war retail developments. The buildings would have been damp and lacking modern sanitation and decent domestic and commercial facilities. The ravages of timber boring insects and decay would also have taken their toll on the structures. In the post war period, the authorities considered that the only way to upgrade the housing stock of Stroud was to demolish and redevelop. The same view was held for the older shops in the town centre. It was only after the 1960's that techniques, materials and skills were developed which would enable the old buildings to be upgraded to modern standards. In the period up to 1970, large areas of the top of the town were cleared. These areas included the Exchange Buildings, both sides of Parliament Street immediately above the Cross, the S side of Parliament Street opposite St Albans Church, buildings in the now Nelson Street car park and most of the S side of Chapel Street. Other parts of the town also suffered, including the loss of virtually the whole of Wallbridge **(Figure 7.1 and 2)**, where some important listed houses were demolished, together with Wallbridge Mill and the Stroud Brewery **(Figure 7.3)**. Some redevelopment did occur, with the construction of the Merrywalks shopping centre and the Police Station/Magistrates Court. However, these buildings added nothing to the character of the town and their construction marked the start of the gradual slide of Stroud towards visual anonymity.

The cleared areas at the Top of the Town and at Wallbridge were left as derelict ground, while plans were drawn up for their redevelopment. This took many years and by the early 1970's plans for further demolitions were announced, in particular the County wished to demolish some of Stroud's most important listed buildings to provide a route for a ring road. These buildings included the Old Police Station **(Figure 7.4)** and Petty Sessional Courts at the end of Merrywalks, The British School **(Figure 7.5)** and 32-34 High Street **(Figure 7.6)**. However, by this time, there had been an influx of new people into the town. They had moved here because they liked the character and feeling of Stroud and these 'incomers' considered that something was going wrong with the way the Planners were treating the town. They could see the cleared, derelict areas, they could see photographs of some of

CHAPTER 7

the good buildings that had been lost and could see nothing of value in what was proposed for the redevelopments. Actions were initiated to stop further demolitions and it is largely due to the activities of these people that the demolitions were halted and Stroud has retained some of its best buildings. All of these have now found new uses and have been upgraded to meet the needs of 21st century users.

Chapel Street

The first activities to halt further demolitions occurred in Chapel Street. In 1976, the Stroud District Council (SDC) vacated the houses on the N side of the street and the remaining cottages at the E end of the S side. They were left to become increasingly derelict and vandalised. Plans for their demolition were actively being considered by the Council. A group of concerned residents formed a group known as Chapscorp and lobbied for the retention of the houses. A booklet, entitled 'Jerusalem on Chapel Street' was published, in 1978, to raise public awareness on the future of the buildings. This contained photographs and poems relating to the plight of the buildings. The SDC decided not to demolish the buildings on the N side and to incorporate them in the scheme for the redevelopment of the area. Unfortunately, those remaining on the S side were demolished. The activities to save the Chapel Street buildings were fairly low key and were confined to lobbying, letters to the paper and raising the profile locally.

The Ring Road

Around the same time, plans were announced for the construction of a ring road for Stroud. This had been at the planning stage for some years and some demolition to clear its intended path had already occurred. The new Police Station had already been constructed next to the route of the proposed road. It was planned to run from the N end of Merrywalks over the spur of the hill next to the Library and Church, through the Cross and then down to join London Road. It was not really a ring road as it divided the town into two separate parts, the commercial centre and the residential part. Visually it was a disaster and its construction required the demolition of some important listed buildings. Following the announcement of the formal plans and the applications to demolish the listed buildings, there was a campaign to prevent the construction of the road and to save the listed buildings. This was far larger and more acrimonious than earlier actions to save Stroud. The Stroud Campaign Against the Ring Road (SCARR) had a large membership, which held fund raising events, organized a petition, did work to raise money and lobbied locally and nationally. Opposing views were expressed by many in the town. Some thought that the campaign against the construction of the road was being organised by protestors from Bristol! Others felt that the whole concept of the road was totally misguided and would have a very negative impact on the life of the town. It stimulated a lively and at times bitter debate on the future of Stroud. The late Claire Toy wrote a parody of the saga of the road as a children's book, entitled 'The Plotter of Gloucester'. In the Foreword to the book, Ian Nairn of the Sunday Times wrote *'This story happens to be about a real town, and a very fine place it is too. But it is a parable for all towns. Especially towns like Stroud, which are undervalued because they don't conform to conventional standards of beauty. My kind of town: your own, maybe'*. Matters were brought to a head when the County Council applied for planning permission to demolish the listed buildings that stood in the path of the road. The opposition was vocal and many letters of opposition were sent, together with a petition, to the Council. The Secretary of State decided that the demolition of the buildings should be the subject of a public inquiry. This was held in Stroud in 1976, over a period of 3 weeks. The case against the demolition (and the rejection of the plans for the road) was made by SCARR and was presented by Alan Ford. The Inspector accepted the views of the Objectors and permission to demolish the buildings was rejected. This meant that the plans for the ring road had to be abandoned and Stroud was saved from this ill-conceived scheme. The listed buildings had been purchased by the County Council, as part of the preparations for the road scheme and all lay empty and increasingly threatened by vandalism. Fairly quickly, the Old Police Station and British School found new uses, but Nos 32 –34 High Street were in a particularly derelict state and they remained empty and under threat for several more years.

The Stroud Preservation Trust

In the late 1970's, plans for a link road were announced by the County, which would connect London Road to the Cross. It was the less contentious half of the old ring road scheme. The benefit of this road was that it would enable the High Street to be pedestrianised and would improve access to the Top of the Town. The downside was that the construction would require the demolition of the buildings on the S side of the Cross. By this time all of the buildings here had been derelict for over 10 years and some were in a dangerous state. The group included 32-34 High Street, which were in the worst state of repair and had already received extensive emergency works to prevent collapse (**Figure 7.7**). However, preliminary investigations by members of SCARR had shown that No. 33 retained substantial elements of an early building. Expert advice had been sought and the initial view was that the building could be medieval in origin and as such was one of the earliest surviving secular buildings of the town. An offer to save the building was made by the County Council to those involved with the Ring Road Campaign. If they formed a building preservation trust to restore the building, then the building would be given to the trust for £1. Clearly a substantial undertaking for those with limited commercial building experience and possibly an act of brinkmanship by the County, i.e. do something or keep quiet. This is how the Stroud Preservation Trust came into existence. The Trust was formed with six initial trustees: Julian Usborne, Ann Mackintosh, Ian Mackintosh, John Thomas, Robin Wichard and Nigel Paterson. Julian was the first Chair of the Trust. The Trust gathered a membership and together moved the work forward. The building was thoroughly investigated and the architectural development worked out. We did not find direct evidence for the early origins that were suggested by the preliminary investigations. However, it did retain substantial parts of a building dating back to the 16th C, or possibly a bit earlier. It had grown with Stroud, with additions and modifications being made throughout its long life. The former presence of a medieval building on the site cannot be ruled out, but so many changes had been made that it was difficult to detect in the present structure. Plans were drawn up for the restoration of the building, by the Fielden and Clegg Partnership (Architects in Bath). The Manpower Services Commission provided the labour through a job creation scheme, as unemployment was high at the time. A loan was obtained from the Architectural Heritage Fund to cover the building costs. The work was managed directly by the Trust and Julian Usborne and Ann Mackintosh ran the day to day activities. A site foreman was employed to organise the building team and do the work. The adjacent buildings were demolished to provide the space for the new road and reclaimed materials were used in the restoration of No. 33. The project was finished successfully in 1982 and the properties were sold on the open market (**Figure 7.8 to 7.11**). The proceeds were used to pay off the loans incurred during the restoration and the surplus funds formed the initial rolling fund of the Trust.

In 1984, the Trust purchased No. 55 High Street (**Figure 7.12-14**). Investigations by Ian Mackintosh showed that it had been built in 1782 and that it had been an important commercial building throughout its life. The former garden to the rear had been fully developed with 19th and 20th C buildings

Chapter 7

(**Figure 7.15**). A loan was obtained from the AHF to assist purchase and to cover the building costs. This time a site manager was employed, who organised the building work. The main building was converted to a large ground floor shop with flats on the first and second floors. This was the first time that accommodation had been generated above a shop in the town for many years (**Figure 7.16**). Since then many more upper floors above the shops of the town have been brought back into domestic use. The rear yard was cleared of the most recent warehousing and a 19th C brick building was retained. A former alley running through No 55 was re-opened to give access to the rear area (**Figure 7.17**), which was converted to a yard containing small shops and a café. This was called Witheys Yard (**Figure 7.18**), after the family that owned the building as a Chemist's for many years. The property market was on the up whilst the work was being done, so a healthy surplus was made on the project, which increased the size of the fund that could be rolled on to the next project.

In 1985 (after 2 years of negotiation), the Trust obtained a forty year lease on the Goods Shed at Stroud Station. Although this was a Grade 2* Listed Building, it had lost its roof covering and the timber roof structure was starting to deteriorate. Also, some of the stonework was in poor condition. Built to a design by Brunel in 1845, it dated from the construction of the railway. It had ceased to be used by the railway in the 1960's. The Trust spent £100,000 in replacing the roof and stonework and restoring the building to its original form (**Figure 7.19**). The intention was to then find a suitable user and convert it for a new use. This has taken far longer than was ever anticipated. Detailed discussions have been held and schemes drawn up with several potential users. However, the conversion costs are very high and this has made it difficult to secure the capital funding, with a relatively short-term lease. Potential uses have included a music resource centre and a restaurant/ café/ music venue. Since the restoration, the Trust has maintained the building at a considerable expense to combat vandalism and to prevent renewed deterioration. There are now hopes (2004) that finally we are moving towards building a financial formula that will enable the Shed to be converted to an arts exhibition centre: fingers crossed!

The Trust's next project was the Toll House at Cainscross. This was owned by the Co-Op, but had lain empty for several years (**Figure 7.20**). In 1987, we purchased the Toll House and the two adjoining brick built houses. The group was restored as three separate dwellings (**Figure 7.21 and 22**). The detail of a painting in the Stroud Museum was used in the restoration of the façade of the building (**Figure 7.23**). The restored houses were sold and again a surplus was made and the rolling fund further increased.

In 1990, the Trust, with the aid of an AHF loan, purchased Arundell Mill House and cottages. These are sited to the S of London Road, below Coulter's Garage. The properties were in an extremely delicate state (**Figure 7.24 - 27**), having been unoccupied for about a decade. They belonged to Michael Bishop, whose family had bought the site in the late 1940's. As the years progressed, family members passed away and nothing was thrown away. Michael was the remaining family member and presided over the final decay of the house and contents. In the mid 1980's, he had to move out of the house, as it had become unsafe to occupy. He boarded up the property and made it as secure as he could. Despite daily visits by him, the house was increasingly subjected to vandalism and theft. It contained some good antique furniture, books and other items, which were slowly mouldering inside (**Figure 7.28 – 30**). In the late 1980's, following an approach from the Trust, he agreed to sell the emptied properties to the Trust for restoration. This was a large undertaking, as without the rapid actions by the Trust, the main house could have collapsed. Emergency works were undertaken to prop up the main house, whilst plans were made for the conversion of the main house to three dwellings and the restoration of the two semi detached cottages. The wing, behind the main house, was leased to a joinery company and work could not start there until the lease expired. The cottages were restored first and sold (**Figure 7.31 and 32**), before work embarked on the main house. Extensive work was necessary, with one part being completely rebuilt. Many good features were uncovered during the work (**Figure 7.33 - 35**) and the split into three houses corresponded to the three main phases of development of the building (**Figure 7.36 and 37**). Small gardens were allocated to each house, with the main grounds being retained as a communal garden. The completion of the work on this part of the project, in 1993, was marked by an opening ceremony, attended by Prince Michael of Kent. The economics of this project were not good. We bought the property at the peak of the late 1980's property boom for £250,000. However, the property market crashed soon after, which combined with the high restoration costs, resulted in a project deficit of some £50,000. This was unfortunate, but the project had saved buildings that would otherwise have been lost and did create some nice homes. The lease on the rear wing expired some four years later. The Trust decided to sell the wing unconverted to minimise the potential for further losses. It was sold for £25000 and has subsequently been sympathetically converted into two cottages.

The Trust has not embarked on any more large projects. We did try to purchase No. 15 High Street and had a feasibility study conducted on its restoration and future use. The restoration costs were very high because of the deteriorated state of the building. We could not develop a viable project at the asking price for the building and the owner would not accept a reduced amount. We could therefore not proceed with the project. The building did eventually sell, but it is noteworthy that it remains in a derelict and deteriorating state and is a blot on the High Street. Presumably, the new owner realised that it was not possible to generate a viable restoration scheme. Or is someone speculating on the general rise in property values at Stroud's expense? It is only in the last year (2005) that the 'new' owner was forced to sell the property (to an unknown buyer). This followed a formal action by the Stroud District Council, who used their powers to ensure something was done to get the building repaired. So, hopefully, in the not too distant future, this building will be restored and will again be able to make a positive contribution to the historic environment of the High St.

Over the years, the Stroud Preservation Trust has also helped out in other issues relating to the conservation and promotion of our local historic buildings. It provided some seed funding to the Woodchester Mansion Trust, it contributed to the restoration of the carrilion of bells at St Laurence's Church in Stroud, played a prominent role in the restoration of the Anti Slavery Arch at Paganhill and has promoted our local buildings through exhibitions and public lectures. It is still working to bring the Goods Shed back into use and could spring back into action should the need arise.

The present Trust Directors are Geoff Beckerleg, Stephen Davis, Camilla Hale, Tim Harrison, Anne Mackintosh, Ian Mackintosh and Nigel Paterson. Other Directors have come and gone over the years and these include Alison Buchanan, Alan Ford, Hugh Barton and Janet Gaskell.

58-62 High Street

In the early 1980's, these properties were owned by Milwards (the shoe company) and they had a shop in No. 58, with storage in the cottages behind (**Figure 7.38**). The other premises had been leased to tenants, but over the years had gradually fallen vacant. Lack of maintenance and structural problems with Nos 60 and 61 resulted in a proposal by the owners, for the demolition of the whole block and the redevelopment with a pastiche in the Cotswold vernacular style. The scheme gained the support of the District Council, who were keen to have the 'unsafe' buildings demolished. The resistance to the demolition of these listed buildings grew rapidly and the Stroud High Street Action Group (SHSAG) was formed. Many activities took place to stop the demolition and again there was an acrimonious de-

Chapter 7

bate between those who sought to save the buildings and the authorities, who wanted them removed. To raise the stakes, the council parked old refuse collection lorries in front of the buildings in the High Street, as it considered that they were in imminent danger of collapse. As you can imagine this did not exactly enhance the street scene and could not be taken entirely seriously! The 'dangerous' state of the buildings was used to justify demolition on the grounds of public safety. 'Not so' thought the objectors and as soon as demolition began, protestors moved onto the rooftops. This direct action stopped the demolition, whilst a High Court Injunction was sought by SHSAG, and obtained, to halt further work. A public inquiry ensued in which the action group argued that the listed buildings had been allowed to fall into disrepair, with the intention of seeking permission to demolish. This made a mockery of listing buildings to ensure that they were protected. The view of the protestors was upheld and permission was only granted for the dismantling of the dangerous parts of the structures and the storage of these parts in preparation for the reconstruction of the buildings. In 1984, Hatton Developments purchased 58-62 High Street and developed proposals for the restoration of the best elements of the buildings and attracting retailers back to the High Street. The proposals were accepted and the street frontages were restored, including the rebuilding of 60 and 61 using as much of the original materials as possible **(Figure 7.39)**. The appearance of the rear elevations was maintained by limiting new build to single storey additions. The scheme was facilitated by the construction of the link road between the Cross and London Road, which enabled the pedestrianisation of the High Street to proceed. It seemed that at last a sensible balance between the conservation of the historic buildings and the enhancement of the character of the town with the needs of modern retailing had been found. The High Street returned to being an active shopping street and the retained buildings give it character and a sense of history.

Hill Paul Building

This building was built in 1898 for Williamson and Tratt and Co, a clothing manufacturer. This firm went into liquidation in 1902 and the building was taken over by Hill Paul and Co, another clothing manufacturer. In 1971, this company was still employing 110 people in the building, but it closed soon after. The building then remained empty and deteriorating for the next 30 years. The building was built with six storeys and is a prominent landmark of the town. There were various suggestions for its re-use following the closure of Hill Paul and Co, including a new museum and conversion to a new magistrate's court, however, none of these progressed beyond the early discussion stage. In the 1980's, planning permission was obtained by the then owners for conversion to apartments. This was granted, as it was hoped that this would give the building as new lease of life. However, the conversion was never started. The granting of planning permission increased the value of the building and it was sold. The new owners left the building to deteriorate. In the late 1990's concern was growing about the state of the building. The roof was leaking badly and the internal floor structures were decaying and rot was taking hold of the building. Also, some of the upper brickwork, adjacent to Cheapside was considered to be in danger of collapse. The building stands in a conservation area, but the SDC did not use its powers to ensure the building was maintained in a weatherproof state. Attempts to get the building listed failed on several occasions.

By this time the building belonged to Harper Homes and they decided that demolition of the building and redevelopment was the way forward for the site. The SDC agreed and granted planning permission for demolition. The Council had also served a dangerous structures notice on the owners. Campaigners formed the Hill Paul Regeneration Group and set about saving the building **(Figure 7.40)**. They vowed to fight the demolition to the end. Significant amounts of money were raised from private individuals towards the cost of buying the building. Some £85000 was raised in the first two weeks of the campaign, but a total of around £1.3 million was needed to secure the building for the future of Stroud, together with the adjacent Graham Reeves site **(Figure 7.41)**. The Hill Paul Regeneration Company was formed by some members of the Group to take on the acquisition and conversion of the building. In December 2000, a wrecking crane was moved onto the site with the intention of demolishing the building quickly **(Figure 7.42)**. Urgent negotiations were held with the owners and against all odds, an agreement was reached. An initial payment was made and monies for further regular payments had to be raised. This saved the building from immediate demolition and the crane was removed. Emergency works were done to remove the hazards and temporary weatherproofing was done. The magnitude of the fund raising task was daunting and very quickly it became apparent that sufficient funds would not be raised to meet the payments. Negotiations were held with Cheltenham Builders, with the aim of their purchase of the Graham Reeves site to reduce the financial burden on the Hill Paul Regeneration Company. However, this would still mean that an 'over the odds' purchase price would be paid for the Hill Paul Building. Negotiations continued and finally agreement was reached with Chelbury Homes that they would purchase the whole site and undertake the restoration and conversion of Hill Paul, together with the redevelopment of the adjacent site. A key factor in their plan was to add an extra two floors to the building and this made the project viable to them. Their plans, after some discussion, were accepted by all and finally Hill Paul had been saved. Building work was completed in 2003, and the converted building is a credit to all those involved in its rescue **(Figure 7.43 and 44)**. The saving of this building was an enormous undertaking (both physically, mentally and financially) for those who were prepared to get involved with the campaign. The building was saved by their efforts and stands as a record of their commitment. Recognition must also go Chelbury Homes, who trod where other developers feared to go.

Chapter 7

Figure 7.1. Wallbridge: Midland Cottages, demolished c.1976.

Figure 7.2. Wallbridge: Kings Arms Inn, demolished late 1960's.

Figure 7.3. Wallbridge: Stroud Brewery in 1966, demolished soon after.

Figure 7.4. The Old Police Station and Courts, boarded up in 1975.

Figure 7.5: The British School in 1975.

Figure 7.6. 32-34 High St in the mid 1970's.

What Happened to Stroud Between 1960 and 2003

Figure 7.7. Stroud Preservation Trust: 32-34 High St, as purchased for £1.

Figure 7.8. Stroud Preservation Trust: 32-34 High St, work in progress.

Figure 7.9. Stroud Preservation Trust: 32-34 High St, restored building.

Figure 7.10. Stroud Preservation Trust: 32-34 High St, restored building.

Figure 7.11: Stroud Preservation Trust: 32-34 High St, restored building.

Figure 7.12. Stroud Preservation Trust: 55 High St, as purchased.

217

CHAPTER 7

Figure 7.13. Stroud Preservation Trust: 55 High St, work in progress.

Figure 7.14. Stroud Preservation Trust: 55 High St, restored building.

Figure 7.15. Stroud Preservation Trust: 55 High St, rear buildings before work started.

Figure 7.16. Stroud Preservation Trust: 55 High St, work in progress on a first floor flat.

Figure 7.17: Stroud Preservation Trust: 55 High St, re-opening the alley.

Figure 7.18. Stroud Preservation Trust: 55 High St, Withey's Yard.

WHAT HAPPENED TO STROUD BETWEEN 1960 AND 2003

Figure 7.19. Stroud Preservation Trust: Goods Shed at Stroud Station, restored.

Figure 7.20. Stroud Preservation Trust: Toll House, before restoration.

Figure 7.21. Stroud Preservation Trust: Toll House, work in progress.

Figure 7.22. Stroud Preservation Trust: Toll House, restored.

Figure 7.23: Stroud Preservation Trust: Toll House, painting in Stroud Museum.

Figure 7.24. Stroud Preservation Trust: Arundell Mill House, as purchased.

219

Chapter 7

Figure 7.25. Stroud Preservation Trust: Arundell Mill Cottages, as purchased.

Figure 7.26. Stroud Preservation Trust: Arundell Mill House, after removal of invasive trees.

Figure 7.27. Stroud Preservation Trust: Arundell Mill House and Cottages after removal of all vegetation.

Figure 7.28. Stroud Preservation Trust: Arundell Mill House, inside, prior to purchase. The clock was stolen within a couple of days of the photo being taken.

Figure 7.29: Stroud Preservation Trust: Arundell Mill House, inside, prior to purchase.

Figure 7.30. Stroud Preservation Trust: Arundell Mill House, bedroom, prior to purchase.

Figure 7.31. Stroud Preservation Trust: Arundell Mill Cottages, work in progress.

Figure 7.32. Stroud Preservation Trust: Arundell Mill Cottages, restored.

Figure 7.33. Stroud Preservation Trust: Arundell Mill House, 17th C window and roof line of earlier building hidden by early 19th wing.

Figure 7.34. Stroud Preservation Trust: Arundell Mill House, 17thC hearth that was discovered.

Figure 7.35: Stroud Preservation Trust: Arundell Mill House, 17th C hearth restored.

Figure 7.36. Stroud Preservation Trust: Arundell Mill House, work in progress.

CHAPTER 7

Figure 7.37. Stroud Preservation Trust: Arundell Mill House, restored.

Figure 7.38. 58 High St, former Milwards Shoe Shop, under threat of demolition.

Figure 7.39. 58-62 High St, saved and renovated.

Figure 7.41: Campaign to save the Hill Paul building.

Figure 7.40. Campaign to save the Hill Paul building.

222

WHAT HAPPENED TO STROUD BETWEEN 1960 AND 2003

Figure 7.42. Hill Paul Building: headlines from Stroud News and Journal.

Figure 7.43. Hill Paul Building restored.

Figure 7.44. Hill Paul Building restored.

223

CHAPTER 8

VERNACULAR BUILDINGS OF CHALFORD

The villages at Chalford on a 1905 postcard (the writer of the card notes that Chalford is a very pretty spot).

CONTENTS OF CHAPTER

HERE, THE settlements and buildings at Chalford are discussed. The origins of the settlements and their strong association with the cloth industry are described, together with a description of the surviving buildings. The area is not fully recognised for its true historic worth. There are so many buildings remaining from its 'industrial past' and these tell the story of the people and its industry. The chapter is divided into two sections: Chalford Hill and Chalford Vale/Chalford St Mary's.

Chalford Hill: Thoughts on the development of the village are given, together with a description of its cottages, which range in date from the mid 17th to the mid 19th C. How the cottages have changed over the years is discussed. Some more detailed descriptions of buildings are given and these have been analysed using the principles given in the initial chapters of the book. Cottages are described along the lanes that lead through the village. A map is given to identify these lanes, together with many photos, mainly taken from the lanes. Be prepared to get lost when walking around the village, it can be confusing if you don't live here!

Chalford Vale/St Mary's: The development of the mills, houses and cottages in the valley is described. This is where the clothiers lived and they controlled the local cloth industry and many of their houses survive, although the mill buildings were largely rebuilt in the 19th C to meet changing production needs. Combined with the buildings are the transport links, which were introduced between the late 18th and mid 19th C. Briefs details of the mills and associated houses are given: these are described moving East along the valley from St Mary's. There are fewer cottages in the valley than on the hill and a general outline of these is given.

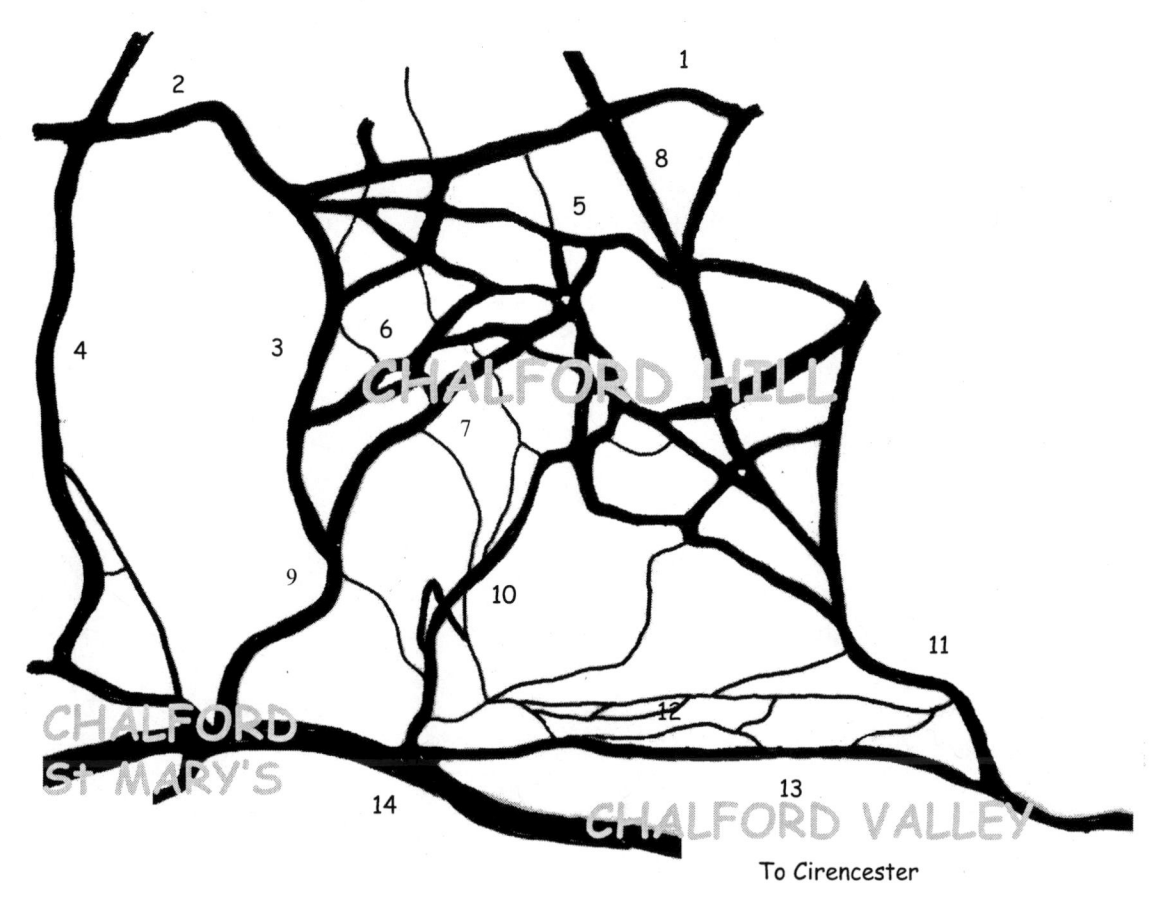

1. Burcombe rd
2. Abnash
3. Skiveralls
4. Old Neighbourhood
5. Midway
6. Silver St
7. Commercial Rd
8. Middle Hill
9. Dark Lane
10. Marle Hill
11. Coppice Hill
12. Rack Hill
13. High St
14. London Rd (A419)

THE LANES AND FOOTPATHS OF CHALFORD

Chapter 8

8.1 Some Background

The cloth making industry had begun to develop in the Stroud area, as early as the 12th C. However, the population was decimated by the black-death in the 14th C and this resulted in the disappearance of the early cloth industry. It was only in the 16th C that it began to recover and many of the villages that are sited along the sides of the Stroud valleys owe their existence to this second development of the weaving industry. Prior to this, in the medieval period, the importance of the wool growing industry grew and created great wealth for the few who owned land and the large flocks of sheep. At that time, wool was mainly exported to mainland Europe for weaving. The earlier local settlements, such as Bisley, Minchinhampton and Painswick are associated with the wool growing industry and they each have an impressive church, built using the wealth generated from the selling of the wool. The Minchinhampton Custumal gives a good picture of the medieval wool growing and cloth industries in the Parish of Minchinhampton and an analogy is probably valid with Bisley Parish. Bisley is the local settlement with the earliest known origin and this can be traced back to at least the Saxon period, possibly earlier. The name Bisley is thought to be of Saxon, or possibly Roman origin and may be derived from the words 'pasture of the does' (*Biss*, a hind or doe and *ley*, a lea or pasture). Mary Rudd provides a fuller discussion on the origin of the name. Here, the settlement developed as a self sufficient, agricultural community in which the importance of wool growing for weaving developed from medieval times. There was earlier occupation in the area. Remains of this include the Roman villa at Lillyhorn, near Bournes Green (**Figure 8.1**) and the important Roman mosaics at Woodchester. The site of the villa at Lilleyhorn was excavated in the 18th C and again in the 19th C and Mary Rudd records some details, but the villa site is not accessible to the public. There are still earlier remains in the form of burial mounds. There are two long barrows from the late Neolithic period (about 4000 years old) at the Camp (**Figure 8.2**) and a round barrow (known as Money Tump) in the field behind Nashend Farm (**Figure 8.3**).

Chalford is the name applied to the area containing the settlements of Chalford St Mary's, Chalford Vale, Bussage (the old part) and Chalford Hill. They grew with the cloth industry in the 17th and later centuries and stand on the ridge, on the fringe of the former Bisley commons and in the immediate valley. The weaving was cottage-based and each cottage would have contained a loom. The cloth (the piece) was sold on to a clothier, who managed the subsequent mill-based preparation stages of the cloth and the sale of the finished material, generally via a factor in London. The cloth industry prospered in the 17thC as witnessed by the large number of cottages remaining from that time (many now in a much changed form).

There were ancient tracks leading through the area and these would have passed through Bisley. One led from Bisley over the common land to what is now Chalford Hill and is thought to have continued down Dark Lane to the crossing point of the River Frome, near Chalford Place. Tracks would also have led to outlying settlements and to other fords across the river. Chalford Vale has an early root in an estate mentioned in the Domesday Book and sited near Chalford Place. It probably developed as there was a crossing point of the river and it was a suitable site for a corn mill. Here, the power in the River Frome was harnessed to drive a water-powered mill. There are other early settlement sites along the valley floor and these too are based on early mill sites and/or river crossing points. There are too many mills noted in early records for them all to have been corn mills and it is likely that some must have been the fulling mills of the early cloth industry. Examples of houses in the valley containing early cores are St Mary's Mill House, Chalford Place and Green Court and these are the houses of the clothiers/mill owners, who developed the industry in the Chalford area. The local cloth industry developed strongly from the early/mid 17th C and the ridge villages originate from this time as settlements of weavers. It is possible that there were a few existing farmsteads incorporated into the new settlements, as a few houses contain remnants of earlier buildings. The settlements continued to develop in the 18th and early 19th C with the continued expansion of the cloth industry. The number of mills increased as the cloth industry grew, so that eventually the valley bottom became crowded with mills and there was competition for the limited water supply from the river and springs.

8.2 Development of Chalford Hill and its Cottages

The villages were established on the ridge as settlements of handloom weavers, where there was a good supply of building stone from both the Inferior and Great Oolite strata and a strong supply of well and spring water (at the junction between the Great Oolite and the Fuller's Earth clays). The valley would have been regarded as being less ideal for settlement because the valley floor was damp and prone to flooding. Also, the light is better on the hilltop, a prime requirement for weaving. The folklore is that the villages initially grew as unplanned squatters settlements of handloom weavers on the edge of the Bisley Common. This is probably true, but the houses surviving from the 17th C are well constructed cottages, with some good, but simple, detail. Perhaps these have replaced the first, earlier and more temporary cottages. The villages developed as self-sufficient communities, so that besides weavers, there were all those needed to provide the requirements of a working community. The stone for the cottages was dug locally. On the valley side and on the hilltop there is much evidence for stone quarrying and a limited amount of mining. This has not been studied in any detail in the Chalford area, but it must have been an industry of an appreciable size, requiring a significant workforce of quarrymen and stone masons. There are extensive areas of quarried land in the area of Rack Hill at Chalford and many workings were formerly present on the top of the hill in all of the ridge villages. Many of the quarries on the top have been infilled and the land redeveloped in recent times, whereas the workings on the valley side have been left as a terrace, with limited development.

The earliest part of the village is built around the head of a small valley eroded at right angles to the main valley of the River Frome. There are active springs here and these feed a small stream that descends over the clay band to be re-absorbed when it reaches the porous Inferior Oolite and Cotswold Sands. Since the last ice age ended (about 10000 years ago), the springs have eroded out the valley in the Fullers Earth clay band, leaving the exposed, overlying Great Oolite to shear and breakaway when it became unstable. The major valley development must have occurred in the immediate post glacial period, when the rainfall and water run off were much higher than today. The early houses were built around the head of the valley, some on the clay and some on the overlying stone. Some were built alongside the course of the stream that runs down Marle Hill. The actual siting of the cottages seems to have been determined by the immediate lie of the land and by the knowledge of the builder. It seems that the original cottages were sited close to the tracks that ran through the area. The present lane that leads from Midway to Commercial Road and on to Dark Lane may be following an early route. There are at least eleven cottages/houses with parts dating from the mid/late 17th C, lying close to this route: these include (starting near Midway), The Old Malt House (**Figure 8.4**), Weavers Cottage, Little France Cottage (**Figure 8.5**), Halstead (**Figure 8.6**), Fleece House (**Figure

Chapter 8

8.7), Fleece Cottage, The Ferns **(Figure 8.8)**, Glenhaven **(Figure 8.9)**, Clematis Cottage **(Figure 8.10)**, Holly Bank **(Figure 8.11)**, The Orchards **(Figure 8.12)** and Elm Cottage **(Figure 8.13)**. Another route may have split from this and passed down Marle Hill and there are at least eight cottages with 17th C origins close to this: these are Grey Cott **(Figure 8.14)**, Farthingcote **(Figure 8.15)**, Hazel Cottage **(Figure 8.16)** (part of the Bunch of Nuts), Mole Cottage **(Figure 8.17)**, The Glen **(Figure 8.18)**, Marle Hill Cottages **(Figure 8.19)**, Steep Cottage **(Figure 8.20)**, Glen Cottage **(Figure 8.21)** and Marle Hill House **(Figure 8.22)**. These two groups of cottages account for the majority of the earliest buildings noted in the village. All of these properties originated as small cottages: some retain their original appearance, others are heavily disguised by later additions. At least two of them started as single storey dwellings, with an attic room. The others appear to have been 2-storeys, with an attic room, from the start. The majority only had one room per floor. The 2-storey cottages are thought to date from the second half of the 17thC. Another track may have led through Abnash and joined the other track running through the village at the top of the steep part of Dark Lane, below Skiveralls House. There are several houses with early origins to the side of this lane. These are Skiveralls House, The Cordieries, Abnash House and Byways **(Figure 8.23)**. Both The Corderries and Skiveralls House are based on smaller houses, rather than cottages. Byways dates from the mid 17th C, but has a reused 2-light lancet window in the front wall. This window could date from the 14th C and strongly suggests that this area had been inhabited for several centuries before the main village developed. Perhaps, there were outlying farmsteads beyond the common land?

The earliest cottages of Chalford Hill were set in individual plots of land with areas of common land remaining between them. Over the 18th and 19th C additional cottages were added on the dwindling amount of common within the settlement. Additions were also made to the existing cottages and further cottages and workshops were built within the early garden plots. Property boundaries were invariably marked by dry stone walls **(Figure 8.24)**. The garden would have been used for growing food, so it was important to prevent animals, from the surrounding common land, invading the garden and eating the crops. Formal 'Rights of Way' were designated to respect the pathways that had developed through and within the settlement, but using the residual common. In 1865, the common lands between Chalford and Bisley were enclosed and the small parcels of residual common within the village were rationalised. This resulted in the construction of more cottages /houses on these plots. The Triangle is built on one such plot. The much told story is that the plot was bought by a villager, who then offered to re-sell it to the owner of Grey Cot at a profit. On principle the offer was rejected and so a house was built to block views from Grey Cot to spite the owner **(Figure 8.25)**. By the mid 19th C the village had become fully developed and the village has retained its present character from that time. The village contains no very large houses and only a few larger houses and even these seem to be formed by the amalgamation of smaller buildings. It developed from a settlement of handloom weavers, to provide housing for those working across the whole spectrum of local industries. It remained in this state until the immediate post Second World War period. By this time the state of many of the houses had deteriorated and they did not contain the amenities and facilities expected in the post war world **(Figures 8.26 and 8.27)**. The authorities will have regarded the cottages as sub standard and new housing was built on the periphery of the old village. There was not the desire, materials or techniques to upgrade the old cottages. New houses were preferred by most. This shift to new housing and the general decline in the industrial nature of the local industry meant that many of the old cottages were left empty for a period and a few were demolished (e.g. in the area of the Wheatsheaves in Chalford Hill). Major changes have occurred in the commercial make-up of the village since the 1960's and it has transformed from a village with a complete suite of shops and services, which enabled the village to be self sufficient to one which is now almost fully dependent on externally supplied goods (although, there is still a butchers shop and an electrical shop, which part meet the demands for these particular goods). This has been accompanied by a shift in the social make-up. The local industries have continued to decline and with it the need for a large local workforce. The industrial workers houses of the village (which is what many of the original weaver's cottages had become) have been 'gentrified'. Cottages have been combined to form larger houses and many extensions have been built. Many new people have moved into the village in the past 30 years and have spent much time and money in renovating/restoring the old cottages. In the main, the character of the village has been maintained, but great care must be taken to ensure that there is not a slow, but continual erosion of its vernacular character. By this, I mean the construction of large extensions, in inappropriate materials, which do not respect the scale and detail of the adjoining buildings. This particularly applies within the part of the village designated as a conservation area.

THE COTTAGES

17th C: Some of the earliest surviving structures show that the earliest cottages were built with a single storey and an attic room, under a steeply pitched roof. Only a couple of single storey cottages now remain (in the Chalford area) **(Figure 8.28)**, but the evidence for more can be seen in the gable end walls of what are now two-storey houses, where the earlier and lower roof lines are still detectable **(Figure 8.29 and 8.30)**. Tentatively, these were built in the earlier part of the 17th C. In the later part of the 17thC, the cottages seem to have been built with two-storeys and attic from the start and there is evidence that single storey cottages could be increased in height to become two-storey cottages, plus attic, in this period **(Figure 8.31)**. Approximately thirty of these 17th C single and two-storey cottages can be counted in Chalford Hill (including the Marle Hill area) **(Figure 8.32)**. They are simple dwellings, well constructed and intended to meet fairly basic needs. They are constructed out of the local stone, probably dug on the site or close to it. The roofs were probably stone tiled from the start, again with locally dug stone (there are good tilestones near Bisley). There are no footings, so over the years, there may have been slight movement, particularly if the cottage is constructed on the Fullers Earth clay. These early cottages are usually built with their fireplace gable end into the bank, presumably to keep the damp out of the house **(Figure 8.33)**. There is invariably a stone winder stair next to the hearth. Many of these hearths and stairs have been uncovered in recent years, when cottages have been renovated. The hearth usually had a bread oven in either a side or the rear wall. If in the rear wall, there would have been a projection from the outside wall to accommodate the area of the oven, whereas if on the side, it was contained within the stonework beside the hearth. The majority of the two-storey weaver's cottages have one room on each floor. The attic was used, as it was floored and was reached by a good stair (a continuation of the winder from ground to first floor). The 17th C dwellings had fairly simple exterior detail and this was limited to a chamfered stone surround to the main doorway and, in some cases, hood moulds above the stone mullion windows. The houses would all have been stone tiled in this area and would all have been limewashed (in a range of shades, ochre, cream, white). Internally the main feature was the hearth with large chamfered (flat) and stopped stone jambs, usually with a large wood lintel (oak or elm), again with a chamfer and stops. Stone hearth lintels were also used (less common), but tended to split under load and from the effect of heat from the hearth. Ash pits forming part of the hearth floor have been noted in several cottages (although these may be later additions). The collected ash could be used in making soap (it's alkaline). The large open fireplaces were designed to be lit all year round and would have been effec-

Chapter 8

tive in keeping the damp out of the end wall of the house. Wood beams are used to support the upper floors and to tie the roof truss in 17th C cottages, and these have flat chamfers and stops. Generally, the earlier the beam, the wider the chamfers.

The placing of the weavers loom is a matter of conjecture. These were cottages of broadcloth weavers and the loom was about 3m wide and required two people to operate it. It would not have fitted in the attic room, which must have been used for storage or sleeping. It was always provided with a reasonable winder stair, so it was an integral part of the 'living' accommodation. The ground and first floor rooms are the spaces with a suitable area for the loom. The ground floor room contained the hearth and would have been used for the main domestic activities. This leaves the first floor room as the most likely candidate within the cottage. Alternatively it could have been sited in an outside 'shed' and certainly there are quite a few examples of stone built workshops in the cottage gardens in Chalford Hill (**Figure 8.34 and 35**). These seem to date from the 18th C, but there could have been earlier examples, which have been removed, or even converted into cottages.

It seems that as the prosperity generated by the cloth industry increased many of the simple, early houses were extended, either by adding upper floors to the single storey cottages or building additions to the rear or side of the two-storey cottages. This process may have been associated with increasing family size or there may have been an economic driver in the provision of extra cottages for rent to house the expanding working population. In most cases, the addition was not directly linked internally with the existing cottage, showing that the number of 'cottage units' was being increased, rather than the size of the individual cottages. The process of expansion continued through into the 18th and early 19th C, so that some of the original small cottages became subsumed in fairly complex groups e.g. The Bunch of Nuts, near Queen's Square. However, the early core of the building will still be identifiable. Each cottage complex had a similar cottage core, but each group now looks very different, because of the wide range of ages and positioning of the added parts.

18th C: New houses built in the 18th C seem to be aligned parallel to the lane or to the hillside (eg, cottage in Silver St, **Figure 8.36**). This change may have been a result of different internal arrangements, associated with different living standards and perhaps a desire to gain more light for the house. 18th century houses have cruder timber-work than those of the previous century. The beams tend not to be chamfered or stopped, are not as well dressed and may be of smaller scantling. They may have been cased in plaster from the start, whereas 17thC beams were intended to be seen originally, but were cased at a later date. The window frames, if they are stone mullions, are without dripmoulds and the area of glass is larger. Later in the century, there is an increasing frequency of the use of wood casements with a timber or stone lintel above in the outside face of the wall. The coursing of rubble stone walling is less well defined and courses may be interrupted by the irregular placing of larger (jumper) stones. In some houses of this date the front and gable end walls may be built with well dressed block masonry, possibly with a string course at the front (eg, The Old Duke of York Inn (**Figure 8.37**) and The Old Builders Arms in Chalford Hill), with the rear wall constructed in rubble stone. The facades of 18th C cottages may be more symmetrical with a centrally placed front door and a through passage, with a room on either side (kitchen and parlour).

19th C: The style of the 18thC cottages seems to carry through into the 19thC, with changes in the detail. **Figure 8.38** shows an example at Oakridge Lynch before it was renovated. Some windows have segmental arch heads (initially in stone, later brick), instead of the outer wood lintel (which tends to rot). Stone mullion frames were also still used, although to a lesser extent, and the side

Vernacular Buildings of Chalford

members can be constructed from a larger number of stones, which may be coursed the stone of the wall. Sash windows were used in the multi pane form in the late 18th and early 19thC, moving to the large paned version in the later 19thC, as the technology of glass making was improved. The use of the 'cottage casement' window was also widespread. The use of the large open stone, cooking hearth continued through to the advent of coal use and the availability of iron ranges/hearths. Existing hearths were then reduced in size and new ones were smaller. This change occurred from the late 18th C onwards, when the canal came into operation and coal could be imported into the area economically. The nature of the hearth opening can be used to give a guide to the date of the building. If there is no evidence for an early wood burning hearth, then it is likely that the building originated after the late 18th C. The nature of the infill of an early hearth gives a guide to the date of the changes to a building. In recent years there has been a tendency to re-open the early hearths as historic features of the building. They certainly do add character and charm to a room and give a sense of the age of the building. However, it does take away part of the historic record of the building and unsympathetic work can spoil a historic feature.

So, if you are contemplating recovering an early hearth, seek advice and record what is found as the hearth is excavated. Keep the information you record in a file containing details of the house. The design of the coal burning grate provides a reliable indication of the date of its installation (but beware, we're all good at re-using things). Some details are given in Chapter 4, but also refer to some references (Chapter 11). Beams fell out of use in the 19th C and the partition walls became load bearing. This change may have been due to a shortage/cost of suitable timber or changing fashion. Another significant change seen in 19th C is that increased mechanisation occurred and stone and timber were both cut by machine rather than by hand. This resulted in changes to the appearance of building materials, as the surface finish became regular (e.g. the regular pattern of the rotating stone cutting blade, compared with the hand chiselled finish). The pitch of the roofs changed with the transition from Cotswold stone tiles to Welsh slates. This, again, was associated with improved transport capabilities by canal and rail. Although, the use of local Cotswold stone for retiling existing buildings, was not discontinued completely until the mid 20th C.

THE DRY STONE WALLS OF CHALFORD

Dry stone walls have been used in the Stroud area since at least the 13thC, and probably for many hundreds of years before that. However, the walls within Chalford Hill and other ridge villages date from the 17thC and later, as this seems to be the earliest date for the development of the main settlements. It is difficult to date a dry stone wall with certainty, as the building technique has remained unchanged over the centuries. Although certain features, such as the style of gateposts and coping stones **(Figures 8.39 to 8.40)**, and the nature of the stone dressing may help for dating purposes. It is probable that the early houses of the villages in the 17th and 18thC were surrounded by walls to mark the property boundary on the common, to retain livestock and to protect garden produce. Some of these wall positions may survive, but the actual walls are likely to have been rebuilt several times. In the mid 19thC, when the remaining common land was enclosed, there was a rationalisation of the property boundaries. Remaining areas of common within the settlement areas were allocated to the former commoners and incorporated into their garden plots. This must have required new walling to mark the revised boundaries. More walls have also been added over the years, as the earlier house plots have been subdivided to generate new building land.

The majority of the walls are built of ragstone (the harder, grey, shelly rock) from the Great Oolite

Chapter 8

series **(Figure 8.41)**. In an original wall the stone should be consistent in its nature, as it will have been quarried from the same section of the rock strata. However, some of the stone in the present walls will have been recycled (several times) and the stones will be mixed with those from other walls and new stone may have been added **(Figure 8.42)**. Part way up the side of the valley, many of the walls seem to have been built of freestone (eg, on Rack Hill) from the Inferior Oolite series and these are now severely perished and some have virtually disappeared **(Figure 8.43)**. This is not a good dry walling stone and care should be taken when re-using such stone, as it may not last well in a new wall.

The size of the stones within a wall depends on the nature of the bed from which it has been removed, and many different sizes can be seen in the walls of the area. But, if properly built, all will have been constructed in a similar way. The stability of the wall depends on it having a good heavy coping to keep the walling stone under compression. The original type of coping will almost certainly have been of upright stones (without mortar) **(Figure 8.44)**. This is the best design as it allows the coping to settle unevenly with the wall. Some houses have dressed coping slabs, mostly flat, although some have a convex or triangular section **(Figure 8.45)**. These probably date from the 18th and 19thC and were probably intended to suggest a degree of status to the property.

There are a few sections of wall within the villages, which are strictly not dry stone walls. These are built of well dressed stones with a regular face, but are laid without mortar. They are called mason's walls, as they were built by stonemasons, not wallers. A fine example is the one at Clematis Cottage in Commercial Road **(Figure 8.46)**, Chalford Hill. This dates from the early 19thC, when the house was occupied by a stone mason.

Other features that can be found in the drystone walls in Chalford Hill include 'pig holes' (to get pigs out of their pens into the lane) **(Figure 8.47)**, angled stones (to protect the wall from damage by carts) **(Figure 8.48)** and water spouts and troughs **(Figure 8.49 and 50)**.

Description of Some Cottages and Houses in Chalford Hill

Some descriptions of selected houses in Chalford Hill are given in this section. Many of them have origins that can be traced back to the 17th C, to a simple cottage. Subsequent additions and changes have resulted in complex houses that look completely different to each other now, but when disentangled, their cottage cores are similar. Also, it is evident that the early additions seem to have been built as separate cottages, without a connection through to the earlier cottage. The buildings grew by addition, so that there could be as many as five cottages forming a group of varying origins around a mid/late 17th C core. Loading doors are not a feature of the cottages dating from the 17th C, but they are more common in those dating from the 18th and 19th C. These have now been blocked up, but their former presence is shown by building lines in the stonework. This must be telling us something about the people who were living and working in the village. The folklore is that the villages grew on the ridge as squatter's settlements of handloom weavers. This is probably nearly correct except that the surviving cottages from the early development of the villages are not squatter's cottages, as they are too well built. It is possible that the early development was more organised, but if so, it must have occurred to provide cottages for an influx of workers involved in the expanding cloth making industry of the area. The growth by addition of the early cottages is showing that the influx of people continued for over 100 years. The absence of loading doors in the earlier cottages suggests that the yarn for weaving was supplied to the weavers in the developing village. The presence of the loading doors in many 18th and early 19th C buildings may be indicating that the spinning itself was also being done within the village at this time. Wool is a low density material and is bulky, hence a large storage area

VERNACULAR BUILDINGS OF CHALFORD

is needed to produce a relatively modest amount of yarn.

The cottages have been described according to their relation with the main routes through the village to the valley. It has not been possible to describe all of the cottages along these routes, but sufficient examples have been given to provide a representative selection of the different types.

ROUTE FROM MIDWAY TO COMMERCIAL ROAD AND DARK LANE

Little France Cottage **(Figure 8.5)**: Well coursed rubblestone walls, with two-light stone mullion window frames and continuous dripmoulds above the ground and first floor windows. The ground floor has a central entrance with flanking windows. The stonework of the gable end wall shows that the wall height has been raised to generate low attic walls. Internally, there is a large gable end hearth with a wood beam and stone slab jambs. Originally there would have been two rooms on each floor, although the ground floor partitions have been removed. The detail suggests an origin in the 17th C, with the wall plate being raised in the 18th C.

France Corner **(Figures 8.51 and 52)**: Originally built as three cottages, probably in the mid/late 18th C, now combined as one house. There are vertical building lines between the separate properties showing that it was built in stages, but close in time. It has three-storeys and is constructed in coursed rubblestone, under a moderately pitched, stone tiled roof. The rear wall has single light windows in each of the separate parts of the building. These have iron frame opening lights, hung on pin hinges and with quadrants. There are 12 leaded lights per frame. There is an external stair against the W gable end, leading to a door to the second floor. This level has a lime mortar floor, which shows a former industrial use. The window details in the front elevation vary between the different phases of the building. At the W end (next to the lane) there are two-light windows on the first and second floors under segmented stone arch lintels. On the second floor, leaded lights (square pane) are present, which must be the original type, whereas, on the first floor there are replacement wood frames (divided into square lights by timber glazing bars). The middle part of the building has three-light windows, but otherwise the detail appears to be the same as in the W part of the building. The furthest part of the building has stone mullion windows (18th C type, with larger area of glass) and no dripmoulds. Internally, there are wood burning hearths on the ground floor: one has a timber hearth beam, with stone jambs and a bread oven (18th C origin).

Halstead **(Figure 8.6)**: This house has developed in four phases between the latter part of the 17th C and the early 19th C. The core of the house is a 2-storey cottage, with a single room on each floor and built with its fireplace gable end facing the hillside. This had ground and first floor 2-light stone mullion window frames. The ground floor room had a large open hearth, with a timber beam and jambs formed from large slabs of stone. There is a modified stone winder stair to the right of the hearth and a former closet to the left (now converted to provide access to a slightly later cottage). In the second phase another cottage was added behind the gable end of the Phase 1 building. This is also thought to be a 2-storey cottage, but the ceiling heights have been modified, so only the ground floor was usable in the late 1990's. The detail suggests it was built in the mid/late 17th C. There is a blocked hearth and possibly a stair in the gable end wall. In the third phase, the Phase 1 cottage was extended to the W, to provide an additional room on the ground and first floors. The gable end wall of this part has 3-light and 2-light stone mullion window frames to the ground and first floors. These have plain chamfered surrounds, without dripmoulds. The roof pitch is not steep. The additional room has a hearth of modest size in the side wall. The detail suggests the additional rooms were added at the end of the

CHAPTER **8**

17th/beginning of the 18th C. The attic space over the Phase 1 and 3 buildings has room partitions, but there was no stair access to these rooms in the late 1990's. In the fourth phase, a wing was added to the S of the Phase 3 extension. This contains an entrance hall with stair and parlour on the ground floor, with a landing and a bedroom on the first floor. These rooms have stone mullion frames (without dripmoulds), with wood frame inserts windows, facing W. It seems to have been built to increase the accommodation in the existing house and to provide a new stair. There is a rounded arch over the front door. The detail suggests that this part was constructed in the early 19th C.

Fleece Cottage **(Figures 8.53 and 8.54)**: This one and a half storey cottage must date from the later 17th/early 18th C, a building line in the rear wall shows that it has been extended to the W. It is one of the few surviving single storey cottages in the area.

The Fleece Inn **(Figure 8.7)**: This consists of several phases of building. The earliest part seems to date from the late 17th C and can be seen from Commercial Road. The original cottage was of 2–storeys, with one room on each floor and an attic. The N gable end wall has a large open stone hearth and a winder stair. The W facing front wall has 2-light stone mullion windows on each floor. The S gable end has a two-light and a one light stone mullion window frame, both without dripmoulds, at the first and attic levels. All stone frames have flat chamfers. There have been additions to the N, SW and to the rear of the original building. The additions to the rear and SW seem to consist of several small attached cottages. All are now combined as one house.

The Post Office **(Figure 8.55)**: This is constructed in rubblestone, under a roof of moderate pitch. This had a stone tiled roof until the mid 1980's. The façade is symmetrical, with three, 2-light stone mullion windows on the first floor, without dripmoulds. There is a centrally placed entrance with flanking shop windows. The building dates from the late 18th C. The plastic window frames were installed in the late 1980's and replaced wood frames with iron opening lights, with leaded lights, pin hinges and quadrants. Internally, there are floor support beams and these are relatively small and have very narrow chamfers.

The Ferns, Commercial Road **(Figure 8.8 and 8.56)**: This building has developed in at least six main building phases. The first phase, which dates back to some time around the mid 17th C, represents one of the earliest cottages of the village. This was a single storey building with a steeply pitched roof **(Figure 8.29)**. The ground floor had two rooms: one had a large open stone fireplace, with an oven in the rear wall of the hearth **(Figure 8.57)**. There was a projection behind the hearth wall that contained the main body of the oven. There was a stone winder stair to one side of the hearth and a closet to the other. The second room was unheated and had several keeping holes in its walls **(Figure 8.58)**. The attic floor would have been used for sleeping and storage. The W facing gable end (facing the side of the valley) had the stepped, inwardly facing chimney-breast for the large ground floor hearth **(Figure 8.59)** and the other gable end had windows at the ground floor and attic levels. There was a well outside the entrance door to the heated room. In the second phase, the single storey cottage was converted to 2-storeys with attics. This was done by removing the early roof, adding more stones to the perimeter walls and constructing a new roof **(Figure 8.60)**. First floor windows in the front and rear walls, and in the W gable end (for the stair and closets) were added and a new attic floor was inserted. Both first and second phase windows were stone mullions without dripmoulds **(Figure 8.61)**. In the third phase, the perimeter walls were raised again to generate half height walls in the attics, so that it became a 2½ storey house. Again a new roof structure was built and this survives in the present house **(Figure 8.62)**. The structure is three bays long and has a pair of large 'A' frame trusses. These sit on the half height walls and therefore are not jointed into a tie beam. There is a single collar on each truss at approximately head height and these are bolted into position. There are beams supporting the attic floor: one is large and has a moderate chamfer and is probably re-used from an earlier form of the house, the other has a narrow chamfer and was probably new when installed. The rafters are hand-cut and are limewashed, showing that they were exposed under the roof slope. The details suggest that the dates for these three phases are mid 17th C, late 17th C and mid/late 18th C. The evidence for these phases shows in the stonework of the E and W facing gable end walls and in the S facing front wall.

In the fourth phase, a cottage was added behind the W gable end wall and in line with the earlier building. This was 1½ storeys tall **(Figure 8.63)**. The segmented stone arch lintel of the ground floor window and the presence of an original coal burning hearth opening (it would originally have been fitted with a range) **(Figure 8.64)** show that this was built at the beginning of the 19th C. The roof structure is simple, with purlins running between the gable end walls of the cottage and earlier house. There are no beams or roof trusses. The floor joists and boards are elm. It was originally built as a separate dwelling, although it has been knocked through to the earlier house in recent years. The rear part of the bread oven in the fireplace of the adjoining, earlier house was removed when this cottage was built, however, the evidence in the stonework shows its former presence.

In the fifth phase a two-storey wing was built to the N side of the Phase 1-3 building **(Figure 8.65)**. This is constructed in machine cut stone, with stone mullion window frames to its E side and on the first floor of the N facing gable end wall. These windows are tall compared with stone window frames of the 17th C and have a flat chamfer surround, without a dripmould **(Figure 8.66)**. There are iron-opening lights and these have long twisted securing stays. There is a tall, stone chimney-stack rising from the wall plate of the W facing side. Inside, there is a hall with a geometric pattern tiled floor and a good pitch pine staircase, with turned newels and balusters **(Figure 8.67)**. There is a single room on each floor, each with a coal burning hearth (although the original mantelpieces and grates have been removed. The ground floor room has a bay window, in pitch pine **(Figure 8.68)**. The details suggest that the wing was built in the late 19th C to provide improved accommodation to a cottage formed from half of the Phase 1-3 cottage. In Phase 6, a single storey addition, with a pitched roof was built off the S side of this part of the building **(Figure 8.69)**. Inside, there is a single room, open to the roof and without a hearth. It is thought that this was a washroom, serving the adjoining kitchen (in the E room of the early cottage, to which a hearth had been added when the Phase 5 building was built).

It is known that at that in the early part of the 20th C the house was divided into 3 cottages: the Phase 4 cottage, the W end of the Phase 1-3 cottage and the E end of the Phase 1-3 cottage with the Phase 5 and 6 wings. In the 1970's, the three cottages were combined to form a single house.

Moseley's ice cream business was operating from the stone built workshop in the garden in the mid 20th C **(Figure 8.70)**. The workshop dates from the early 19th C and may originate with a use associated with the cloth industry. It has a crude coal burning hearth, which could be an addition.

Glenhaven **(Figures 8.9 and 8.71)**: This is sited well below the road level, in the middle of its garden plot. It has three main building phases. The original cottage (W end of the front part of the house) consists of a two-storey cottage with an attic, under a steeply pitched roof. There is a three-light stone mullion window on the ground floor of the front elevation and two-light frames on the ground, first and attic levels in the W gable end wall. All frames have flat chamfered surrounds and are without

CHAPTER 8

dripmoulds. The first floor of the front wall has an early 19th C style wood window frame, which does not seem to have been inserted in an earlier opening. Presumably, before this time the first floor only had the gable end window. The walling consists of well-coursed rubblestone, with a couple of jumper stones. There is a large hearth in the E gable end wall (blocked when viewed in 1992), with an adjacent winder stair. The detail suggests it was built in the late 17th C. The original cottage has been extended to the E with a 2-storey addition, without an attic, as the ceiling heights are higher than in the original phase. The first floor window forms a part dormer in the roof. The walling consists of coursed rubblestone, with some jumper-stones. The detail suggests this part was built in the latter part of the 18th C. The third main phase is a large extension to the rear and built in the late 1990's. There is also a small stone built addition, with a pitched roof, at the W end of the building, which was used as a bathroom prior to the early 1990's. This also contained a well. There is a lean-to on the E gable end, with external access. Both of these additions probably date from the 19th C.

Clematis Cottage (**Figure 8.72**): Until the mid 1960's, this was Commercial Road Stores (**Figure 8.73 and 8.74**). The shop occupied the right hand, ground floor of the main range of the building facing onto Commercial Road. The owner lived in the left hand part and in the wing set back from the lane. The house and shop were combined when the house was 'modernised' in the late 1960's. Some of the work was redone and restoration work was conducted in the early 1980's. The following notes have been written from evidence collected during this work.

The house shows four main building phases, starting with a 2-storey cottage, with one room/floor, in the late 17th C. This cottage was constructed in coursed rubblestone with large quoin stones and a moderately pitched roof. Its rear part can be seen projecting, as a short wing, behind the rear wall of the present house (**Figure 8.75**). It was built gable end into the bank, with the hearth and winder stair at that end. The front wall, facing S, had ground and first floor 2-light stone mullion window frames, with dripmoulds (**Figure 8.76**) and a doorway, with a stone surround, which has a flat chamfer and scroll stops. There was a large internally projecting, stepped chimney-breast passing through the first floor to the attic and stack. There was not a hearth on the first floor. A stone lined well (approx 2m to water level and 3 m water depth) was constructed in front of this cottage. No other detail of this cottage has survived, having been removed by later phases. In the second phase, another 2-storey cottage was added to the front of the original cottage. This was positioned so that the ground and first floor front windows of the original cottage were not obscured (**Figure 8.77**). It stands parallel to the bank, with the rear ground level near the top of the first floor. The front wall of this addition was built in large ashlar blocks, without an inner skin of rubblestone or brick. A large stone block bridges the well, leaving about half the area of the well exposed outside the wall. It is thought that this addition was built as a separate cottage, as there has never been a connection through to the original cottage on the ground floor. There was a large hearth in the single ground floor room and this has a wood lintel and stone jambs (**Figure 8.78**). The hearth has survived and is shallow and there are no chamfers or stops, which shows that the cottage was added in the 18th C. The floor was laid with large stone flags, placed directly onto the clay (**Figure 8.79**). The rear wall has two wide recesses with stone vaults behind stone arches (**Figure 8.80**). These are about 1.5m deep and pass beneath the upper part of the rear wall and project into the hillside beyond. Their function is not clear. When built, they must have been damp and thus not suited for storage. A previous owner of the house called them 'donkey holes' because they were used as stable, but this cannot be proved. The floor of the upper storey had been replaced, when the building was 'modernised' in the late 1960's, and therefore the former site of the stair is not known with certainty. It was not next to the hearth, but was probably a wooden, straight flight stair laid against the wall of the Phase 1 cottage. Lodgings in the stone work of the front and rear walls showed that there was formerly a ceiling beam **(Figure 8.80 and 81)**. The first floor room retains the original ceiling beam and joists. These are oak. The beam has narrow chamfers, but no stops and the joists sit in lodgings in the top of the beam. The front wall of the room had two window openings, beneath stone lintels. The window frames are of the casement type. The set of joists in the first floor ceiling is complete, so there was not a stair to the attic room when the cottage was built. Instead, the attic was entered from the outside, via the wide door, under a gabled roof, in the rear wall **(Figure 8.82)**. There are half height walls in the attic, supporting the roof to the front and rear. The gable end wall of the attic room had a small hearth, with a dressed stone surround and an arched stone lintel. The original, oak, roof structure is still in place **(Figure 8.83)**. This consists of a single truss, with the principals rising from the top of each of the half walls. Each has a post that stands next to the wall and transfers part of the load from the underside of the principal to the tie beam at floor level. A short horizontal timber plate ties the foot of each principal to its post. The plate/post joint is secured with a forelock bolt. Forelock bolts preceded the development of threaded bolts and were used in the 18th C. The timber post and plate help to oppose the outward thrust of the roof. It is not a common form of roof structure, but it has been seen in at least one other house in Chalford Hill (The Old Builders Arms). There is one purlin per roof slope that sits in a trench on the back of the principal. The function of the attic room is not clear, it has a small hearth, a wide entrance door, but no evidence for an original window. If it was intended as a workroom, some form of window would be expected. It cannot have been domestic as there is no access to the lower floor, unless it was connected through to the attic of the original cottage. Although a possibility, this cannot be proved as the whole roof structure of the 17th C cottage was replaced as part of the next building phase.

In the third phase, the S gable end and rear wall of the 17th C cottage were removed and a substantial new stone building was constructed parallel to the road. This now dominates the whole building, with the rear part of the original cottage surviving as a small wing projecting to the rear. This contains the early fireplace, which was modified to support the new roof and a coal-burning hearth. The winder stairwell of the original cottage was infilled at the ground floor level, but survived as a wood winder leading from the first floor to the 'new' attic floor. The new attic was linked to the attic over the Phase 2 cottage (even though the floor levels are different) and this may reflect a more historic connection. The Phase 3 building is well constructed, with rubblestone walls (a shelly stone, probably from the Great Oolite series) with dressed lintels and quoins. Each lintel is constructed in parts with a central, flush, plain keystone. The front elevation has a near central front door, with flanking ground and first floor, 3-light wood mullion windows with leaded lights (square pane). Each has a central iron opening light, hung on pin hinges. The opening lights have 2-turnbuckle handles and sprung quadrants. There is also a first floor 2-light window, above the front door. All lights have an internal, narrow, quarter round moulding. These windows were restored in 1983 to the original pattern, reusing much of the original ironwork and glass **(Figure 8.10)**. There was formerly a wide dormer window rising off the wall plate (this shows on photos taken in the 1930's). The ground floor window opening to the right of the entrance door is larger than the other openings and yet is original work to this phase. For many years, this part of the building was Commercial Road Stores, with the owner's accommodation to the left and upstairs, together with the adjoining cottage (which is thought to have contained the stair). The larger window opening here, strongly suggests that the building was originally constructed to contain the shop on the ground floor and that it had a shop window in this position. There was a proper shopfront present in the photographs taken of the building in the 1930's.

CHAPTER **8**

The S facing end wall is comprised of the front wall of the early cottage but raised to the present height. It has a hipped roof. The original first floor 2-light stone mullion window is present in the wall, but the lights are blocked in and now partially hidden by a later entrance hall. The original ground floor window members are also still there, but the window was removed and the stone used to block up the opening completely to form an arched recess in the living room of the new addition. The original stone frame of the entrance door to the cottage is also present, but hidden behind an early 19th C reeded timber architrave.

The hearth of the original cottage was rediscovered in 1982 and uncovered **(Figures 8.84, 85 and 86)**. It had been converted to a coal burning hearth and the style of the fire surround suggested this had been done at the beginning of the 19th C. The surround was in dressed Cotswold stone and had reeded sides and top, with square corner blocks containing roundels. A plain mantelshelf sat on top of the surround. The original open stone fireplace retained its original jambs and wood beam. The beam had a narrow chamfer and scroll stops. The jambs were not chamfered. There was an intact bread oven in the in the side of the hearth. Its existence was indicated by a large stone slab forming the outer wall of the fireplace **(Figure 8.87)**. When uncovered it was found to contain a broken spoon and a clay pipe lain together on the floor of the oven: presumably a good luck token. The opposite side of the hearth was not uncovered as a stone column had been constructed here to support the upper flue wall, which in turn supported a truss for the later roof. The flue itself was large and could be climbed up to the mid first floor level for sweeping.

In the early 19th C, an entrance hall was constructed in dressed stone to provide the shop owner with a more private entrance to his house and also to link the ground floors of the Phase 2 and 3 buildings **(Figure 8.88)**. The entrance doorway has a fanlight **(Figure 8.89)**. The original well was found under the rotting wood floor of this hall during the renovations in the early 1980's. The architraves around the door and windows in the entrance hall and in the room at the W end of the Phase 3 addition (adjacent to the shop) have the same detail **(Figure 8.90)**. They have a reeded moulding to the sides and top, with corner blocks containing a moulded plaster flower decoration. The door from the entrance hall to the lounge is a heavy six-panel door, with a narrow moulding, fixed near the edges of the panels. The reed moulding of the architraves is similar to that of the coal burning hearth surround (now removed) and is consistent with an early 19th C origin. This must also indicate the date when the entrance hall was added.

The roof structure over the third phase of the building has detail, which suggests it originated in the late 18th/early 19th C. It is 4 bays long and consists of wide 'A frames, supported on low front and rear walls **(Figure 8.91)**. The timbers forming the principals are large, hand sawn and there is a pegged, diagonal mortice and tenon joint linking the tops of the principals. There are tie beams in the floor, but these are not structurally part of the truss. The collars are set at about 5 foot above the floor and are fixed across the face of the principals by large threaded bolts. There are 2 rows of butt purlins on each roof slope and these are jointed through the principal with the pegged, fish plate type of joint. At least one of the purlins is re-used timber, from some sort of machine (a loom?).

The attic floor has regular, machine cut joists that are laid between cross ceiling beams. The beams are pitch pine and have flat chamfers (about 25mm) and triangular stops. They are regular in profile and have an almost polished surface. The beams and joists are thought to have replaced the original floor of this phase, probably around the end of the 19th C. In contrast the three ground floor ceiling beams are hardwood and are irregular in profile. They are without chamfers or stops. These are the style of beam expected in an 18th C building and were probably intended to be plastered or cased.

Vernacular Buildings of Chalford

Hollybank **(Figure 8.11)**: Probably originated as a two-storey cottage in the late 17th C. There is a two-light stone mullion window, surviving on the first floor and facing Commercial Road. There are additions to the early cottage and extra cottages have been added to the W.

Jacobs Cottage **(Figure 8.92)**: This dates from the early 18th C and has a symmetrical façade, with flanking two-light stone mullion windows on the ground and first floor. It looks like it was originally detached, but has been incorporated into the group with Hollybank.

Cleeve Cottage **(Figure 8.93)**: The detail suggests it dates from the early/mid 19th C. It has two-storeys and attics, under a moderately pitched roof. The windows are in the front elevation and these have been converted to a pair of two-storey bay windows (possibly in the late 19th C). The front wall is rendered to hide the modifications necessary for the construction of the bay windows. The gable end and rear walls are constructed in rubblestone. The N gable end has a first floor entrance door and an adjacent blocked window. This part may have formerly had a commercial use. The rear wall has no windows. Internally, there are only coal burning hearths and no structural beams. The house is narrower than some of the earlier cottages.

Rose Cottage **(Figure 8.94)**: This has two and a half storeys and the detail of the stonework of the front elevation shows that it has developed in phases. The earliest part seems to date from the early 18th C and is represented by the more regular block stonework on the lower floors, in the central part of the present house.

Hillside (1 and 2) and Prospect Terrace **(Figure 8.95)**: These cottages are built of rubblestone. There are building lines in their rear walls, which shows they were not all built at the same time. However, the similarity of style shows they are close in their date of origin. Prospect Terrace has stone mullion windows, without dripmoulds, and coal burning hearths, which indicate an origin in the early 19th C. Hillside (detached from the Prospect Terrace) has cottage style casement windows, with stone arched lintels and coal burning hearths. These were probably built by the mid 19th C. No. 1 Hillside originally had two ground floor rooms: a kitchen with a hearth suitable for a range and a parlour with a small coal burning hearth. There are no structural beams.

Abnash to Dark Lane

Abnash House (Abnash Farm in the early 20thC) **(Figure 8.96)**: This is one of the larger houses in Chalford Hill. It is built of coursed rubblestone and is three storeys tall, under a stone tiled roof of moderate pitch. The stonework of the front wall shows that it has been altered from a house with two gabled dormers to the present form, by infilling the gap between the dormers and building up the wall to either end. The original windows of the façade have frames with rebated, flat chamfer surrounds. A slightly larger window has been added on the second floor between the original dormers and this has a plain, flat chamfer surround. The second floor windows have dripmoulds. There is a continuous dripmould above the windows on the ground and first floors. This form of dripmould has been seen in several larger local houses (e.g. The Mount, Coppice Hill). There is a central entrance door, with flanking three-light windows. The first floor has similar windows, but with a two-light window above the door. The gable end, facing Abnash, shows the lines of the roof changes and a pair of owl windows set outside the stonework of the original gable end.

Chapter 8

Mary Rudd notes that the farm, which stands on the W border of the Avenage Tything, is of ancient origin. An early mention of land in the area is in the Bisley Manor Court Rolls of 1401, which notes that William Boun holds of the Lord one messuage and one ferundal of land in Abenesse (another form of the name Abnash), formerly Whithed's. The title deeds of Abnash House date from 1651 and Rudd records some detail of ownership through to the late 18th C. She also notes that the house, with its adjacent barns, suggests a farm of great antiquity, the oldest part of the building being that at the S end, which has a very ancient chimney and thick walls. She suggests that the house was much added to and rearranged in the early 17th C, when a fine stair was added and the building was extended to the N. I guess by the term 'ancient' Rudd is thinking of a medieval building as she is specific in naming the 16th and 17th C's. The notes given here suggest that this is an early occupied site in Chalford, what remains (and is visible from the outside) shows a building of 17/18th C origin, but there is clearly a memory of an earlier root.

Documents of the 15th and 16th C also mention Abenashe. The will of William West of Abenesse, dated September 1562, states that: '....To his son James, his great crock, great panne, and the bedstead he now lies upon. The cobbard, three of his best sheep, a coffer and the brode lome with apparel, paying to his brother 16s 8d, are to be delivered to him on the death of his mother.....'. Further bequests of sheep to other family members are made in the will. It is clear that he was a weaver, but that he also kept sheep. It shows weaving and agriculture progressing hand in hand and that the weaving was active in the 16th C. The will does not record where William West lived, other than it was in Abenesse.

Byways **(Figure 8.97 and 8.98)**: This stands on the N side of Abnash, nearly opposite Abnash House. It is comprised of a good two-storey building, with attic, under a steeply pitched roof. The walling is well coursed rubblestone, without jumpers. The windows have two-light stone mullion frames, with reserved, flat chamfer surrounds and dripmoulds. This style of window is not common in Chalford, where the majority of the stone frames have plain surrounds. However, in Stroud, the reserved chamfer is common throughout the 17th C, but seems to disappear by the late part of the century and is replaced by the version with plain surrounds. The ground floor also has a three-light window, without dripmould and a plain surround. This dates from the 18th C and will have replaced the earlier form of frame. The rear of the property has the central section of the wall built up as a dormer. This possibly provides headspace for a stair. In the front wall there is a small lancet window with two-lights. Rudd dates this to the 13th C and is re-used, probably from an earlier building on the site or close-by. Several of these early windows are known in the area: in Stroud (Ivy Cottage, Bowbridge Lane) and in Bisley (Magnet Cottage). They must have been regarded as special, when their original buildings were demolished, hence their re-use. There is a lower addition to the W of the main house, which has some windows of a similar form to those on the main house. However, this is likely to be a slightly later addition, as it just clips across a single light stone window frame in the gable end of the house.

The Corderries **(Figures 8.99 and 100)**: Rudd notes that adjacent to Abnash is an estate known as the Corderries, which was formerly known as Skiveralls. Since she wrote her book, the estate has been broken up, so that there is now a large house known as the Corderries and an adjacent building (which documentary evidence suggests originated as a building associated with the weaving industry), surrounded by large gardens. The adjoining land has been partly developed as housing in the 1970's, but much remains as woodland along the side of the valley formerly known as Pathcombe,

VERNACULAR BUILDINGS OF CHALFORD

but now generally known as Old Neighbourhood. The origin of the name, Skiveralls, is not known, but is first found in the Bisley Court Rolls for 1586 and again in 1592. A messuage called 'Skeveralls' is mentioned in the 1592 document, but it is not certain whether this refers to what is now called the Corderries or that now called Skiveralls, further down the lane. The title deeds for the Corderries start in 1665, which record the purchase of the property by Richard Saunders, freemason of Bisley, who bought it from Daniel Webb. In 1680 he sold it to Jasper Corderoy, clothier of Minchinhampton. It seems that at that time the house was called 'Long Tunn'. The Corderoys were a Hugenot family and their surname must be the origin of the present name of the property. Rudd traces the ownership of the house through to the early 20th C. She notes that the oldest part of the house dates from the 17th C and the adjacent building, which she calls a wool-store or drying house, dates from the late 18th C.

A recent investigation (2005) has revealed more about the development of the house. The building called a wool store or drying oven by Rudd, was built as a good quality house. It has ground and first floor two-light stone mullion window frames, with a central ground floor entrance. There is a continuous dripmould over the ground floor windows that steps up over the door lintel. There is a moulded eaves cornice. Internally, there is a large ground floor hearth in the W gable end wall, which has a large stone lintel and jambs built of stone blocks. The hearth opening does not have chamfers or stops. There is a domestic-scale bread oven adjacent to the hearth opening and this has its own flue, above the front of the opening to the oven chamber. This presumably joins the main flue. There is a first floor hearth in the same wall, smaller in size, but with similar detail. The roof has four bays and the trusses are of the same design as described for the addition to Clematis Cottage. The truss timbers are secured together using forelock bolts and there are rough assembly marks visible on some of the timbers. The floor support beams are either without, or have a very minor chamfer. All of the details are consistent with an origin in the first part of the 18th C (i.e. earlier than suggested by Rudd). It is probable that at some stage it ceased to be used primarily as a house and was used as part of the business operation of the owner, the documentary evidence suggests both a wool store and a drying house are options. The E gable end of this house shows a ghost roof line and a vertical building line for a single storey building with a steeply pitched roof that must have stood to the E of the present building until fairly recent times (as the residue of the pointing to weatherproof the tile to gable end join is still visible). The current main house has a dominantly early 19th C character. The front wall has a central entrance with a Venetian window above, which intrudes slightly into an eaves cornice. This, in turn, is overlain by a parapet. There are flanking multi pane sash windows on the ground and first floors. Each is of the Venetian style, but with a square head, rather than an arched head over the central light. The detail of the walling shows that these windows were inserted into an existing wall. Internally, there is much timber and plaster detail, which dates from the same period as the windows. The detail includes six-panel doors with reeded architraves and corner blocks, dado rails and ornamental plaster ceiling coving (one room has acanthus leaf decoration). There is a good oak stair (semi circular), with plain balusters. It appears that an existing house was extensively (and expensively) remodelled in the early part of the 19th C. It seems that the house was also extended to the S, by one room at this time. The parapet concealing a valley gutter will date from this time. The eaves cornice beneath this probably dates from an earlier form of the house, which dates from the same period as the 'wool store' house. Internally, there are some hidden features which either date from this period or from a 17th C form of the house. These include plastered ceiling beams, which appear to have chamfers and stops (replicated in the casing plaster) and a large blocked hearth in a cross wall (possibly originally a gable end wall). The hearth shows as a thick section of wall on the ground floor and as an internally projecting, stepped chimney-breast within the attic. There are two additions to the rear (W side) of this

Chapter 8

house: both seem to date from the 19th C, but they have different detail. One addition has multi-pane sash windows with dressed stone block surrounds and internal detail that has an early 19th C character. The second has several stone window frames with arched heads and recessed spandrels, which have a 16th C flavour, but seem to be 19th C copies. There is a detached, 11/2 storey outbuilding sited slightly to the NW of the main house and this seems to be of industrial rather than domestic origin. It has a blocked three-light stone mullion window with dripmould in one gable end, with one vertical iron bar/light. The attic has a two-light window in one gable end and a wide sliding sash in the other gable end. There is a stone chimney-stack rising off the side wall plate, but no evidence for a ground floor hearth. It is thought there may be a blocked first floor hearth concealed beneath plaster. The roof truss (one only) does not have a tie beam, and the principal rafters sit on half height attic walls. There is a collar. The detail of the windows, stonework and roof suggest an origin in the late 17th C, with the sash being added in the 19th C. Perhaps it is another detached weaving shed?

Skiveralls House: This has several building phases. It is comprised of two cottages, probably built in the early 18th C. One cottage is larger, with originally two rooms per floor with attic, the other had one room per floor. The wall height has been raised over both cottages to form a long attic space, with three-light windows in the front elevation and what seems to be a large loading door in the rear wall. The 'new' areas of walling, within the attic, have never been plastered and the space has an industrial flavour. The walls were probably raised in the 18th C. There are additions to the rear.

Elm Cottage **(Figure 8.13)**: A two-storey cottage with attic under a steeply pitched roof. The walling is coursed rubblestone. There is one room per floor in the original part of the cottage. There is a two-light stone mullion window (plain surround, with flat chamfer) in the front wall of each floor. The original cottage has been extended to either side: on the right the addition appears to be modern, that on the left is a garage, which may have been formed from an earlier outbuilding. The detail of the original cottage suggests an origin in the late 17th C.

Lanes from France Corner to Queen's Square and Marle Hill

Grey Cot (known as Gordon House in the early 20thC) **(Figure 8.14)**: This is based on a 17th C cottage, but has been enlarged. The detail suggests this was done in the 18th C. Mary Rudd says that the house was originally occupied by Huguenot weavers. She records that the title deeds begin in 1673 with the conveyance of house and shop (this may be a loom shop) by Philip Davis (broadweaver) to his son William, also a broadweaver. She records the changes in ownership through to 1912. The important point about the deeds is that they show that a house was in existence by 1673.

Cotspur **(Figure 8.101)**: This is sited above the lane, behind Grey Cot/Cotswold Place. It seems to have been built as two cottages, now combined. The larger cottage (to the N) has a symmetrical façade with a near central front door with flanking, fairly tall, two-light stone mullion window frames. These have plain, flat chamfers, with a continuous dripmould that steps up over the door. It terminates on the outer side of each window. The first floor has shorter windows, which otherwise are of the same form as the ground floor windows. Again there is a continuous dripmould of the same form, but without the step up. There is a blocked first floor opening above the front door, which has dressed stone side members. These look original and the opening seems to be a former taking-in door. There is a large ground floor hearth with a deep stone lintel and slab stone jambs. The lintel has a narrow chamfer. There is a bread oven to the side of the hearth wall. There is also a winder stair (in stone) to the side of the fireplace. A building line marks the junction with the smaller cottage (the direction of the line shows that the larger cottage was built first). It has ground and first floor, two-light stone mullion windows, with plain chamfer surrounds and no dripmoulds. The roof is continuous over the whole property and the pitch is moderate. The detail shows that the earlier cottage was built in the late 17th/very early 18th C. The attached cottage seems to be close in date.

Cotswold Place **(Figure 8.102)**: A group of 18th C cottages. The main property is set back from the lane. It is aligned parallel to the hillside. There is a central entrance and three-light stone mullion window frames without dripmoulds. The windows have a larger area of glass than is seen in typical 17th C windows. The roof pitch is shallower than that of Oakley (adjacent cottage, gable end seen from the lane). The comparison serves to highlight the difference in the roof pitch seen in 17th and 18th C cottages in Chalford. There is a stone built 'workshop', with stone mullion window frames bordering the lane. There are several examples of detached workshops in Chalford Hill (there is another at the Old Duke of York Inn and a much larger and later one, adjacent to the Old Builders Arms.). Originally, they are thought to have been linked with the cloth industry, possibly as detached weaving sheds (shops).

Oakley **(Figure 8.103)**: The house is built of coursed rubble stone, with a steeply pitched roof. There are two floors and an attic. It is aligned roughly E-W and the E gable end faces into the hillside. There is a building line in the S (front) elevation, which shows that it was built in two phases. The first is the part to W end of the current building. The detail suggests that was built in the mid to late 17thC and consisted of a cottage of two-storeys plus attic, with its hearth in the gable end facing into the hillside. The second phase is that part of the building to the right of the building line in the front elevation. The internal detail suggests it was constructed in the early 18thC date at the latest. Originally, the two parts must have been intended as separate dwellings, as they each have a large hearth and stair. They have been combined in recent years.

There are two chimney-stacks, one in the gable end of the first phase building (now within the cottage) and the other in the E gable end. There are two, 2-light stone mullion windows at the first floor level in the S facing elevation. These have plain chamfers and are without dripmoulds. They seem to be of the same style, but one is placed in each phase of the building. This either suggests the two phases are close in date or perhaps the window in the second phase part was reused. The ground floor windows in this elevation are different in each phase: neither are original. The window at the W end (first phase) has a segmented arched lintel with a wood casement window and is of a style typical of the late 18th/early 19thC. The window at the E end is modern, although the opening must date from the initial building of this phase. It has been reduced slightly in width, by the addition of stonework. The current front door is in the near centre of this elevation (within the phase 1 part) and enters into a narrow lobby next to the phase 1 hearth and this may not be the position of the original entrance. There was formerly a separate entrance into the phase 2 building, next to the current front door, but this has been converted into a window. The W gable end has 2-light stone mullion windows with dripmoulds at ground and first floor levels. These have plain chamfers. There is a single light window with a short dripmould (no returns) in the gable. The N elevation is partly obscured by an addition (probably 18/19thC) with a sloping stone tiled roof. There are no windows showing at first floor level. The E gable end has a single light window (serving the stair that was formerly sited next to the hearth.

CHAPTER 8

The ground floor room of the Phase 1 cottage has a large open stone fireplace with original wood beam (with narrow chamfer and no stops), stone jambs (with narrow chamfers). There is no oven showing in the hearth. To the left of the hearth is a space, which probably originally contained a winder stair. Most cottages of this date in Chalford Hill have a stone stair in this position. There is a cross ceiling beam with approx 25mm chamfer and scroll stops.

An entrance to the room on the ground floor of the second building phase has been created by removing the rear wall of the entrance lobby (i.e., through gable end wall of phase 1 building). This room also has a large open stone fireplace, with original plain wood beam. The right hand jamb is formed of a stone slab (with a bread oven behind it) with a further vertical dressed stone beneath the slab. This type of construction is also present in the oven at Clematis Cottage (Commercial Road). There is a further oven in the rear wall of the hearth, this would have originally projected beyond the outside face of the rear wall. It is thought unlikely that the two ovens are contemporary with each other. The entrance to the side oven has been blocked, perhaps when the rear one was added. There is a semi circular recess to the side of the hearth, with a single light stair window in the rear wall. This would have formerly contained a winder stair. There is an axial ceiling beam, of slender proportions and a very narrow, rough chamfer. The end of the beam has been cut off to allow the insertion of the present stair.

The roof structure over the Phase 1 building has a pair of roughly cut principal rafters with a morticed collar and a diagonal joint at apex of principals. There are two rows of trenched purlins/roof slope. There is an inward projecting semi circular chimney-stack. The roof structure over the Phase 2 building is similar except that there is a single row of purlins /roof slope and the chimney-breast is shallower.

Laurel Cottage **(Figure 8.104)**: This was formerly Pincott's shop. The windows openings of the front façade have been modified. A photograph of the early 20th C shows that it used to have stone mullion frames without dripmoulds **(Figure 8.105)**. The stonework of the front wall shows that the building has been enlarged several times. There is a vertical building line showing that it has been extended to the N and a horizontal building line shows that the wall height has been raised to form low walls in the attic. There is a rear wing, with a gable end hearth. There are several stone built outbuildings around a courtyard to the rear of the building. Early in the 20th C some of these were commercial premises. The house was built in the 18th C, with additions and modifications later in the century.

The Old Duke of York Inn **(Figure 8.106)**: The Duke of York has seen many changes over its life. There are five major building phases and these are fairly easy to see and form the basis of the text. However, within each part of the building there have been many other minor changes and these make the overall interpretation of the building rather complicated. The earliest standing phase can be dated to the early 18th C and the present form of the building was completed by the early 20th C. There is reused structural timber in the rear part of the building and these seem to date from around the mid 17th C. This suggests that there may have been an early building present, but this has been removed as part of later work and the materials re-used. The details suggest these materials were re-used during the early part of the 19th C. A plan of the property in a deed dated 1895 shows that there was formerly a wing passing towards the lane from the NW side of the building **(Figure 8.107)**. This must have been removed soon after, as the wall detail here suggests that the present section of wall was built around this time. The details are the use of grey mortar, the use of machine cut stone, the style of the stone bay window and the window above **(Figure 8.108)**. The building has been a private house since the

VERNACULAR BUILDINGS OF CHALFORD

early 1990's and the name reflects its former use. The Duke of York was closed as a pub **(Figure 8.109)** by Whitbread Breweries in 1990 and the building sold at auction. It was bought by the owner of the Old Neighbourhood Inn (formerly The Mechanics Arms) and plans prepared for its conversion to a private house. The building was re-sold prior to this conversion and the Author has subsequently done the conversion work over the past decade. Much information has been gleaned about the history of the building over this period from evidence remaining in the structure, from documentary evidence and by word of mouth.

Phase 1: The earliest standing part of the building (Phase 1) is on the S side facing Queen's Square. It dates from the early 18th C. The front wall is constructed in hand dressed masonary blocks (not ashlar), with an intermediate string course, a central ground floor entrance and flanking ground and first floor 3-light stone mullion windows **(Figure 8.110)**. These windows are without dripmoulds and have flat chamfered surrounds. Originally they were fitted with leaded lights attached to horizontal bars (4 per light). They have a larger area of glass than is present in windows of the 17th C. A 2-light stone mullion window had been added above the entrance early in the 20th C in rather a poor fashion: this was removed in 2004 and the stonework restored. The original building had a carved stone porch hood above the entrance **(Figure 8.111)**, but this was removed by Whitbread Breweries in the 1960's and an ugly storm porch added. The latter has now been demolished and a simple stone tiled hood constructed. This sits on oak brackets made by Freeman's at the Camp in the 1930's. The original hood has not been lost. It was reclaimed by a concerned villager, stored and then sold to the owner of Rodney House, who had it installed over the front door there. The gable end walls are also of well-coursed masonary **(Figure 8.112)**. The E gable end wall has a flue for the large ground floor hearth. The W gable end wall has 2 single light stone window frames (now concealed by the Phase 2 extension), which originally provided light to the attic **(Figure 8.113)**. The stone of the rear wall is more random. On the ground floor it is rubblestone **(Figure 8.114)**, whereas at the first floor level, it is still rubblestone, but the coursing is better and there are jumper stones (suggesting an 18th C date) **(Figure 8.115)**. There is a blocked doorway on the ground floor, which is in line with the entrance in the front wall, showing that there was originally a through passage. It is possible that the stonework of the rear wall of the ground floor is a remnant of the original building on the site.

Internally, the ground floor of the Phase 1 building was divided into two rooms, together with a front to back corridor. The room to the E end has a large open hearth with stone jambs and a wood lintel **(Figure 8.116)**. The hearth was uncovered in the 1970's and the present lintel was fitted then. The jambs are original and are without chamfers, there is a seat behind the S jamb. The stonework to the rear of the hearth is unusual (but is as discovered). It has a small oven with a rear flue to one side of the hearth back and a couple of niches for keeping things dry to the other side. The fire sits in a recessed channel in the back of the hearth between the stonework of the oven and the niches. There is an inner stone lintel bridging the top of the channel where it opens into the large straight up flue. A similar oven has been seen at Rose Cottage, Bisley and this cottage has a datestone of 1720. There is a well-worn, stone winder stair to the left of the hearth with its original door frame (and a reclaimed door) **(Figure 8.117)**. Stone winders were not built after the early 18th C. There was formerly a fireplace in the other gable end wall, but this was removed in the 1960's, when extensive work was carried out by Whitbread Breweries. A combined Public and Lounge Bar serving area was created by removing the ground floor section of the W gable end wall and supporting the upper wall on steel girders **(Figure 8.118)**. The hearth must have been small as the space for the flue is limited to within a normal wall thickness.

Chapter 8

The ceiling structure is original and there are 2 ceiling beams. One is a half beam and is sited to the left of the entrance **(Figure 8.119)**. It formerly had a partition wall (probably studs with lath and plaster) beneath it and the position of the door into the room at this end can be identified by the discoloured part of the beam (where it had been painted above the door). The other beam (to the right of the door) is a full beam **(Figure 8.120)** and there are no signs of a wall beneath it, perhaps there was a more transient tongue and groove timber partition here or a simple draught screen by the door. The main beam does not have chamfers or stops, whereas the half beam has a rough, narrow chamfer to one side (and no stops). The ceiling joists sit proud of shallow cutouts in the top of the beams and are not fixed in position. The joists are hand sawn, irregular and are approximately 100mm x 75mm in section **(Figure 8.121)**. Until the early 1990's, the ceiling structure was hidden by a plasterboard ceiling. However, when this was removed the joists above, particularly at the fireplace end of the room, appear to have been blackened by soot staining. There were also marks and nail holes showing that a lath and plaster ceiling had been present at some stage. Remains of early plaster (almost like daub) were also found in the wall area between the joists, within the former ceiling space **(Figure 8.122)**. This plaster had been painted with several coatings of lime wash. This detail must show that the joists were exposed in the ceiling during the early life of the building. Perhaps, the plaster ceilings were only added when finances allowed. At the W end of the ground floor ceiling the support for the hearth-stone for a first floor fireplace is present **(Figure 8.123)**.

The first floor was originally divided into 2 rooms and the line of the original partition is indicated by the plaster/limewash staining on the set of original ceiling joists (which again suggests that the joists were exposed in the ceiling) **(Figure 8.124)**. There was a stairhead room and an inner room, each was of approximately the same floor area. There are two elm ceiling beams, which are not chamfered or stopped **(Figure 8.125)**. The joist detail is the same as in the ground floor ceiling, except that the joists are slightly smaller in section. A second section of winder stair (in elm) continues to the attic floor **(Figure 8.126)**. The attic consists of a single long space, with a pair of single light windows in the W gable end wall. The windows are separated by the flue, which serves the hearths on the lower floors. The roof structure is not the original one, although it probably copies the earlier pattern. There are two principal rafter trusses, without collars, which sit on tie beams that also support the floor **(Figure 8.127)**. There is a single row of butt purlins on each roof slope. The purlins are jointed, using a pegged timber fish-plate, across the back of each truss. The structure is thought to date from the early 20th C, it has been limewashed and some parts covered with wallpaper. Many coins were found under the attic floor, when the floorboards were replaced in the mid 1990's. Most were half pennies dating back to the mid/late 18th C and were of UK origin, although one was from the Dutch East India Company and another from Hibernia. It seems that the attic was used for sleeping and the coins must have fallen from pockets in clothing.

Phase 2: Soon after the Phase 1 building was completed, it was extended to the W. The new section of S facing wall continued the architectural detail (string course, 3-light windows and hand dressed masonary) of the original building **(Figure 8.128)**. A vertical building line marks the junction of the two parts. This new part has a roof structure at right angles to that of the existing cottage and it continues back beyond the line of the rear wall of the earlier part, so that when first built it had the appearance of being a wing, when viewed from the back of the building. The W facing side wall at the S end is built of large masonary blocks, that are similar (but less well dressed) than those of the front wall **(Figure 8.129)**. There are no windows in this wall and it contains a wide flue for a large stone fireplace. The N end of this wall was rebuilt around the beginning of the 20th C. The new section of wall is built of machine-cut stone, bedded in a grey ashy mortar. On the ground floor there is a good bay window constructed in cut stone **(Figure 8.108)**. This may have been built as a shop front, as there was a sweet shop in this part of the building in the early 20th C. The N gable end is built of rubblestone, with some larger stones forming the wall within the roof angle and containing a single light window **(Figure 8.130)**. There is a loading door, converted to a window on the original first floor level. The E side wall (the rear part that formed the side of the wing that projected to the rear) is now an internal wall. However, when building work was being done in the 1990's, it was apparent that the outer face was constructed in well dressed stone (as would be expected for an outside wall) and that there were two doorways into the ground floor of the building, each with outer stone and inner wood lintels. It seems that when originally built, there may have been a separate workroom at this end of the Phase 2 addition.

Most of the original roof structure of the Phase 2 addition is still present and consists of two principal rafter trusses, without collars and a single row of purlins per roof slope **(Figure 8.131)**. The original tie beams were removed in the early 20th C, when the ceiling heights were raised and replaced with modern timbers at a higher level (within the attic space) and with various iron tie rods **(Figure 8.132)**. The ridge timber sits on sections of timber board nailed to the faces of the trusses. The front truss has a third principal, which passes from the apex of the truss to the W corner of the building **(Figure 8.133)**, so that from the front of the building, the roof has the appearance of being hipped. When first built, this phase had two floors with an attic. The attic must have been used, as there is a single light window in the N facing gable end wall (now converted to a flue). However, all of the internal floor structure was removed when the ground and first floor ceilings were raised and the usable attic floor was lost.

There is only one original hearth in the Phase 2 addition and this is on the ground floor at the S end of the W wall **(Figure 8.134)**. This has a stone lintel (in two pieces, each slightly inclined and joined with an iron staple) and stone jambs (each in 2 slabs of hand dressed stone), which are without chamfers. The hearth is wide, but not deep. On the ground floor the chimney-breast projects into the room by only approximately 15 cm, whilst at the first floor level, the flue is contained within the normal wall thickness. There is a relieving arch above the stone lintel. This fireplace was uncovered in the 1990's. The infill material showed that it had been infilled in stages. First, it had been reduced in width using stone and then the reduced hearth had been infilled with a coal burning grate **(Figure 8.135)**. It was also apparent that there was an ash pit in front of the original hearth, however this was not restored. The chimney-stack is built off the wall plate of the first floor. There is a recess in the S wall of the addition, close to the hearth. This is shallow and was probably intended for shelves to store china. There is a similar recess in the room above and this has panelled doors **(Figure 8.136)**. The N end of the addition did not contain any original hearths. Although the N gable end wall now contains blocked coal burning grates on the ground and first floors. These predate the change in the floor levels (as the hearthstone of the first floor hearth is below the current floor level) and probably dates from the mid 19th C. It is not possible to say whether the Phase 2 addition was built to extend the accommodation of the existing cottage or whether it was separate accommodation. On balance, it seems more likely that it was a separate dwelling with a workshop, as it is difficult to see how the rooms could be linked on the ground and first floors to the Phase 1 cottage. The continuity of the detail in the front façade does, however, suggest that it was in the same ownership.

In Phase 3, an addition was made behind the Phase 1 cottage, such that it butts against the wing formed to the rear of the Phase 2 addition **(Figure 8.137)**. It gives an overall rectangular plan to the

Chapter 8

building. The first floor window surround detail suggests it was built in the late 18th/early 19th C, reusing much structural timber work from an earlier building (pre Phase 1). All of the internal partition walls are modern. The E gable end wall, now nearly hidden by the Phase 4 lean-to, contains a first floor loading door. The lintel over the door is a reused end section of a beam, with a 100mm flat chamfer and a step, draw stop **(Figure 8.138)**. The detail suggests the original beam was early 17th C. Because of the rise in the ground level, the loading door is only about 1.5 m above the outside level. There are no windows or hearths in this wall. The rear wall has two first floor windows with large stone blocks framing the surround and stone cills. The frames are modern, but the original frames would have been in wood and probably of the cottage casement type. There are flues within the wall thickness, between these windows, serving ground and first floor hearths. The ground floor hearth has been largely removed by later work, when it was converted into a window (to serve the Gents toilet in the final form of the Duke of York Inn). The first floor hearth was uncovered in the early 1990's. It has a rough hand dressed stone lintel and jambs and formerly housed a coal burning hob grate **(Figure 8.139)**. There is a vertical building line marking the junction with the Phase 2 addition. The quoin stones forming the W side of the line show that the rear part of the Phase 2 addition was formerly free standing. The stone courses of the Phase 3 addition butt against these quoin stones. There are jumper stones in the coursed rubble stone outer face of the rear wall. There is a ground floor entrance, with a group of wood lintels above it. These show that when this phase was first constructed, the door was directly next to the Phase 2 part and there was a window next to the door. At some stage, probably in the early 20th C, the door was moved slightly to the E and a column of stone added next to the building line and the window was lost. The present ground floor windows and their reconstituted stone lintels were introduced by Whitbread Breweries in the 1960's, when the pub was last upgraded. The Phase 3 addition shares its S and W walls with the earlier phases. The ground floor has two large ceiling beams with 100mm flat chamfers, but no stops. Later style timbers act to spread the load under these beams in the rear wall of the Phase 1 building **(Figure 8.140)**. The beams are very well dressed, are straight and have lodgings for moderately large joists on their top-side. These are re-used beams. The ends, containing the stops have been cut off or are hidden within the wall. One beam end may be present as the lintel over the loading door. The joists present in the early 1990's were degraded and thus removed. They consisted of various pieces of timber. Mixed in with some reasonable joists were bits of purlin, collar and principal rafter from an early roof structure (the parts could be identified by the nature of the mortices, cut-outs and peg holes in the timbers). There was formerly a stair against the W gable end wall (nb. this wall is also the E side-wall of the Phase 2 addition. However, this cannot have been original to the phase, as its landing was in front of a coal burning hearth (now blocked). This hearth has a smoothed stone lintel and stone jambs **(Figure 8.141)**. To the right of the hearth, there is a blocked doorway leading to the original first floor level of the Phase 2 addition **(Figure 8.142)**. This retains a rather roughly constructed doorframe, with a bead moulding around the opening: this possibly dates from the original construction. The roof structure is 3 bays long and contains a pair of principal rafter trusses, without collars and with the tie beam above the ceiling level **(Figure 8.143)**. Both ties are reused timber. One is a half beam with a 100mm flat chamfer and a step draw stop at one end **(Figure 8.144)**. The other tie is a rectangular beam with regular spaced mortices in its top (narrower) side: it is probably the bottom member of a good stud wall **(Figure 8.145)**. There is a single row of staggered, cut back, butt purlins on each roof slope. The ridge board is supported on fillets of timber nailed to the faces of the principals. The joists are not original (probably replaced in the mid 20th C and are not intended to be load bearing. A valley gutter separates the roofs over the Phase 1 and 3 parts of the building. The amount of early timbers that have been re-used strongly suggests that a cottage was demolished close to here or on the site, prior to the construction of this addition. The origin use of this addition is rather confusing. It had a ground floor hearth, two first floor hearths and a first floor loading door. All of these seem to be original to the phase. It is possible it was added as another cottage to the existing group and the whole has now become the Duke of York. The presence of the loading door suggests that it had a part industrial use and probably contained a workroom associated with the cloth industry.

In Phase 4, a lean-to was added across the E gable ends of the Phase 1 and 3 parts of the building **(Figure 8.146)**. There is a blocked doorway near the centre of the E wall. The former opening is now partly below the current inside and outside ground levels. Although, it is known that the internal floor level was raised by approx 0.6 m during the renovation of the building in the 1960's. The walls are constructed from rubblestone and inside the walls have never been plastered **(Figure 8.147)**. The roof structure is constructed from machine cut timber and was probably replaced some time in the 20thC. The internal space is currently a garage/workshop. In the later days of the working Duke of York Inn, it was divided into two rooms, one was a coal store and the other was a bottle store. An elderly resident of the area, in the early 1990's, said he could remember that this part of the building was occupied by a mother and daughter in the 1920's. Its original function does not seem to have been domestic as there are no hearths or windows (or their former positions) visible. The wide chamfer on the stonework **(Figure 8.148)** at the entrance (to the now garage) may indicate a cart or wagon was formerly manoeuvred there, so a storage/industrial use is most likely.

There is a detached two-storey building behind the Duke of York, which contains a single room on each floor **(Figure 8.149)**. The detail of the stonework shows that the wall heights have been raised. This was probably done in the late 19th C, as the upper quoin stones are machine cut. The present windows in the W facing front wall and the loading door in the S gable end wall must originate from the time when the walls were raised. Also, the present high ceiling on the ground floor (which fits with the large ground floor window) must also date from this time. It is thought that the earlier form of the building was also two-storey, but with a lower ceiling height and a more steeply pitched roof. There is a hearth in the N gable end wall, which is of the correct size for a small coal burning range **(Figure 8.150)**. The existing range here was removed from the Post Office at France Lynch, when it was renovated several years ago. Next to the range there are two small flues in the wall, which appear as small openings near the floor level **(Figure 8.151)**. A single flue of this type has been seen in other cottage outhouses where it is used by the fire under a copper for heating water. The presence of two flues of this type suggests that separate fires for different purposes were needed. The stonework shows that the hearth and pair of additional flues date to the original phase for this building. The configuration of the floor joists showed that when the ceiling was raised in the late 19th C, there was no provision for a stair linking the two floors. The entrance door to the first floor in the N gable end wall and the present roof structure all date from the mid 20th C. The original function of the building is not known, but the presence of the multiple flues in the gable end wall and the loading door suggest that it was not a domestic building. It was probably built as a detached workshop. Several others have been noted in Chalford Hill, e.g. at Cotswold Place and the Ferns. It is plausible that they housed broadlooms for the cottage based weaving industry.

The Duke of York has developed in stages from an initial cottage in the early 18th C. There is some evidence which suggests there was a 17th C building on or near the site and that this survived until the late 18th C, when it was completely removed or remaining evidence of it well hidden in later building phases. The early 18th C cottage is well constructed with some good detail. Over the next

Chapter 8

100 years, two additions were built to generate the rectangular form of the house that still exists. Each seems to have been built as a separate dwelling and each has a taking in or loading door. This suggests a link with the local weaving industry and there is a strong possibility that they were homes for cottage based handloom weavers. Their intimate relationship with the original early 18th C cottage suggests that they were in common ownership. The presence of the two-storey outbuilding also suggests a link with the local industry. Over the years the building has been split into separate dwellings in different ways. In the early part of the 20th C it contained an inn (Duke of York), a sweet shop and two separate cottages. In the 1960's all were merged to form the Duke of York Inn on the ground floor, with an apartment for the publican upstairs. In the 1990's it was converted to a private house, with some minor adjustments to the internal layout.

No documents have been found that give further information on the early history of the complex, during which it was developing. However, information does exist from 1821 onwards. Prior to this date the property belonged to William Yarnton Mills, who was a lay rector at Bisley. He owned properties in the Stroud area and the whole portfolio was placed in a family trust for the benefit of his grandson, Thomas Mills Goodlake. The abstract of title of the property, written in 1891, when the trust was being wound up and the properties were being sold, gives details of the trustees and transactions undertaken on behalf of the trust, but little detail of the properties themselves. Thomas Mills Goodlake had died in 1877 and one of his daughters and her husband, the Marquis and Marquisse de Lasterie had acquired the ownership of the whole package of properties. They were then sold. The Duke of York Inn and the White Hart Inn (now Hartsop Cottage, Bisley) were purchased for £905, by Albert Crook, who lived at Marle Hill House **(Figure 8.152)**. In 1895, he sold the Duke of York to the Stroud Brewery Company for £850 **(Figure 8.153)**. The title of sale contains a site plan and this shows a wing passing out to the lane, where there is now car parking and the house is now terminated by a stone bay window (this is late 19th C in origin). The details also mention a brewhouse, stables and cottage. The cottage is known to be part of the original cottage, but the locations of the brewhouse and stables are not known with certainty. The lean-to across the E gable ends is likely to be the location of one of them. Interestingly, the outbuilding is not shown, but the building detail suggests something must have existed, which was extensively rebuilt in the late 19th C. Perhaps this was the brewhouse. The Stroud Brewery Company owned the building until the 1960's, when it was transferred to West Country Breweries and then Whitbreads, who sold it in 1992.

Spring Cottage and Friars Cottage: These have an origin in the latter part of the 17th C as a single dwelling. It consisted of a two-storey house with two rooms on each floor, under a fairly steeply pitched stone tiled roof. The walls were of coursed rubblestone. The original ground floor hearth remains in the gable end wall facing into the side of the valley. This retains its original wood fireplace beam and stone slab jambs, but the depth of the hearth is reduced slightly. There is a stone winder stair beside the hearth. The building was extended to the E with an additional cottage in the first half of the 18th C. This has a hearth of moderate size on the ground floor, in the gable end wall and this has a slightly projecting, external chimney-breast. The architectural details (stonework, windows, string course) of the addition are similar to that of the Old Duke of York Inn and the Old Builders Arms. A further extension was made to the W in the late 20th C and by this time the house was divided into two dwellings.

The spring which gushes out of the wall in the lane between Spring Cottage and the Old Duke of York Inn, marks the junction of the Fullers Earth Clay and the Great Oolite. This is also evident in the slight rise in the lane as you move from the clay, onto the rock strata.

Chalford Hill Stores (now The Old Stores) **(Figure 8.154 and 155)**: This has developed in stages. There seems to be a two and a half-storey cottage (with three-light ground and first floor windows, of the larger type, without dripmould) built behind the three-storey block that forms the larger part of the property. The detail of the cottage suggests an early 18th C origin. The three-storey block consists of two parts, with their own roofs and separated by a valley gutter. There is no building line, which indicates they are contemporary with each other. There is a first floor loading door (now blocked) in the W facing gable end of the three-storey block. The window frames are mainly two-light stone mullions, without dripmoulds. The S part of the three-storey block has a blocked ground floor entrance door and has gable end hearths at the E end, which shows that this part must have been built as living accommodation. However, it is speculated that the rear part of this block was originally constructed for industrial purposes and the most likely use is for looms. There are several examples of three-storey buildings in the village with taking in doors for the upper floors. These are not domestic in origin. The garage to the rear is also stone built and may also be linked to the original use of the building. The detail suggests that the majority of the building was developed by the latter part of the 18th C.

The Bunch of Nuts: A group of cottages sited below Spring/Friars Cottages. Not seen in any detail, but seems to consist of a late 17thC cottage, which has grown by the addition of three further cottages between the 18th and early 19th C. It has been suggested that the name refers to the former use of one of the cottages as an alehouse.

Cottages on Queen's Square: The first group (adjacent to Chalford Hill Stores) are all aligned parallel to the slope of the ground and are set back from the lane **(Figure 8.156)**. They are of two-storeys, under a moderately pitched stone tiled roof and are constructed in well-coursed rubblestone, with large quoin stones. A vertical building line shows they were built in two stages (a terrace of three, with one added). However, the similarities in the style show that they are close in date of construction. The original window frames are three-light mullions, without dripmoulds and with plain, flat, chamfer surrounds on both ground and first floors. These have a relatively large area of glass. The group originated as four cottages, each with a large ground floor hearth with a wood or stone lintel. The detail suggests they were built in the early 18th C.

The second group (Well Cottage and Willoughby) follows the first group and is built much closer to the lane **(Figure 8.157 and 158)**. There are two, two-storey cottages, with attics. The walling consists of well-coursed rubblestone, with some jumper stones. Although, there are not any vertical building lines, there is a discontinuity in the stonework coursing, which indicates that there were two stages of construction. The windows are two-light stone mullions, with plain, flat chamfer surrounds, but no dripmoulds. Again the detail suggests an origin in the 18th C, although Well Cottage may be of earlier origin (information from the owner).

A third group of cottages stands on the W side of the lane **(Figure 8.159)**. There are currently two cottages, one with a recent addition. The core of the group is a 17th C cottage, aligned at right angles to the lane. The cut down E gable end of this cottage remains as the dormer window, with the two-light stone mullion window, with dripmould. The W gable end remains facing into the garden. The adjoining cottage, aligned parallel to the lane probably dates from the late 17th C. The walls of this cottage are built of well-coursed rubblestone and there does not appear to be jumper stones. Internally, there is a large hearth with stone jambs and a wood lintel in the gable end wall that is adjacent to the sidewall of the other cottage.

Chapter 8

The three groups of cottages in the Queens Square area were all probably built as weaver's cottages and were all in existence by the early part of the 18th C.

Rodney House and the Old Builders Arms: This building began as a cottage in the late 17th C and evolved during 18th C to form the house that survives today. In the mid 20th C, the whole was a single dwelling, but has subsequently been split into two properties. There is also a large detached 'barn' that was converted to a house in the late 1990's. This, in all probability, was built for some manufacturing purpose, possibly as a weaving shed in the mid 19th C. The original cottage (Phase 1) is sited in a wing, behind the main front part of the house. The ground floor has a large fireplace in the N gable end wall, with the remains of a stone winder stair to its side. The hearth retains the original wood lintel with a carved date of 1689. Phase 2 **(Figure 8.160)** (the front range, now the Old Builders Arms) has good detail with a lower and an upper stringcourse. There are three, three-light stone window frames and one two-light stone mullion window frame on the first floor. The ground floor has three, three-light windows and the main entrance. The stonework is of a good quality and comprised of well-dressed stone blocks. There is an off centre front door with a hood and surround with classical details. The roof structure has similar detail to that seen in the roof of the Phase 2 part of Clematis Cottage **(Figure 8.161)**. This detail includes roof trusses sited on low attic walls, with a vertical post jointed into the underside of the principal and linking to the tie beam, joints secured with forelock bolts, purlins cut back at the junction with the principal, and collars fixed across the side faces of the principal rafters. It is thought that this phase was built in the early part of the 18th C. In Phase 3, the Phase 1 building was extended to the S. This part has a large ground floor hearth in a cross wall, near the S end. The ceiling beams are of a moderate size and the detail suggests that Phase 3 was built in the mid/late 18th C. Phases 1 and 3 form a consistent range of building with two-storeys and attics (the two parts are now Rodney House) **(Figure 8.162)**. It has coursed rubblestone walls, with mainly wood casement windows of a late 18th/early 19th C style, under wood lintels. The S gable end wall has 2-light stone mullion frames. There is a first floor loading door in the W facing side-wall (now converted to a window). The current front door has the porch hood that was removed from the Duke of York in the late 1960's.

The 'barn' **(Figure 8.163)** may have been built to serve the cloth industry in the village. It originally did not contain any hearths and had ground and first floors. The first floor was not present in the early 1990's, but has subsequently been replaced as part of the conversion of the building to a house. There are rows of ground and first floor windows. These have timber frames under stone lintels (which are machine cut). There is a loading door at first floor level, at the W end and facing the lane. There was formerly a large window, with a stone cill in the gable end facing W. The roof trusses are elm and the timbers, relatively thin and have bolted collars. There was formerly a stable at the W end, which retained its cobble floor. It is suggested that the building is a weaving shed. The detail suggests it was built in the mid 19th C, at the end of the cloth making period in the area.

Wychbury **(Figure 8.164)**: This is one of the later houses of the immediate area and dates from the late 19th C. It has sash windows with large panes in the front façade. Much of the walling stone is machine cut.

Cottages on Marle Hill

There are at least seven 17th C cottages on the side of the small valley that runs down Marle Hill. Because of their position on a steep slope, they have generally not grown so much by addition, compared with some of the groups on the flatter land at the top of the hill. They have been extended, but most have maintained more of their original external character. In addition there are cottages built in the 18th and 19th C.

Fir Tree Cottage and Christmas Cottage **(Figure 8.165 and 166)**: Both are built with their rear walls directly bordering the lane that now runs down Marle Hill. This suggests that the lane was established when these cottages were built. The earlier cottages are randomly sited in respect to the lane, which indicates that the way down the valley was less formalised when they were built. Both cottages are built in rubblestone, with roofs with a fairly low pitch. The windows are wood casements in the cottage style. There are not any windows in the rear walls. All the detail suggests they were originally built around the mid 19th C. Each cottage has a building line in its rear wall, showing that they developed in two stages (each phase as a separate cottage).

Mole Cottage **(Figure 8.17)**: The original cottage is built gable end into the hillside, with the hearth at that end. It has two-storeys and an attic, under a steeply pitched roof. There is one room on each floor and the floor areas are modest. It is difficult to see how it can ever have housed a broadloom. The walls are constructed in coarsed rubblestone, with 2-light stone mullion windows (with flat chamfer surrounds) on the ground and first floors, in the W facing gable end. There is a single light window in the attic. There were probably windows in at least one of the side walls, but these must be hidden by the later additions to both sides. The ground floor hearth has stone slab jambs and a wood hearth beam. There is a stone winder stair to the right of the hearth. The roof structure is of two bays, with a central truss, with tie beam.

Brendan House **(Figure 8.167)**: This dates from the mid 19th C. It has a symmetrical façade, with multi pane sash windows. It was built following the closure of the adjacent stone quarry.

A lane leads off Marle Hill below Brendan House. This follows the contour of the hill to Rack Hill, which was a former cloth drying area for the mills in the valley below. However, there is also much evidence to show that this was an important quarrying area prior to the mid 19th C. The freestone of the Inferior Oolite was dug from here. There are several cottages along the lane, which are known to be quarryman's cottages. There are small stone mines in the hillside behind them (these are now closed up). Mines are said to have been dug, when the limit of the quarry land had been reached. Extra stone was grabbed by burrowing under the adjacent land. Rock House (further along and below the path) is built on a quarried out shelf and has a quarry face in the hillside behind it. This also has small mines dug into it. Part of this house dates from before the early 18th C, which shows that stone was being quarried here from early times. The Inferior Oolite must have been used for the drystone walls along Rack Hill and after 150 years or so, some are now badly perished.

Fernleigh **(Figure 8.168 and 169)**: Constructed as three cottages with a dressed stone front wall and rubblestone rear and gable end walls. The roof has a moderate pitch. The front elevation has two-light stone mullion window frames, without dripmoulds. One ground floor hearth is exposed and this was built for coal burning and has the name R.Cox and 1826 scratched on the flanking stonework. This most probably indicates the build date, as the writing would have been covered by plaster in the finished building. The date is consistent with the absence of beams and the presence of the coal-burning hearth. The cottages had been combined by the early 1980's. An extension was added in the early 1990's.

Chapter 8

Glen Cottage **(Figure 8.21)**: This stands on the valley floor and the original cottage has been extended to either side, in the late 18th/early 19th C and again, in the late 20th C. The original cottage is very similar to Mole Cottage, but with slightly larger area. There is a large ground floor hearth, built in the gable end against the valley side. The front of the hearth wall has a recessed area between the stair and the jamb of the hearth. The function of this is not known, it could be a keeping hole. A similar feature has been seen in a cottage at Waterlane. The detail of the original cottage suggests a late 17th C building date. The gable end windows of the original cottage have dripmoulds.

Steep Cottage **(Figure 8.170)**: This cottage was extended in the early 1980's **(Figure 8.171)** . Prior to this, it consisted of a 11/2 storey cottage, which had been extended with a wing containing an extra room on each floor **(Figure 8.172)**. The cottage is constructed in rubblestone with a steeply pitched roof. The roof structure of the original cottage sits on the half height walls **(Figure 8.173)**. It consists of a central truss, without a tie beam, but with a collar that is bolted across the face of the truss. There are two rows of butt purlins on each roof slope and these are cut back at their junctions with the principal. Pairs of purlins overlap each other through each principal. There is a diagonal mortice and tenon joint at the top of the pair of principal rafters and the ridge timber is housed in a notch in the principal. The original rafter set is still in place, even across the junction with the roof over the later wing. There is a hearth on the ground floor with stone jambs and a wood lintel, the jambs are formed of rough stone blocks and these are not chamfered **(Figure 8.174)**. The hearth beam has a narrow chamfer. There is an axial ceiling beam with a flat chamfer that is approximately 50mm wide, but without stops. The detail of the roof structure and hearth suggest it was built in the early 18th C, with the wing added later on in that century.

The Glen **(Figure 8.18)**: The outside evidence suggests this has been built in two phases, which are in line with each other. The rear part has two-storeys and attic under a steeply pitched roof, whereas the front part has two and a half storeys under a less steeply pitched roof. It is possibly that the walls of the front part of the building have been raised to form the low height walls in the attic. Each part has a rear gable end fireplace. The E facing gable end has a three-light window on the ground floor and two-light windows at the first and attic levels, all with dripmoulds and plain chamfer surrounds. There are similar frames in the side elevation of the building. Both parts originate in the latter part of the 17th C, probably as separate cottages.

Field Cottages: This consists of a cottage with an attached mill (now itself converted into a separate cottage). The original cottage dates back to the latter part of the 17th C, as it has a gable end hearth and winder stair, typical of the period. It seems that the early cottage has been refronted, with windows that are early 19th C in style (with segmented stone arch heads and cottage casement windows (replacements)). The mill had an internal wheel, as the blocked, arched openings for the leat can be seen in the front and rear wall. The wheel was powered by the active springs from the Fullers Earth Clay/Great Oolite spring line.

Marle Hill House **(Figure 8.22)**: This has a datestone of 1712. The house seems to be based on several two-storey cottages, with the earliest being gable end into the bank. This part has stone mullion windows with rebated surrounds and ovolo chamfers in the gable end. To the N of this there is another cottage parallel to the bank and this has the larger type of stone mullion window frame, with rebated surround and plain chamfers.

SILVER STREET TO SKIVERALLS

This lane contains cottages of a diverse character, which date from the 17th to 20th C. All of the pre 20th C buildings are constructed in stone. Those built in the post mid 20th C are built of reconstituted stone. These notes are confined to the pre 20th C vernacular cottages. The main development occurred along the along the N side of the lane with the cottages facing S, there is limited development on the S side and here the cottages are built with their backs onto the lane, with gardens on their S side. The following notes describe several of the cottages along the street.

Cliff House **(Figure 8.175)**: Constructed in coursed rubblestone, without jumper stones, and aligned at 90° to the lane. It has two-storeys under a shallow pitched roof. There are two-light stone mullion window frames, without chamfers. There is a large ground floor fireplace, with a timber hearth beam, in the N gable end wall (i.e. against the bank). There is a two-storey addition (in brick) along the W side of the earlier cottage. The earlier part of the cottage must date from the latter part of the 17th C and it seems that the roof pitch has been reduced in more recent times. The addition was probably built in the late 19th C.

Cliff Cottage **(Figure 8.176)**: An early 18thC cottage, built of coursed rubblestone with a moderately pitched roof and aligned parallel to the lane. The front is not symmetrical. The front door is at the W end, and this has a flat stone canopy supported on short stone brackets. The door frame is comprised of stone quoins, without a chamfer, laid alternately on the front face of the wall and in the reveal of the door. There is a stone lintel between the porch brackets. To the right of the door, there is a two-light stone mullion window under a continuous dripmpould. There are two, two-light stone mullion windows on the first floor, without dripmoulds. All windows are relatively large in area and have plain, flat chamfer surrounds. The E gable end has a blocked single light stone frame, which was probably intended to give light to a stair well and to the attic. There is a vertical building line marking the junction with an addition to the W. This is also constructed in coursed rubblestone and has a three-light window frame on the ground floor and a two-light window on the first floor. The frames are constructed in timber and the detail suggests an origin in the late 18th C.

Quail Cottage **(Figure 8.177)**: This cottage is built with its gable end bordering the lane. It is one and a half storeys tall and is built of coursed rubblestone. It has a steeply pitched roof. The ground and attic floors, of the S facing gable end, each have a two-light stone mullion window, with dripmould and a plain, flat chamfer surround. There is an owl window in the apex of the gable, which (if original) suggests an origin in the late 17th C. The rear (N facing) gable end should contain a large hearth and a winder stair. The rear part of the W facing side-wall has similar windows to those in the S gable end, except there are no dripmoulds. The front end of this wall has what appears to be a large chimney gable. In reality, this is most likely to be the gable end wall of a demolished, adjacent cottage. It seems that there was a hearth and flue in this wall that was used by Quail Cottage and the wall had to remain when the major part of the cottage was removed. There would originally have been two ground floor rooms, one heated, the other unheated (until the adjacent cottage was built). The original cottage at The Ferns would have looked similar to this.

Chapter 8

Hedges and adjoining cottage **(Figure 8.178)**: This is a tall, two and a half storey building, built of coursed rubblestone under a moderately pitched roof. Part of the roof retains its stone tiles. It consists of a pair of cottages, which appear to be of unequal size. The larger cottage has ground and first floor three-light stone mullion frames without dripmoulds, with an additional two-light window on the first floor. The other cottage has a two-light window on the ground and first floors. The front doors are sited towards the centre of the front elevation. The whole appears to be of one build, as there are no building lines evident. The vertical height between the windows shows that the rooms are tall. All of the windows have similar detail, with plain, flat chamfer surrounds, lights of a 'large' area and similar sized windows on each floor. There are gable end chimneys. The detail suggests an origin in the early part of the 19th C.

The Cottage **(Figure 8.179)**: This is built on the corner of land between the S side of Silver Street and the lane that links to the top of Commercial Road. It consists of two phases of building. The earlier part has a rear gable end that directly borders Silver Street. This has an externally projecting, stepped chimney-breast. This part has two-storeys and an attic. The walls are built of roughly coursed rubblestone, which has some jumper stones. The roof pitch is steep. There is a two-light stone mullion window frame without a dripmould on the ground and first floor of the side elevation. These have plain, flat chamfer surrounds. This part was probably built by the early 18th C. It has the orientation expected for a 17th C cottage, but the external chimney-breast suggests a slightly later date. A further cottage was added at 90° to the W side of the original cottage some time around the early 19th C. This part has two-light stone mullion window frames in the front elevation.

Lane to top end of Commercial Road

Vine House: Originally constructed in the mid 18th C, as a pair of cottages (one larger than the other). The original windows had stone frames, those in the larger part have been replaced with sash windows.

Prospect Cottage **(Figure 8.180 and 181)**: This has developed in several phases. The current front of the cottage (facing E) has stone arched lintels over the windows, which suggests a date in the early 19th C. However, the gable end beside the lane, shows the ghost building line for a steeply pitched roof of a single storey building with attic. This earlier cottage was orientated at right angles to the lane and had a large hearth (surviving) in its N gable end wall. In plan, it was probably similar to the one already identified at the Ferns in Commercial Road. This was then adapted, in the early 19th C to a cottage facing E, with a symmetrical façade and the windows with the arched lintels. An extension, with a catslide roof, was then added to the rear of this building, again in the 19th C. This form of the cottage shows in some of the books containing early photographs of Stroud and the surrounding villages. More recently, the addition with the catslide roof has been converted to two-storeys with a pitched roof.

Bakery Cottage **(Figure 8.182)**: Building lines in the front elevation show that this has been formed by the extension of an earlier smaller cottage. The 3-light stone mullion window frames with a large area of glass in the modified façade, suggest that the changes were complete by the late 18th C.

Further along Silver Street:

VERNACULAR BUILDINGS OF CHALFORD

Walton Cottage **(Figure 8.183)**: This cottage has a near central front door, with flanking stone mullion window frames, that to the E side has three-lights. There are two, two-light windows on the first floor above the ground floor windows. The window frames have flat chamfer surrounds, without dripmoulds. The walls are comprised of coursed, well-dressed rubblestone. The roof has a moderate pitch and there must be low height walls in the attic. Originally the ground floor would have been divided into two rooms, with a central corridor/stair. The detail suggests that the cottage dates from about the mid 18th C. There is a single storey addition, which has a tall three-light stone mullion window, a small gable end hearth (with a stone lintel and rubblestone jambs) and a fairly steeply pitched roof. The detail also suggests an 18th C origin, either as a weaving shed or a cottage.

Cottage next to Cyprus Villa **(Figure 8.184 and 185)**: Built in coursed rubblestone, there is a definite vertical building junction showing in the rear wall. However, the junction is not apparent in the front wall. The front wall has stone mullion window frames (mixture of three and two-light windows, one is modern). It is possible that a small late 17th C cottage has been extended and that at this stage a consistent new front was constructed. This work included the rebuilding of the existing side wall of the early cottage, which now formed part of the front of the extended property. The 'new front' has a good porch hood slab on stone brackets. This cottage was photographed in the early 1900's and used in the book entitled 'Old Cottages, Farmhouses and Other Stone Buildings in the Cotswold Region' **(Figure 8.186)**.

Cypress Villa **(Figure 8.187)**: Tall, two and a half storey house with attics. There is a central front door with flanking large pane sash windows. Similar windows on the first floor, together with a third window above the door. The central window has coloured glass around the edge of each sash frame and is most probably a landing window. There is a pair of matching dormer windows built half within the height of the walls to light the attic floor. The walling is well dressed, coursed stone. There is a good cast iron fence, sitting on a low, stone wall to the front of the property. The detail suggests an origin in the late 19th C. There is an attached lock-up shop (formerly Homefitters, then Chalford Vale Meats, now vacant).

The Wheatsheaves: Local authority housing built in reconstituted stone in the 1950/60 period, on the site of the demolished Wheatsheaves public house **(Figure 8.188)**. The footpath to the side of the houses that passes up to Skiveralls has some cottages that range in date from the late 17th to 19th C.

OVERVIEW OF THE DEVELOPMENT OF CHALFORD HILL

Chalford Hill developed as a settlement of handloom weavers. It was sited there for a number of reasons: there was a good supply of fresh water and building stone, the position is sheltered and it was lighter than in the valley. The latter would have been an important consideration for a weaver. It is also probably true that the land was less suited to agriculture because of the steepness of the hillside. There are a few larger houses in the Skiveralls area and there may have been an early farmstead here, around which the village developed. The earliest cottages, which are generally accepted as having been built either by or for weavers are of 17th C origin. Some of the earliest ones had a single storey with attic under a steeply pitched roof. Some at least had two rooms on the ground floor. Cottages built towards the end of the century generally had two-storeys and attic, under a steeply pitched roof. These had one room per floor. Several single storey cottages have been identified in the early core of the village, but they have been increased in height to form two-storey cottages at different times.

Chapter 8

There are more cottages which were originally two-storey, than were originally single storey and this is probably reflecting increased economic development in the later part of the century. The early cottages are sited along tracks that pass from the Bisley Common down to the crossing points on the River Frome (near Chalford Place and the bottom of Coppice Hill). There is no formal plan, the cottages seem to have been built where the land appeared best suited. They share many common details in terms of fireplaces, beams, windows and roof structures and are well constructed. They remain structurally sound, despite being built without foundations. The 17th C cottages were built gable end into the bank, with the hearth at the bank end, which presumably helped to keep the building dry and ensured that windows could be sited in the opposite, lighter gable end. Each was surrounded by a large garden and a dry stone wall. The provision of food must have been important to the weavers during the early development of the settlement. The wall would have been needed to keep sheep away from the crops. Most of the 17th century cottages have grown by the addition of further cottages, as opposed to the extension of the original accommodation. These cottages appear to have been built as separate dwellings, albeit directly attached to the original lodgings. The motivation seems to have been to provide extra cottages for additional weavers and their families, rather than to increase the accommodation in existing properties.

In the 18th C, the development of the village continued in the area of the early core, with some expansion further up the hill into the area of Midway. 18th century cottages have a different form to those of the 17th C: externally, they tend to be aligned parallel to the bank, have less steeply pitched roofs and tend not to have dripmoulds over the windows (although these were not universally used in the 17th C either). They also tend to be more symmetrical with a central front entrance with flanking windows that serve two ground floor rooms. Internally, the beams tend to be rougher in their finish and do not have chamfers or stops. Large hearths were still used, although they were not as deep and the surrounds and beam were not chamfered or stopped. These cottages are mixed in with the 17th C cottages, sometimes attached, sometimes separate. The core of the village has the feeling of being random, with no planning, apart from an association with the historic routes through the area now developed as the village. Midway represents a more planned development of the village, with the cottages (mostly of late 18/early 19th C origin) and gardens being sited in an ordered fashion along the lane. Many of the cottages that originated in the 18th C have taking-in doors. Sometimes, they appear to have parts of the building with an industrial rather than a domestic origin. It gives the feeling of an expanding community in which industry played a role in many of the households. There is evidence that some houses were associated with small factories (which were most likely weaving sheds). These include (Fleece House, France Corner, Old Duke of York Inn, The Old Stores (Chalford Hill Stores), Rodney House and Suffield Cottages. Perhaps these small domestic/industrial complexes in Chalford Hill are the premises of minor clothiers, who were employing weavers/renting looms in the 18th C. This is an area that would justify some more research.

Some limited further development occurred in the 19th C within the early part of the village. Again these were either attached to existing properties (some of which by this time were showing several phases of addition) and as detached cottages. These properties tend to be narrower in width than the earlier cottages and this may be reflecting a change in the use of the buildings from domestic/work to purely domestic. This would have occurred because in this century, attempts were made to shift the weaving activity to the new mills in the valley bottom to improve the efficiency of the industry. However, this was followed by a fairly rapid decline in the cloth making industry, so that it had virtually died out at Chalford by the mid 19th C. These cottages tend to have coal-burning hearths, which are smaller than the earlier wood burning hearths. In this period, there was also some development along Midway and farther out in Burcombe Road.

Development in the 20th C has continued, but mainly outside the confines of the early part of the village. There has been some infilling using non-vernacular materials and styles, but the extent has been limited and has not detracted from the character of the place. The main 20th C developments have been along Burcombe Road, Avenesse, Dr Middletons Road, various closes off Middle Hill and in the area of Downview and Aston View.

CHAPTER 8

Figure 8.1.. Site of Roman villa at Bournes Green.

Figure 8.2.. Long barrows at The Camp.

Figure 8.3. Money tump, behind Nashend Farm.

Figure 8.4.. The Old Malt House Cottage. *(2006)*

Figure 8.5: Little France Cottage. *(2005)*

Figure 8.6. Halstead. *(2006)*

VERNACULAR BUILDINGS OF CHALFORD

Figure 8.7. Fleece House, formerly the Fleece Inn.

Figure 8.8. The Ferns. *(1990)*

Figure 8.9. Glenhaven. *(1990)*

Figure 8.10. Clematis Cottage, formerly Commercial Road Stores.

Figure 8.11. Holly Bank.

Figure 8.12. The Orchards.

CHAPTER 8

Figure 8.13. Elm Cottage. *(2006)*

Figure 8.14.. Greycot. *(2006)*

Figure 8.15. Farthingcote. *(2006)*

Figure 8.16. Hazel Cottage. *(2006)*

Figure 8.17. Mole Cottage. *(2006)*

Figure 8.18. The Glen. *(2006)*

VERNACULAR BUILDINGS OF CHALFORD

Figure 8.19. Marle Hill Cottages. *(2006)*

Figure 8.20. Steep Cottage, Marle Hill. *(1984)*

Figure 8.21. Glen Cottage. *(2006)*

Figure 8.22. Marle Hill House. *(2006)*

Figure 8.23. Byways. *(1995)*

Figure 8.24. Dry stone boundary walls. *(2006)*

267

CHAPTER 8

Figure 8.25. The Triangle and Greycot. *(2006)*

Figure 8.26. Basic pre war kitchen, in use until 1980. *(Westview, Brownshill, 1999)*

Figure 8.27. Cottage range (early 20thC) in use until the 1960's.*(Westview, Brownshill, 1999)*

Figure 8.28. Single storey cottage with attic, France Lynch. *(1994)*

Figure 8.29. The Ferns: roofline of single storey cottage. *(1990)*

Figure 8.30. Prospect Cottage: roofline of single storey cottage. *(1989)*

VERNACULAR BUILDINGS OF CHALFORD

N.B. Figure 8.32 on next page

Figure 8.31. Two-storey cottage at Fleece House. *(2006)*

Figure 8.33. Cottage in Silver St built gable end into the hillside. *(1990)*

Figure 8.34. Stone built shed behind the Old Duke of York Inn. *(1999)*

Figure 8.35. Stone built shed in front of Cotswold Place. *(1999)*

Figure 8.36: Early 18th C cottage in Silver St, parallel to the lane. *(1990)*

Figure 8.37. The Old Duke of York Inn, Chalford Hill, with string course. *(2006)*

Chapter 8

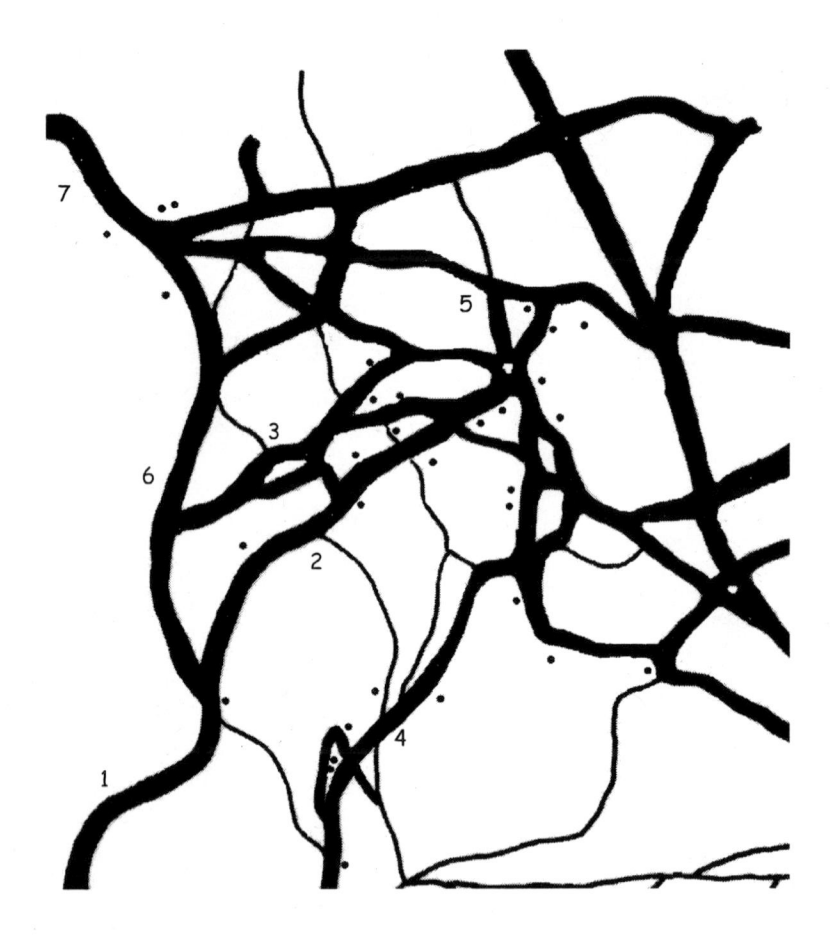

1	Dark Lane
2	Commercial Rd
3	Silver St
4	Marle Hill
5	Midway
6	Skiveralls
7	Abnash

Figure 8.32. Distribution of buildings with a 17th C origin in Chalford Hill

VERNACULAR BUILDINGS OF CHALFORD

Figure 8.38. Early 19th C cottage at Oakridge Lynch. *(1991)*

Figure 8.39. 18th C gatepost. *(Duke of York Inn, 2006)*

Figure 8.40. Late 19th C gatepost on Rack Hill. *(1999)*

Figure 8.41. Typical drystone wall, with one type of stone. *(1999)*

Figure 8.42: Drystone wall, with mixture of stones. *(1999)*

Figure 8.43. Badly perished drystone wall on Rack Hill. *(1999)*

CHAPTER 8

Figure 8.44. Coping formed of upright stones, laid dry. *(1999)*

Figure 8.45. Shaped coping slabs (mid 19th C). *(Baptist Chapel, Coppice Hill, 1999)*

Figure 8.46. Masons stone wall. *(Clematis Cottage, 2006)*

Figure 8.47. Pig hole. *(Fleece House, 1999)*

Figure 8.48. Angled stone to protect wall. *(Duke of York Inn, 1999)*

Figure 8.49. Water spout. *(Duke of York Inn, 1999)*

Vernacular Buildings of Chalford

Figure 8.50. Trough supplying spring water in wall of Uplands House in Commercial Road. *(2006)*

Figure 8.51. France Corner. *(2006)*

Figure 8.52. France Corner (rear view). *(1988)*

Figure 8.53. Fleece Cottage. *(2006)*

Figure 8.54.. Fleece Cottage. (rear view) *(2006)*

Figure 8.55. The Post Office. *(2006)*

Chapter 8

Figure 8.56. The Ferns. *(1990)*

Figure 8.57. The Ferns: Winder stair, fireplace and former closet. *(1989)*

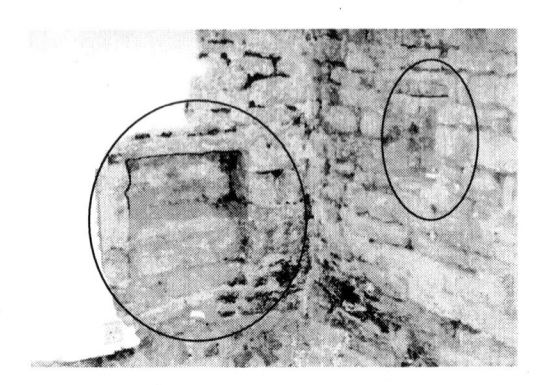

Figure 8.58. The Ferns: keeping holes being uncovered. *(1989)*

Figure 8.59. The Ferns: stepped chimney breast on the first floor. *(1989)*

Figure 8.60. The Ferns: Phase 2 roof line. *(1986)*

Figure 8.61. The Ferns: first floor stone window frame. *(1989)*

VERNACULAR BUILDINGS OF CHALFORD

Figure 8.62. The Ferns: Phase 3 roof structure. *(1990)*

Figure 8.63. The Ferns: cottage added in phase 4 (early 19th C). *(1990)*

Figure 8.64.. The Ferns: hearth opening for a coal burning range in phase 4 cottage. *(1989)*

Figure 8.65. The Ferns: Phase 5 addition, late 19thC. *(1989)*

Figure 8.66. The Ferns: window detail in phase 5 addition. *(1989)*

Figure 8.67. The Ferns: stair and tiled floor in phase 5 addition. *(1989)*

CHAPTER 8

Figure 8.68. The Ferns: bay window in phase 5 addition. *(1986)*

Figure 8.69. The Ferns: Phase 6 addition. *(1989)*

Figure 8.70. The Ferns: stone built workshop in the garden. *(1989)*

Figure 8.71. Glenhaven: rear view with recent addition. *(2006)*

Figure 8.72. Clematis Cottage: front view during renovation. *(1983)*

Figure 8.73. Commercial Road Stores, circa 1930, now Clematis Cottage.

Figure 8.74.. Commercial Road Stores.

Figure 8.75. Clematis Cottage: Phase 1 as wing behind main part of present building. *(1983)*

Figure 8.76. Clematis Cottage: top of original (phase 1) window. *(1983)*

Figure 8.77. Clematis Cottage: Phase 2 cottage. *(1983)*

Figure 8.78. Clematis Cottage: fireplace in phase 2 cottage. *(1983)*

Figure 8.79. Clematis Cottage: floor in phase 2 cottage. *(1984)*

Chapter 8

Figure 8.80. Clematis Cottage: stone vaults and beam lodging in rear wall of phase 2 cottage. *(1984)*

Figure 8.81. Clematis Cottage: former beam lodging in front wall of phase 2 cottage. *(1983)*

Figure 8.82. Clematis Cottage: door into attic of phase 2 cottage. *(1983)*

Figure 8.83. Clematis Cottage: Phase 2 cottage roof structure. *(1983)*

Figure 8.84.. Clematis Cottage: coal burning fireplace added in early 19th C. *(1983)*

Figure8.85. Clematis Cottage: removal of coal burning hearth to reveal original (phase 1) fireplace. *(1984)*

Figure 8.86. Clematis Cottage: Phase 1 hearth restored. *(1984)*

Figure 8.87. Clematis Cottage: bread oven in original fireplace. *(1983)*

Figure 8.88. Clematis Cottage: early 19th C porch with fanlight. *(1983)*

Figure 8.89. Clematis Cottage: detail of early 19thC fanlight.

Figure 8.90. Clematis Cottage: early 19th C architraves, dado rail and door (and the author's family). *(1983)*

Figure 8.91.. Clematis Cottage: early 19th C roof structure in phase 3 part of building. *(1983)*

CHAPTER 8

Figure 8.92. Jacob's Cottage. *(2006)*

Figure 8.93. Cleeve Cottage. *(2006)*

Figure 8.94.. Rose Cottage. *(2006)*

Figure 8.95. Prospect Terrace *(2006)*

Figure 8.96. Abnash House. *(2000)*

Figure 8.97. Byways. *(1991)*

VERNACULAR BUILDINGS OF CHALFORD

Figure 8.98. Byways, rear view. *(1991)*

Figure 8.99. The Corderries: main house. *(2005)*

Figure 8.100. The Corderries: 'weaving barn'. *(2005)*

Figure 8.101. Cotspur. *(2005)*

Figure 8.102. Cotswold Place. *(2006)*

Figure 8.103. Oakley. *(1991)*

CHAPTER 8

Figure 8.104. Laurel Cottage, formerly Pincotts shop. *(2004)*

Figure 8.105. Laurel Cottage as a sweet shop in approximately 1920

Figure 8.106. The Old Duke of York Inn. *(2005)*

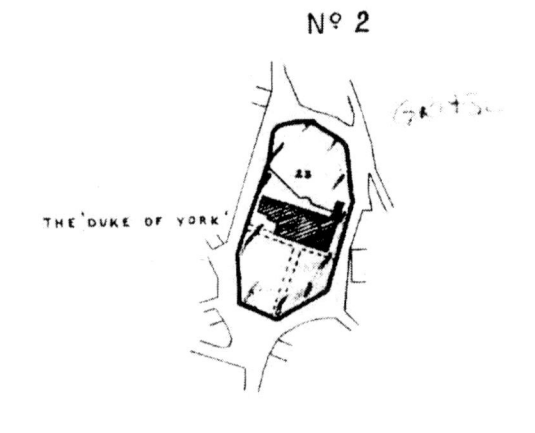

Figure 8.107. Plan of Duke of York in the late 19th C.

Figure 8.108. Old Duke of York Inn: late 19th C bay window and machine cut stone. *(2006)*

Figure 8.109. Old Duke of York Inn: as a public house in the late 1980's.

VERNACULAR BUILDINGS OF CHALFORD

Figure 8.110. The Old Duke of York Inn: Phase 1.

Figure 8.111. The Old Duke of York Inn in the 1950's.

Figure 8.112. The Old Duke of York Inn: stonework of west gable end wall. *(2006)*

Figure 8.113. The Old Duke of York Inn: gable end window of Phase 1 building. *(2006)*

Figure 8.114.. The Old Duke of York Inn: ground floor stonework of rear wall of Phase 1 building. *(2006)*

Figure 8.115. The Old Duke of York Inn: first floor stonework of rear wall of Phase 1 building. *(2006)*

CHAPTER 8

Figure 8.116. The Old Duke of York Inn: ground floor fireplace in Phase 1 building. *(2006)*

Figure 8.117. The Old Duke of York Inn: original stone winder stair. *(2006)*

Figure 8.118. The Old Duke of York Inn: lounge and Public Bar area of the pub. *(1992)*

Figure 8.119. The Old Duke of York Inn: half beam on ground floor of Phase 1 building. *(2006)*

Figure 8.120. The Old Duke of York Inn: ground floor ceiling beam (full beam). *(2006)*

Figure 8.121. The Old Duke of York Inn: joist lodgings in first floor ceiling. *(2006)*

Figure 8.122. The. Old Duke of York Inn: remains of early plaster between joists. *(2006)*

Figure 8.123. The Old Duke of York Inn: hearth stone support in ground floor ceiling. *(2006)*

Figure 8.124.. The Old Duke of York Inn: position of original first floor partition. *(2006)*

Figure 8.125. The Old Duke of York Inn: first floor ceiling beam. *(2006)*

Figure 8.126. Old Duke of York Inn: winder stair to attic. *(2006)*

Figure 8.127. Old Duke of York Inn: attic over Phase 1 building. *(2006)*

CHAPTER 8

Figure 8.128. The Old Duke of York Inn: Phase 2 addition. *(2006)*

Figure 8.129. The Old Duke of York Inn: W facing side wall of Phase 2 addition. *(2006)*

Figure 8.130. The Old Duke of York Inn: Phase 2, N gable end wall. *(2006)*

Figure 8.131. The Old Duke of York Inn: roof structure over Phase 2 addition. *(2006)*

Figure 8.132. The. Old Duke of York Inn: modification of Phase 2 roof to raise floor levels. *(2006)*

Figure 8.133. The Old Duke of York Inn: Phase 2 roof showing third principal of front truss. *(2006)*

Figure 8.134. The Old Duke of York Inn: ground floor fireplace in Phase 2 addition. *(2006)*

Figure 8.135. The Old Duke of York Inn: infill in the fireplace of the Phase 2 addition. *(1994)*

Figure 8.136. The Old Duke of York Inn: cupboard on first floor of Phase 2 addition. *(2006)*

Figure 8.137. The Old Duke of York Inn: Phase 3 addition. *(2006)*

Figure 8.138. The Old Duke of York Inn: re-used beam end as a lintel. *(2006)*

Figure 8.139. The Old Duke of York Inn: first floor fireplace in Phase 3 addition. *(2006)*

CHAPTER 8

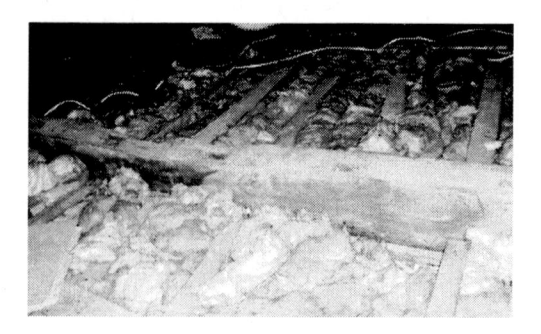

Figure 8.140. The Old Duke of York Inn: re-used beam in Phase 3 addition. *(2006)*

Figure 8.141. The Old Duke of York Inn: first floor hearth in Phase 3 addition. *(2006)*

Figure 8.142.. The Old Duke of York Inn: former doorway formerly linking Phase 2 and 3 additions. *(2006)*

Figure 8.143. The Old Duke of York Inn: roof structure of Phase 3 addition. *(2006)*

Figure 8.144.. The. Old Duke of York Inn: re-used half beam in roof of Phase 3 addition roof. *(2006)*

Figure 8.145. The Old Duke of York Inn: re-used beam in Phase 3 addition roof. *(2006)*

VERNACULAR BUILDINGS OF CHALFORD

Figure 8.146. The Old Duke of York Inn: Phase 4 addition. *(2006)*

Figure 8.147. The Old Duke of York Inn: roof structure and unplastered walls of Phase 4 addition. *(2006)*

Figure 8.148. The Old Duke of York Inn: chamfered jamb in Phase 4 addition. *(2006)*

Figure 8.149. The Old Duke of York Inn: outbuilding, possibly a former weaving shed. *(2006)*

Figure 8.150. The Old Duke of York Inn: re-used range in fireplace in outbuilding. *(2006)*

Figure 8.151. The Old Duke of York Inn: pair of flues next to fireplace in outbuilding. *(2006)*

CHAPTER 8

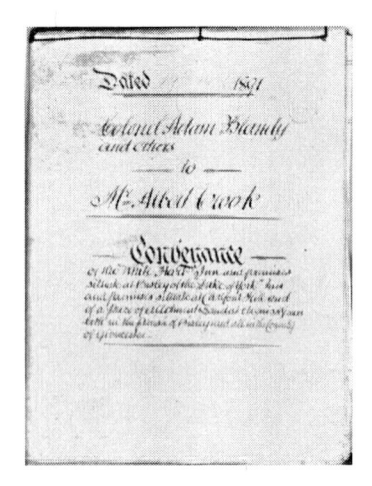

Figure 8.152. The Old Duke of York Inn: conveyance to Albert Crook.

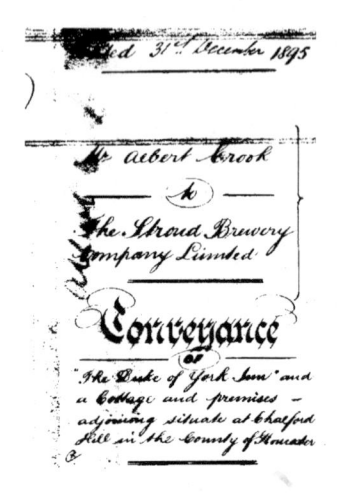

Figure 8.153. The Old Duke of York Inn: conveyance to the Stroud Brewery Company.

Figure 8.154.. Chalford Hill Stores: front elevation. *(2006)*

Figure 8.155. Chalford Hill Stores: rear view. *(2006)*

Figure 8.156. Cottages in Queens Square (first group). *(2006)*

Figure 8.157. Cottages in Queens Square (second group). *(2006)*

VERNACULAR BUILDINGS OF CHALFORD

Figure 8.158. Cottages in Queens Square (second group). *(2006)*

Figure 8.159. Farthingcote (in Queens Square). *(2006)*

Figure 8.160. The Old Builders Arms. *(2006)*

Figure 8.161. The Old Builders Arms: roof structure. *(1988)*

Figure 8.162. Rodney House. *(1950's and 1990's)*

Figure 8.163. Possibly former weaving shed at Rodney House. *(2006)*

CHAPTER 8

Figure 8.164.. Wychbury. *(2006)*

Figure 8.165. Fir Tree Cottage. *(2006)*

Figure 8.166. Christmas Cottage. *(2006)*

Figure 8.167. Brendan House. *(1930's)*

Figure 8.168. Fernleigh. *(1940)*

Figure 8.169. Fernleigh. *(2006)*

Vernacular Buildings of Chalford

Figure 8.170. Steep Cottage. *(2006)*

Figure 8.171. Steep Cottage. *(early 1980's)*

Figure 8.172. Steep Cottage. *(1930's)*

Figure 8.173. Steep Cottage: roof structure.

Figure 8.174.. Steep Cottage: fireplace. *(1980's)*

Figure 8.175. Cliff House. *(late 1990's)*

CHAPTER 8

Figure 8.176. Cliff Cottage. *(1992)*

Figure 8.177. Quail Cottage. *(1992)*

Figure 8.178. Hedges and adjoining Cottage. *(1992)*

Figure 8.179. The Cottage. *(1992)*

Figure 8.180. Prospect Cottage. *(1991)*

Figure 8.181. Prospect Cottage: early roof line *(1991)*

VERNACULAR BUILDINGS OF CHALFORD

Figure 8.182. Bakery Cottage. *(2006)*

Figure 8.183. Walton Cottage. *(2000)*

Figure 8.184.. Cottage next to Cyprus Villa. *(2006)*

Figure 8.185. Next to Cyprus Villa: rear view. *(1992)*

Figure 8.186. Cottage next to Cyprus Villa. *(1902)*

Figure 8.187. Cyprus Villa. *(2006)*

Chapter 8

Figure 8.188. Wheatsheaves Cottage (demolished 1960's). *(1930's)*

8.3 Development of Chalford and its Cottages, Houses and Mill Buildings

In using the name Chalford in the title of this section, I refer to the settlement in the valley bottom and its lower slopes, so it includes Chalford St Marys and Chalford Vale. The settlements at Chalford Hill and Chalford are separate and each have distinctive characteristics. The early transport routes lay across the valley, rather than along it, so tracks led down from the direction of Bisley to cross the River Frome at several points. It is at these crossing points that the earliest areas of settlement in the valley are found. These early routes are still used and are now marked by roads that descend from the area of Chalford Hill to the valley bottom. There is Old Neighbourhood and Dark Lane **(Figure 8.189)**, which joined to cross the river and form the route up Hyde Hill, Marle Hill, which just ran down to the valley bottom **(Figure 8.190)** and Coppice Hill, which runs down to St Stephens Bridge to cross the river and continue on up Marley Lane and then on to Gypsy Lane **(Figure 8.191)**. At each of the crossing points there is a concentration of buildings surviving from the 17th C and possibly earlier, particularly at the bottom of Coppice Hill. The early houses along the valley bottom are larger than the cottages found in Chalford Hill, which suggests they were economically and industrially distinct settlements. Chalford Hill must have done the spinning and weaving, whilst other stages of the cloth making process were done in the mills in the valley bottom. It is known that the clothiers owned the mills and controlled the whole weaving industry. The clothier bought cloth by the piece from the weavers, using yarn that they had supplied. The larger houses in the valley are those built for clothiers and their size reflects their greater prosperity compared with that of the weaver (in his small cottage). Over the centuries the S facing valley side became developed with cottages roughly aligned along several terraces. These cottages seem to date mainly from the 18th and 19th C. They are built close to the spring line formed at the junction of the Cotswold Sands and the Lias Clay. The latter forms the floor of the valley, which is why the river survives above ground. From early times, before the Domesday Book was compiled, there have been water mills extracting power from the river. The earliest mills would have been corn mills. However, by the 11th C, there are too many mills listed for them to be all corn mills and some must have been fulling mills, associated with the early cloth making industry. The early industry was effectively destroyed by the plagues of the 14th C and none of the mills from this period have survived. They would have been small and not suited to the industry that developed later. The cloth making industry of the Stroud valleys developed again from the late 16th C, with a boom following the end of the Civil War. This is presumably the reason why so many of the surviving early buildings of the valleys seem to date from the later part of the 17th C. The industry continued to prosper during the 18th C and into the early 19th C. Many mills were built along the valley bottom and in some of the subsidiary valleys in this period. In the early 19th C there were substantial developments and some large new mills built and earlier sites re-developed. These were built because the clothiers were converting the industry from a cottage-weaving base to a factory-based industry. It was thought that this would improve the efficiency of the industry by taking advantage of technical developments, albeit at the expense of jobs and the independence of the weavers. The clothiers over extended themselves with large loans and the moves to improve the efficiency did not have the desired effect on the competitiveness of the local cloth industry. By the mid 19th C, there were bankruptcies amongst the local clothiers and the rapid decline in the prosperity of the lo-

CHAPTER 8

cal cloth industry meant that it had ceased to operate in Chalford by this time. However, the area has been left with a rich legacy of the buildings of the cloth industry. Many of the mill buildings survive today and most have found new uses in both the industrial and domestic sectors.

The main transport routes are now along the valley, rather than across it. The original narrow, steep lanes have been surfaced, but left mainly in their original form. It is only in recent years that they have begun to suffer from over use by cars and vans, with the consequent erosion of the lane side areas (particularly by unnecessary 4x4's). The canal was the first transport link along the valley and this was completed by the late 1780's. It must have had a dramatic effect on life in Chalford when first constructed, as it meant that goods could be moved in and out in bulk, rather than by cart and packhorse, using the narrow steep lanes. The canal always suffered from difficulties in retaining water above Chalford, where it rises over the Cotswold stone and the puddling of the canal bed with clay required continual maintenance. There was a particular problem at times of high ground water pressure, as erupting springs could displace the clay lining. The new turnpike road was completed by 1818 and further improved the accessibility to the new mills being built at Chalford in this period. This is now widened and has become the A 419. The final transport link was provided with the construction of the railway and this was built by 1845. This must have had a very negative impact on the economics of the canal operations. But it did introduce a means for the rapid transport of goods and people within the area and beyond. It is ironic that the cloth industry in Chalford was in terminal decline as the railways were in their ascendancy.

BUILDINGS IN CHALFORD

Mill Buildings: It is not intended to give a detailed description of the mill buildings in the Chalford part of the Frome valley. The buildings and sites have already been described in other publications, particularly books by Jennifer Tann and Stephen Mills/Pierce Riemer. Ian Mackintosh has also carried out much research as part of his work for the Stroudwater Textile Trust. The majority of the surviving mills date from the early 19thC development of the industry and almost all are many storied and built in Cotswold stone. There are some later brick additions, possibly associated with more recent uses of the buildings and in the introduction of steam power to the original water mills. The later built mills themselves may incorporate some brick in their construction, for instance in the arched window lintels. They are well built and show many vernacular features, such as the use of the local stone and in the window detail. They are all water mills, some of which had the power supply supplemented by the addition of a steam boiler and engine. With so many mills constructed in the valley, there must have been great competition for the water supply. Those higher up stream had the ability to throttle the supply from the mills further downstream. Conversely, those downstream could throttle their sluices and cause water to bank up too much in the river, which would prevent the proper operation of water wheels upstream. Two methods of supply were used: either dedicated mill-ponds, or water that was backed up in the river overnight. Other mills used water from the very active springs that exist at Chalford. No very early mills survive, which is a result of the substantial changes that occurred in the running of the industry in the early 19th C. Prior to this time the weaving was cottage based and this had generated an independent population of local weavers. However, advances in technology and a desire by the clothiers to have a greater control on the weaving itself led to the industry shifting to weaving factories (loom shops) from the early 19th C onwards. This meant that much larger premises were required and a boom in reconstructing the local mills.

The following lists the mill buildings that survive along the River Frome in the Chalford Parish, starting at Chalford St Mary's (which is actually in Minchinhampton Parish).

St Mary's Mill: This can be traced back to 1338, when a water mill (with other property and land) was donated to the Chantry of St Mary, the Virgin, at Minchinhampton. There are several mill buildings surviving on the site. One has been derelict for many years and this is based upon a house that dates from the late 17th C **(Figure 8.192)**. This part has three-light stone mullion windows with dripmoulds. The ground floor of the house is now below ground level, as the mill yard has been infilled with ash from the coal-fired boiler that supplied steam for the engine in the main mill building. The top of the ground floor entrance can be seen towards the end of the building. A vertical building line shows that it was extended to the W and the style of the windows, in the newer part, suggests an early 19th C date. The walls have also been raised to generate an extra floor level. An 18th C document refers to this building as 'cottages converted into workshops'. The large factory mill building was built by 1820 and has five storeys and stone window frames in a local industrial style: stone surrounds with slightly arched lights and divided by mullions (there are similar windows at Ebley Mill) **(Figure 8.193)**. It is 30 foot wide and this provided space for looms and other machinery associated with cloth making. It was built by the Clutterbuck family, on the site of an old fulling mill. It is a fine example of an early 19th C mill building, in near original state. Internally, on the lower floor, there is a surviving undershot water wheel. This is thought to date from around 1840, when the mill was refurbished for new tenants. Originally there were two water wheels, which in 1834 generated 30 hp. A Tangye steam engine (now without its boiler) was installed (secondhand) by the Chalford Stick Company in the early 20th C to supplement the unreliable water-power supply. The upper floors retain their timber floor structures, one floor has had the beams strengthened using iron tension bars. Additional wood posts have been added at some stage to provide extra support for the floors. The roof, with the long dormer window, was reconstructed in recent years following a fire. It use is uncertain, but clearly the window provided a generous amount of light. Perhaps it housed looms or perhaps it was used for mending? This building is well maintained and in commercial usage. There are two other large, single storey stone buildings (circa 1840) adjoining the early 19th C mill. One has a hipped roof. The survival of the greater part of the mill complex at St Mary's is due to the dedication of the Reynolds family. The mill site is early and the house (see later) is thought to be of medieval origin.

Clayfields/Ballingers Mill **(Figure 8.194)**: This was much rebuilt by the Thames Severn Canal Company. It has four storeys, the lower two date from the 17th C and the upper two are of 19th C origin. The water supplying the wheel came from springs on Brownshill. It was converted to a house some years ago, after having a range of industrial uses.

Iles Mill **(Figure 8.195)**: The surviving mill building dates from the early 19th C and there was a fire here in 1913, which destroyed the earlier parts of the mill. A postcard of the valley from the 1920-30 period shows the 19th C mill without a roof **(Figure 8.196)**. It was subsequently repaired and was used for wood and bone turning, and as a flock factory. In more recent years it has been converted into two cottages. One of the gable ends of this building is thought to date from the 17th C.

Belvedere Mill (formerly known as Chalford Mill and Taylors Mill): This is thought to be another of the earliest mill sites in Chalford and records go back to the 16th C. The large, three storey, surviving mill building has three storeys and is constructed in stone under a Welsh slate roof and dates from the early 19th C **(Figure 8.197 and 198)**. It is of double pile construction and has cast iron, multi pane

Chapter 8

windows, with segmented stone arched lintels. The walls are built from semi dressed, coursed stone. There is a low brick arch, which fed the millstream to an internal water wheel (now removed). There is a vertical building line between the E and W facing parts and this shows that the W facing part was built first. It is well maintained and in commercial usage (currently Heber Ltd.).

Bliss Mills: This is a complex of five, originally independent, mills **(Figure 8.199)**: these were formerly known as Bliss Mill, New Mill, Mugmore Mill, Spring Mill (earlier names Wood or Randalls Mill) and Wood Mill. Bliss Mill itself is an ancient site, but now is largely demolished. The group now form the Chalford Industrial Estate. Most of the mill buildings were demolished in the mid 20th C, when the site was taken over by Fibrecrete Ltd (used asbestos to make building materials). However, one large mill does survive. This is New Mill and was built in the early 19th C and rebuilt in the 1890's (probably following a fire) for William Dangerfield's stick company. It is a long building (19 bays), constructed in stone, under a Welsh slate roof and has three storeys. This is now occupied by Chalford Building Supplies **(Figure 8.200)**. Internally, the original beams survive: these are large, roughly dressed and without chamfers. Originally, Bliss Mill was supplied by water from the River Frome, the other mills were supplied by the active spring, called the Black Gutter.

Woolings Mill (including Sevills Upper Mill) (formerly close to Sevillowes House): The mill formerly existed as a wing to the NW of the surviving house called Sevillowes. In 1826 it was described as being part very ancient and part new. It was supplied with water from a spring running off the hillside (this still flows under Dark Lane House in a stone lined culvert). It ceased operations in 1841 and the premises were for sale. The mill buildings were demolished as a source of building materials.

Smarts Mill (also known as Stoneford Mill, Bidmeads Mill, Hoptons Mill and Hallidays Mill at earlier times): Another early mill site, known as Stoneford Mill, is first mentioned in a deed dated 1170. The current mill building dates from the 19th C. The two lower floors are in stone and the two upper floors are in brick **(Figure 8.201)**. In the 1920's it was the workshop of Peter Waals. Behind the mill is an early bridge across the River Frome. This is covered in undergrowth and is in a poor condition. It is not accessible to the public.

Sevilles Mill **(Figure 8.202)**: This had origins in the 17th C, but was demolished by the early 1970's and is currently being re-developed with houses in a sympathetic, vernacular style.

Valley or Mortons Mill **(Figure 8.203)**: This is recorded in the late 18th C. It stood in the area now occupied by a garage in the corner of the Valley Playing Field. It is beside one of the early crossing points of the river, possibly St Stephens Bridge. It was demolished by 1972, but there is some residual stonework associated with the sluices, beside the river. A postcard, dated 1912, shows that it was a small mill. It had two-storeys with three, three-light stone mullion windows, without dripmoulds on each floor. The window detail suggests it was built in the early 18th C.

Ashmeads Mill **(Figure 8.204)**: This has not been found recorded before the early 19th C. There was formerly a large three storey mill building, but this was demolished piecemeal by the mid 20th C. All that remains is an early 19th C brick building and some stone outbuildings.

VERNACULAR BUILDINGS OF CHALFORD

THE LARGER HOUSES IN THE VALLEY

The clothiers who controlled the cloth making industry in Chalford lived near their mills, so it is normal to find early houses, sometimes of a substantial size amongst the mill buildings, on the valley floor. It was common for the mill to be named after the owner and so the name of individual mills does change with time. There are several local families of clothiers who appear in surviving documents over many generations and they inter-married and sold premises amongst each other. Some common names are Tayloe, Ballinger, Blackwell, Smart, Davis, Iles, Clutterbuck, Innel and Toghill (this is not an exhaustive list). In the 19th C, the clothiers built their houses along the lower slopes of the S facing valley side. None are grand houses, but they are substantial as would be expected for those running the local industry. In the valley there are at least fourteen of these large houses of various dates of origin, which is in marked contrast with Chalford Hill (the weaving settlement) where there are very few. Some of these large houses have grown by the addition of later parts, sometimes with the refronting of the earlier part. With the mills, it is evident that complete rebuilds occurred to meet the changing needs of the industry, whereas with the associated houses, modification and upgrading seems to have been the norm. It appears that the owners wanted the houses to look 'up to date' from the front and in the main living accommodation, but the lesser parts of the buildings were left in their original form. The houses are described from W to E along the valley.

St Marys Mill House: These notes have been partly taken from Pesvner. An early house, which dates from the 16th C was refronted in about 1720 **(Figure 8.205)**. The new front, which faces W, has the detail expected of an important local house of the period. It has three storeys, with a central front door, with a fine shell hood on carved brackets and pairs of flanking multipane sash windows. There are rows of five sash windows on each of the first and second floors. Each window is surrounded by a moulded stone architrave with a projecting keystone. The second floor keystones run up into the eaves cornice. The eaves cornice is surmounted by a parapet, which is comprised of a stone balustrade. In about 1820, lower, slightly forward projecting wings were added to either side of the remodelled earlier house. This was done by Samuel Clutterbuck as part of the major work on the site. The detail of the wings is much plainer: the parapet is plain and there are no moulded architraves or projecting keystones around the windows. Behind the 1720 façade, there are remnants of the earlier form of the building. The upper floor contains some arched headed doorways and there is a five bay roof structure with moulded rafters, cambered collars and windbraces. This detail is what would be expected for a house dating from the 16th C. The ground floor detail dates from the 18th and 19th C. It is unfortunate that this part of the house has been without a proper roof for over 20 years. It is only hoped that no permanent damage is resulting to the historic fabric of this important local house. Further additions have been made to the W side and rear of the house, mainly as separate cottages, which date from the late 17th C **(Figure 8.206)**. They have stone mullion windows, with rebated, plain surrounds and with continuous dripmoulds over the windows of each cottage. The cottages are constructed in well coursed rubblestone, under a steeply pitched roof. There is a vertical building line showing that they were not constructed at the same time. The intimate relationship between mill, owner's house and workers cottages at St Mary's is a reflection of the close control that the clothier exerted over his business and workforce.

Brookside **(Figure 8.207)**: This has three storeys and two-light stone mullion windows and seems to date from the late 17th C. The projecting wings (onto the lane) have early 18th C detail (moulded ar-

Chapter 8

chitraves around the windows with projecting keystones). In the early 19th C, a wing was added to the S: this was a mill. By the late 19th C, the mill wing had been demolished.

Iles Mill Cottages **(Figure 8.208)**: Built as a single house and subsequently split into two cottages. The presence of the cross windows and the hipped roof suggests a late 17th/early 18th C origin and it was probably built for the owner of the adjoining mill.

Belvedere Mill House: This is a fine looking house **(Figure 8.209)** which on superficial outside evidence appears to date from 1789 (the date on the pediment of the porch) **(Figure 8.210)**. It has three storeys and is built from well-dressed stone. It has a modillion cornice, surmounted by a plain parapet on the front and N side, whereas the rear and S sides do not have a parapet **(Figure 8.211)**. The roof is hipped. The present roof is a taller version of the one that survived from 1789 until the recent conversion to flats **(Figure 8.212)**. The windows are multi pane sashes with plain surrounds. There is a central ground floor entrance, with a porch with classical detail. It has ionic columns and pediment. The pediment is marked with the year 1789, which must be the year the house was remodelled. There is a fanlight above the door, with a decorated cast lead frame **(Figure 8.213)**. There are two pairs of flanking sash windows on the ground floor and rows of five windows on each of the first and second floors of the front wall. There is a continuous dripmould above the ground floor windows, which only passes around the front and the N side of the building. The fenestration of the rear and S side is irregular, but again is multi pane sash windows. The house is of double pile construction. Closer inspection shows that there are differences in the character of the stonework: that of the lower two floors of the front and all three floors of the N side (front end) is similar, but different to that of the second floor front, rear and S side. There are also blocked window openings in the first and second floors of the N side (front end) wall **(Figure 8.214)**. The building was converted into flats in the early 1980's and in this process much damage was done to the historic fabric of the building. It gave the opportunity to work out the history of the building, but the developers did not understand how to treat the building in a sympathetic way. The blocked window openings contained a pair of late 17th C stone mullion windows with transoms (i.e. cross windows) on the first floor **(Figure 8.215)**: it is not certain whether these were retained. A fine oak staircase with carved brackets to the tread ends was removed and parts of it burnt. Many large structural beams, some retaining evidence of wood panelled partition walling were removed **(Figure 8.216)**, some was sold, but much seemed to be burnt. All of these details were consistent with an origin in the late 17th C. There was a stone spine wall separating the front and rear halves of the building and this contained many blocked window openings. It was clear that the original house occupied the front half of the present house, with a wing to the rear, at the N end (where a continuous dripmould has been noted). It must have been an impressive looking structure. The size of the window openings suggests that there were cross windows on the front, rear and N gable end. The S gable end, which presumably contained the original hearths was rebuilt in 1789 (this is indicated by the nature of the stonework). New hearths had been added in front of the blocked cross windows of the former N gable end, when the house was remodelled **(Figure 8.217)**. The hearths had wide openings and plain wood lintels, although they had been infilled with coal burning grates. The roof structure of the original house was retained when the building was remodelled in 1789. This consisted of four 'A' frame trusses **(Figure 8.218)**, formerly with morticed collars and tie beams with relatively narrow chamfers. However, it was removed when the roof was heightened and an iron supporting structure installed in the early 1980's. There was formerly a statue in classical style in the garden **(Figure 8.219)**.

Chalford Place (formerly known as the Companys Arms): This is one of the earlier houses in the valley. Built as a mill owners/clothiers house, it became an inn in the 19th C. In the late 18th C, Chalford supplied much cloth to the East India Company and this is the origin of the name 'Companys Arms'. The East India Company had gone bankrupt by the early 19th C, it remained as an inn until it closed finally in the 1960's **(Figure 8.220)**. In the 19th C, it was the focal point of the Chalford feast. In the 1870's, 'there were roundabouts and other amusements in the yard of the inn and stalls outside'. The last feast was held just before the Second World War. After the closure of the inn, it fell derelict for a time, before being bought for renovation. It now reverted to its earlier name of Chalford Place. Several owners have conducted much work on the building since the 1970's, however, these schemes were not completed because of the extent of work required and a lack of sufficient funds. It is only now that Chalford Place at last seems to have found an owner, who is able to invest the funds necessary to restore this fine and unusual house. The restoration is currently in progress. The site is ancient and is referred to in documents of the early 13th C and is where William of Chalford had his house. It stood next to a crossing point of the river and was part of an estate, which by the early 16th C, amounted to 67 acres with various properties, including a house, water mill and two fulling mills. In 1523, the estate was given, by Bishop Richard Fox, to his foundation at the newly established Corpus Christi College, Oxford. The College retained the lands and property until 1872, when the estate was broken up. The long ownership by the College has meant that early documents relating to the site have survived. The name 'Chalford Place' is referred to in documents of the early 16th C. It was a clothiers house until the early 19th C, when it was converted to an inn, by its clothier owner, Thomas Cox. This presumably coincided with the loss of the Chalford trade with the East India Company. It remained as a Stroud Brewery Company inn until 1964, when it was closed.

The current house dates from the 16th C, but with major phases of work in the 17th and 18th C and with many minor changes throughout its life: the result is a house of mixed architectural styles. The elevation facing the lane has three gabled dormers, with stone mullion windows on each level **(Figures 8.221 and 222)**. Inspection of the stone-work shows that the stones forming the W gabled dormer and the floors below are smaller than the rubblestone forming the remainder of the elevation. There is a vertical building line marking the change in the nature of the stone and the direction of the line shows that it belongs to the part of the building containing the W gabled dormer. The line represents the former corner of the building, which must be earlier than the rest of the elevation. Inspection of the window surrounds shows that the current stone mullions are not all in their original positions. The ghosts of the earlier ones can be seen in the modified stone-work and in the apices of the gabled dormers. Also, the first floor window under the W gabled dormer (the older one) is set lower than the two under the central and E dormers, where the stonework shows they have been moved to a slightly higher level. There are gable end chimney-stacks and a large central stack on the axis of the roof of this part of the house. This side has a late 16/17th C character and at that time, it would probably have had a similar looking elevation on the opposite side of the house.

In the early 18thC, the S half of the house was reconstructed, from near to the line of the axial ridge of the roof. A new S side was constructed using elements of the latest architectural fashion, but combined in a somewhat quirky way **(Figure 8.223)**. The work does not seem to have been finished. This new part is deeper than the part of the earlier construction that it replaced. Looking from the garden side, it is difficult to believe it is the same house. The newer part is taller. It has three full storeys and the central section breaks forward from both ends and this has a hipped roof. There are pairs of multi pane sash windows on the ground and first floors of the central part. Each has a shouldered,

Chapter 8

moulded stone architrave, with a projecting keystone, which runs into a plat band. The plat bands run across the front and sides of the central part, but not across the end sections. The edges of the central part are formed by pilaster quoins. The second floor window is a sort of Venetian window, with a central arched light and flanking square headed lights. Each has a moulded stone frame, but only the central light has a projecting keystone and this runs up into the projecting, moulded eaves cornice. There are three good diagonally set chimneys to the side (W) of this part of the building. The eaves cornice is consistent across the whole elevation, which suggests that the elevation is of one construction. However, below the eaves, there are dissimilar and odd windows to either side of the central part. Each side has a stack of windows occupying nearly the full height of the building and sited close to the side-walls of the central wing. To the W, the window is three-lights wide and is comprised of stone mullions, with regularly spaced transoms **(Figure 8.224)**. Alternate rows of lights, between the transoms, are blind, the others are glazed. The top row of lights have flattened arch heads and they seem to be integral with the eaves cornice stonework, which suggests they are contemporary with each other. The window is thought to be unique and although it has an early flavour, it is thought to date from the 18th C building phase. On the other side of the central part is another tall arrangement of windows, but of a completely different form to those just described. Here, the 'window' consists of a stack of four, multi pane sash windows, each with the same form of moulded architrave as described for the central part. Only the top light has a projecting keystone, which runs up into the eaves cornice. Each light is separated horizontally by a moulded stone cill. This flight of windows in the 'new' entrance hall is thought to be intended to light a stair, although this must have been removed many years ago (if it was ever installed). There is a ground floor entrance to the immediate right of this window and this has a solid stone segmental pediment on carved brackets **(Figure 8.225)**. Above the hood, the walling is plain and similar in character to that of the central part. The building breaks forward again to the E of the entrance **(Figure 8.226)**. This forms a short wing and it has a hipped roof, set lower than the eaves cornice of the main roof. The upper part of this section of wall has similar architectural detail to the other parts of the elevation. It has a moulded eaves cornice, which is slightly smaller in scale to that of the main roof. There is a large multi pane sash window, set between the levels of the first and second floor windows of the central part, but with a similar shouldered architrave and cill. Below the level of the window the stonework is changed and a cut for roof flashing in the wall shows that there has been a pitched roof addition here, which has been demolished. The addition must have been later than the rebuilding of this part of the main house as the roof cuts across the large sash window (Mary Rudd says this addition is of 19th C origin). The W end of this part of the building is constructed in good masonry and the stonework runs into the stonework of the gable end of the remaining earlier part of the house. The outer walling stone seems to date from the early 18th C phase. On the ground floor, there is a tall and wide blocked doorway, which formerly led into a wide stone winder stair. On the second floor level, there is a blocked taking in door, with a flat slab hood on carved stone brackets. This must be showing that the second floor of the newer part of the building was used as a work/storage space when it was first built. The detail of this part of the house, including the window architraves, the projecting keystones, the string courses and the eaves cornice, are all consistent with an early 18th C origin for the construction of this part of the house. The form of the tall windows to either side of the central part is most unusual and it is difficult to see the logic behind the design. In particular, it is difficult to see why the style of the two tall windows is different: that to the E matches the detail of the central part, but that to the W is more in keeping with the 17th C stone mullion type of window, yet they both seem to be contemporary.

Internally, there were formerly three main rooms, arranged along the N facing side (the gabled elevation) of the house. These are thought to be a central hall, with a parlour at the E end and a kitchen at the W end. This is a 17th C arrangement. Each room has a large hearth, each modified to different degrees. The hearth in the parlour has moulded jambs, which seem to be re-used, possibly from an earlier form of the house. The roof structure is complex. It retains the original roof structure over the N facing elevation containing the gabled dormers. The roof to the S side has been grafted onto this, with an elaborate structure, to enable the construction of the higher roof over this side. As originally conceived there seems to have been an extra floor in the S part. But this has been removed and its presence is indicated by redundant joist lodgings on the beams.

This house retains an air of mystery about why it has been added to in such a quirky way, whether it was ever finished and how it actually functioned.

16th C House at the entrance to Chalford Industrial Estate

This is the earliest standing domestic building in Chalford that retains some of its original external character **(Figure 8.227)**. It has not been used as a house for some years and up to the mid 20th C there was an industrial building added to its front wall **(Figure 8.228)**. The W end of the building (i.e. next to the lane that runs down to Chalford Place) is the early part. It is constructed in well dressed masonry blocks with very fine mortar joints **(Figure 8.229)**. The front, W gable end and rear walls retain their origin stone mullion windows frames, which have round arch headed lights with recessed spandrels, recessed surrounds, concave chamfers to the window openings and heavy dripmoulds. The rear wall has a three-light window of this form on the first floor **(Figure 8.230)** and a two-light window on the ground floor. The front wall has a four-light window (opposite the rear three-light window), with a central king mullion on the first floor **(Figure 8.231)** and no evidence for a window of this form on the ground floor, although there are a couple of later windows (18/19th C). The gable end has a pair of two-light windows on the first floor and a pair of single light windows at the attic level. These are sited on each side of an externally projecting chimney-breast for a first floor hearth **(Figure 8.232)**. The wide chimney-breast rises from corbels built out at the bottom of the first floor and the chimney-breast diminishes in width towards the stack. The important features, the windows and the gable end hearth, are on the first floor and this may be showing that this was a first floor hall when originally built. It has been written that Chalford Place and St Mary's Mill House were also originally first floor halls, but with this house the evidence must be most strong. Perhaps this was the form for the early houses of the clothiers in the valley, where they are built directly on the damp and prone to flooding valley floor? There is a two-storey entrance porch towards the centre of the front elevation. The stonework is similar to that in the area of the 16th C window frames, which suggests that they are contemporary, although there has been some reconstruction along the E side of the porch. There is a two-light window on the first floor and a single light window on the ground floor, both are of the same form as the other arch headed windows, but with the addition of iron grilles. The entrance is to the side of the porch. The walling to the right (E) of the porch has been completely rebuilt in recent years and there are modern window frames. This rebuilding must indicate the part where the industrial building was demolished and this presumably also accounts for the disturbance of the stone to this side of the porch. Superficially the stonework of the rear wall looks of the same build, however towards the centre of the rear wall there appears to be a vertical discontinuity, where the stone courses do not marry together. The E gable end has pairs of ground and first floor multi pane sash windows, with moulded stone surrounds and projecting keystones **(Figure 8.233)**. There is a smaller window, with similar detail at the attic level. The detail of the stonework shows that the whole gable end was reconstructed when these windows were added and the style shows an early/mid 18th C origin. The

Chapter 8

quality of the workmanship is very good and the mortar joints are fine. It is suggested that the E end of the rear wall was rebuilt at the same time. The W gable end wall is not constructed at right angles to the side-walls. The usual explanation for this is that the building has been constructed along a property boundary, e.g. a lane, but it does seem odd that an important house would be constructed in such a position. There is a painting in Stroud Museum, which may show this house in the early 19th C, when it was associated with a mill **(Figure 8.234)**. There are similarities, but also differences in the detail of the building, so whether there is artistic licence or whether it is another, now removed building in Chalford, is not known with certainty. But, it does illustrate the intimate relationship between houses and mills in Chalford.

Skaiteshill House: This dates from the mainly early 19th C, although it is based on an earlier cottage. The house was built by Charles Ballinger, following his purchase of the original property from William Sevill in 1800. Mary Rudd suggests the site is of ancient occupation.

Sevillowes: This is the house associated with Sevilles Upper Mill, which was formerly attached to the NW side of the house. The mill was demolished in mid 19th C the materials sold. The current house is named after two previous owners, Seville and Lowe. The house dates from the late 18th C, with modifications in about 1830. It is built of ashlar and has two-storeys, with a modillion cornice and parapet **(Figure 8.235**. There is a porch with a pediment and Tuscan columns. The end bordering Dark Lane has a canted bay window, the W end of the front wall has a two-storey bow window. The windows have louvred storm shutters, which date from the early 19th C. The garden is terraced and presumably these were formerly used for cloth racks.

Wickham Grange: This has three storeys and is of double pile construction **(Figure 8.236)** and is built of ashlar. The front part is earliest and this has a modillion cornice and pediment: it dates from the late 18th C. A two-storey bow window has been added to the W side of the front elevation, probably in the early part of the 19th C. There is a veranda across the remaining part of the original ground floor of the façade. This has wrought iron supports and a leaded roof. The windows are large, the bow window has curved large pane sash windows and external louvred, storm shutters. The second floor has relatively small sash windows. The ground floor of the original part of the front elevation has full height opening windows and the first floor has sash windows. Internally, there is a good late 18th C stair and some coal burning hearths with marble surrounds. There is a large addition (19thC) to the rear. The main house was split into two houses (front and back) in the early 1980's. Before this time it had been used as offices by Lickfolds (printers), who occupied the whole site. Adjoining the main house is another house, with ashlar walls, mullion windows and external strengthening ribs. It looks similar in construction to Mount Cottage (further W towards Stroud). This is thought to predate the main house. The coach house (also converted to a separate dwelling in the early 1980's), at the entrance to the site, has segmental stone lintels over the windows and is dated 1812. Wickham Grange was known as Beaumont House in the late 19th C and was the home of William Dangerfield who manufactured walking sticks at the Bliss Mills complex. In 1778, it was purchased by Charles Ballinger from Hester Tayloe (who owned Tayloes Mill).

The Grove: This stands at the foot of Marle Hill and has been the home of many clothiers. The rear of the building contains the original house. The present front rooms and the classical façade were added in the early 19th C **(Figure 8.237)**. The house was originally called the 'Blackhouse' and was linked to the Blackwell family until the early 19th C. Mary Rudd gives details of the ownership up to the 1920's. The Regency façade is stuccoed and has two-storeys, with a moulded cornice. The centre part of the front elevation has a pediment and this breaks forward with four fluted pilasters on the first floor and four Tuscan columns on the ground floor. There is a large fanlight over the front door (early 19th C origin).

Chestnut House (Smarts Mill House): This is associated with the adjacent mill. The house has three storeys, under a hipped roof **(Figure 8.238)**. There is a parapet to the front elevation, with a stepped out eaves cornice. The front elevation is rendered, whilst the side walls are exposed stone and these are constructed in rubblestone. The windows are multi pane sashes (12-light on the ground and first floors and 6-light on the second floor). Each window has a simple moulded surround and a sill on small brackets. There are no projecting keystones. There is a central front door with a surround with simple classical detail (Tuscan columns and a pediment). The detail suggests an origin in the early 19th C.

Vale House: This is constructed in ashlar and has three storeys, with a parapet on the W (front) and S sides (the sides that can be seen) **(Figure 8.239)**. It has a central entrance with flanking large pane sash windows. These have stone architraves, but no keystones. The porch has ionic columns. There are string-courses above the ground and first floors. The rear of the house is plain and there are no architraves, parapet or string-courses. The house was built in the mid 19th C. It is not known to be associated with a mill.

Springfield House: This is described as newly erected in 1838 and was owned by the Davis family (clothiers). It is constructed in ashlar with a hipped roof and a wide, overhanging eaves **(Figure 8.240)**. The front elevation has a central entrance, with a porch with classical detail (with Ionic columns).

The Mount: This has two-storeys and is constructed in coursed rubblestone **(Figure 8.241)**. There is a continuous dripmould across the width of the façade above both ground and first floor windows. There is a central front door and flanking sash windows, which are 19th C replacements of the original stone mullion frames. The first floor has a pair of flanking three-light stone mullion window frames and a central two-light window. Each has the same detail: rebated surround with plain, flat chamfers. The façade used to have a pair of gabled dormers (the evidence for this can be seen in the present roof space). As such, it would have been a typical clothiers house of the mid/late 17th C. A doorway bears the date 1684 and this could be the build date. The house has been extended to the W and a vertical building line shows the junction of the two parts. There is a courtyard of former cottages behind the main house. These were presumably originally rented out to handloom weavers.

Green Court: This is comprised of two main parts. The front (W facing) part dates from the early part of the 19th C. This part was built for the Innell family who owned Sevilles Mill at that time. This has three storeys, each with a string course and large pane sash windows **(Figure 8.242)**. The central part breaks forward and this has windows, which are Venetian in style. Each of these has a large central window and flanking narrow windows. There is a central ground floor entrance, with fluted pilasters and a reeded frieze, with corner rosettes. The rear part of the house is late 17th C in origin and has two-storeys under a hipped roof **(Figure 8.243)**. The windows are large pane stone mullions. Mary Rudd notes that internally there is evidence for an earlier house dating from the 16th C. It has been the

CHAPTER 8

home of many clothier families, including Smarts, Batt, Seville and Bliss (in chronological order).

The Old Valley Inn (formerly 'the Clothiers Arms'): The house is constructed in coursed rubblestone, under a stone tiled roof **(Figure 8.244)**. The front elevation (facing S) has two gabled dormers, each with a two-light stone mullion window frame, surmounted by an oval window. The first floor has a continuous dripmould over the first floor windows. There were pairs of two-light windows under each gabled dormer on each floor. Those to the W end of the first floor have been replaced (probably in the 19th C). This is one of the most original clothiers houses remaining in Chalford and dates from the latter part of the 17th C. There is a rear wing (projecting towards the canal) and this has details that show it was added in the 19th C. The inn closed in the late 1960's. Up to that time it had been a Brimscombe Brewery inn.

SOME SMALLER HOUSES IN THE VALLEY

Mount Cottage: These notes were made when the house was for sale in the early 1980's. The building has an unusual construction. The S (front) and gable end walls are built of large, well dressed (hand finished) stone slabs, approximately 9 inches thick **(Figure 8.245)**. There is no inner stone skin and the wall is strengthened with three external stone ribs **(Figure 8.246)**. There is a porch, which is composed of a classical pediment on short stone brackets **(Figure 8.247)**. It spans between two of the ribs. The W (gable end) wall has a small, square external chimney-breast for a corner hearth **(Figure 8.248)**. This retains the original stack. The rear wall is built of rubblestone and is thicker. There is a coved eaves cornice. The windows are all stone mullions, with plain surrounds and flat chamfers. The lights have a relatively large area and there are no dripmoulds or string-courses. It was built as two cottages. The larger one has a central entrance (with the pediment over the top) and flanking three-light windows on the ground floor and a pair of two-light windows on the first floor. The adjoining part has an entrance and a two-light ground floor window. On the first floor, there is a four-light window (with two-lights blocked). Internally, some of the partition walls are comprised of stone slabs and these project to form the ribs that strengthen the front elevation. There is a rear wing behind the larger cottage. The side-wall is constructed in the stone slabs and it has a ground floor entrance and a first floor two-light window, formed out of the stone slabs with a mullion post. The rear wall is built into the bank. Internally, the beams (approximately 20cm square) have rough chamfers (2.5 cm) and no stops. The doors are a mixture of 2 panel doors with H-L hinges (original) and 4 panel doors with ordinary hinges (replacements). All of the hearths were infilled, although the large chimney-breast in the attic shows the presence of wood burning hearths. The attics are of three and two bays and are separated by the chimney-breast for the large ground floor hearth. Each attic has a similar roof structure and is comprised of principal rafters, with tie beams, but no collars. The apex joint of each principal rafter pair is a pegged mortice and tenon joint. There is a single, butt purlin on each roof slope, these are cut back at their junction with the principal. All principals have been cut, so they are curved at their bases, presumably to give a little extra height in the attic. The detail shows that this house was built in one phase in the early part of the 18th C.

Dark Lane House **(Figure 8.249)**: This has two-storeys and is constructed of masonary blocks. There is an eaves cornice with a leaded gutter and a moderately pitched roof. There are two entrance doors. The best one has a moulded stone architrave with a pediment. The other is blocked and has a plain surround. This suggests that it was built as a larger and a smaller cottage, but it has been a single house for many years now. There is a plat band above the ground floor windows. There are three, three-light stone mullion windows on both ground and first floors: these do not have dripmoulds and have a relatively large light area. The surrounds are plain and the chamfers are flat. The detail suggests an origin in the first half of the 18th C.

Thanet House **(Figure 8.250)**: This is a tall house of five storeys (including the lower ground floor). It seems to have been built with domestic accommodation on the lower floors and storage on the upper two floors. It is built of coursed rubblestone under a moderately pitched roof. It is built into the bank, such that the ground three floors of the N gable end form part of the retaining walling for the lane. The upper two floors of the N gable end have taking-in doors, with their early plank and ledge doors. The front elevation has an off-centre ground floor entrance with flanking cross windows, with the transom in the upper part. These have plain, flat chamfer surrounds and a continuous dripmould across the elevation that terminates at the outer side of each flanking window. The windows retain their square pane leaded lights (6 panes in each lower light and 4 in each upper light). The first and second floors have windows with the same detail, with the addition of a central light. The windows at the S end are in line on each floor, whereas the windows at the N end are set-in over the ground floor window (the impact of the off-centre entrance). The top floor windows (floor 5, including the lower ground floor) are set directly under the eaves and are plain two-light stone mullion windows. This floor has been added as the stonework at this level appears to be slightly different. However, the style of the windows suggests that this must have been done fairly early in the life of the building. There is a blocked oval window on the third floor and disturbed stonework on the lower two floors below this window, suggesting their former presence there as well. These must have formerly provided light for a winder stair, beside the gable end hearth. The S facing gable end wall has the entrance to the lower ground floor with an adjoining cross window and a continuous dripmould over both door and window. Originally, there was no connection with the upper floors and when inspected, the basement contained spring fed water tanks. The detail suggests this part of the house was built in the late 17th C, with the roof modifications in the 18th C. A rear lean-to wing has been added and this is again of rubblestone construction, but with large multi pane sash windows. These have stone lintels and stone block sides. The detail here suggests an origin in the 19th C.

Houses formerly to the E of Thanet House: Some 17th C houses formerly stood backing onto the High Street on either side of the New Red Lion Inn. These were demolished in the 1960's. One was the Bell Inn and this was built with its back directly against the lane **(Figure 8.251)**. Part of its rear wall, with hearth and stairwell can be seen retaining the lane in the rear garden of Thanet House. The Bell Inn had some cross windows, with continuous dripmoulds on both the ground and first floors and must have been of a similar date to Thanet House. It looked as if the height of the building had been raised, as the second floor had multi pane sash windows. The inn had an assembly room, which was used by Chartists in the 1830's, when the local cloth industry was in steep decline. In the retaining wall, to the side of the site of the Bell Inn, there is an arched, semi circular recess (about 1.5m wide and 2.5m tall). It is constructed in well-dressed stone and has an 18th C character. Several of these have been noted along the S facing valley side and built into retaining walls. The folklore suggests these are sulpur-burning stoves, used to bleach the cloth. This is most unlikely, since the burning of sulphur under moist conditions would have generated sulphurous gases and these would have attacked the stone, but the stone is in excellent condition. It seems more likely that these are sheltered sites for seats, where more delicate work could be done, or perhaps they are simply garden features. In the area of

Chapter 8

the present car park of the New Red Lion there was a tall house, sited with its gable end into the bank (Figure 8.252). This had three storeys and an attic floor, under a steeply pitched roof. There were two-light stone mullion window frames, with dripmoulds, on each of the W (front) and S (gable end) walls. The detail shows an origin in the latter part of the 17th C. There was a wing added to the rear of the building, in rubblestone and wood window frames (probably 18th C). Details of these buildings can be seen in some early 20th C postcards of the valley. In front of this group of buildings is one of the hidden charms of Chalford: a narrow packhorse bridge crossing the river. It is in a dangerous state, so look, but do not attempt to cross it!

The New Red Lion Inn (Figure 8.253): The front elevation has the size of opening required for sash windows, although the current frames are modern. The N facing gable ends of the double roof are constructed in stone (lower part) and brick (upper part), which suggests there have been some significant modifications.

Tankard Spring House (Figure 8.254): This is constructed in coursed rubblestone and has three storeys under a relatively shallow pitched roof. The front elevation has a central front door with flanking multi pane sash windows. These have plain stone surrounds and lintels and projecting stone cills. There are three first floor windows of the same size (12 pane) and three, second floor windows, which are less tall (6 pane). Internally, much of the structure has been renewed, but there are coal burning hearths only. The detail suggests an origin around the mid 19th C.

Tankard House (Figure 8.255): This is constructed in coursed rubblestone, with the occasional jumper stone and has ground and first floor wood frame windows, under three-piece stone lintels with a flush keystone. On the first floor there are flanking three-light windows and a central two-light window. On the ground floor there is a central entrance, with flanking three-light frames. Each window has similar details and has one opening light, which in the original form would have had an iron frame on pin hinges, with a strap stay bar and quadrants. The detail suggests an origin by the early 19th C.

Cyprus House (Figure 8.256): This is constructed of coursed rubblestone and has three storeys, under a relatively shallow pitched roof. There is a parapet. The second floor windows are markedly different to those of the lower floors (which are themselves consistent) and this shows that the wall has been modified. The second floor has three, two-light stone mullion windows, with plain surrounds and flat chamfers, without dripmoulds. The presence of the parapet suggests a date no earlier than the mid/late 18th C for this modification. The ground and first floors have rows of stone mullion windows. On the first floor there are two groups of pairs of two-light windows, each under a continuous dripmould, together with a three-light window under a dripmould. Each of the windows has a plain chamfer surround and flat chamfers. A single light window, which is an obvious insert, has been added between the three-light and the groups of two-light windows. The ground floor has a three-light window beneath the first floor window of the same size, a group of two, two-light windows and a continuous dripmould under a similar group on the first floor and a five light window (two-lights are blocked) under the second group of first floor, two-light windows. The window detail is the same as on the first floor. There are two entrance doors, that next to the E gable end has a chamfered stone surround and looks original. There are no obvious vertical building lines in the front elevation, suggesting the ground plan is of a single phase. The presence of continuous dripmoulds indicates a late 17th C build date, with the modification of the original attics to form a proper second floor in the later part of the 18th C. The window grouping (i.e. pairs of two-light windows under a continuous dripmould) is the same as that on the Old Valley Inn. It is also possible that the building originally had gabled dormers, as were also formerly present at the Mount. It is also possible that this was originally constructed as several dwellings.

Anchor House (formerly the Anchor Inn) **(Figure 8.257)**: This is built in well-dressed stone and has two-storeys, under a moderately pitched roof. There is a central entrance, with flanking two-light windows, each with a plain surround and wood frame. There are three openings on the first floor, all with two-light windows. The present frames are modern, formerly each wooden frame would have had an iron opening light on pin hinges and proper square pane leaded lights. There are is a continuous course of lintel stone above the ground and first floor windows, with keystones (flush) at the centre point of each opening. These are same construction as in Clematis Cottage (Chalford Hill). There are low attic walls. The build date is thought to be in the early part of the 19th C.

Sevilles Mill House **(Figure 8.258)**: This has developed in several stages. The original house is built of coursed rubblestone and the front wall (W facing) has a pair of three-light stone mullion windows on the first floor under a continuous dripmould (terminates at the outer side of each window). The rear wall has two, two-light windows on the first floor. All of the windows in this part of the house have rebated surrounds and plain chamfers. The original house has gable end chimneys. The N stack (the valley-side end) serves a large ground floor hearth, with a fine stone lintel and large stone jambs. The hearth opening has a relatively narrow chamfer with scroll stops with bars on the jambs. The underside of the lintel over the hearth has a slight camber and this is replicated in the lintel over the entrance doorway. There is a stone winder stair adjacent to the hearth. The details (relatively narrow chamfers and continuous dripmoulds) suggest it was built in the latter part of the 17th C. The S gable end of this part has a sash window on the ground floor, which has a moulded stone surround and keystone. The window was probably added in the first half of the 18th C. The roof of this part has been raised and the building also extended to the N, such that the N gable of the extended part supports the lane. There is a taking in door to the attic of this part at the level of the road (it retains its early door). The front wall of the extended part has an unusual stone window frame. This has two-lights, with each light having a double arched head. The surround has a concave chamfer. Not sure of the date of this window, the addition seems to date from the 19th C, which is probably the date of the frame.

Bubblewell House **(Figure 8.259)**: This shows a similar development to Sevilles House and this can be clearly seen in the stonework of the front (W facing) elevation. It is based on a small, two-storey cottage, with a moderately pitched roof. This is constructed in well-coursed rubblestone. It has an entrance to the N end and two-light stone mullion windows on each floor (the ground floor window is a replacement). These have plain surrounds with flat chamfers. The ground floor window has a dripmould, whereas there is not a sufficient space under the eaves for one on the first floor. The S facing gable end wall has three-light stone mullion window frames on the ground and first floors. These have a larger light area than those on the front elevation. They have rebated surrounds with flat chamfers and dripmoulds. There is a two-light window with similar detail in the attic gable. The cottage has been extended to the N along the same line and a vertical building line marks the junction of the two parts. The newer part is also constructed in coursed rubblestone and has a ground floor entrance, next to the building line (not a good place structurally). There is a three-light window on the ground floor, with a rebated surround, flat chamfers and a similar light area to those in the

Chapter 8

gable end of the original part. The dripmould has been cut-off next to the doorway, which suggests that this has been created at a later date. There is a two-light window on the first floor, with similar detail to that on the ground floor, but without a dripmould. This marks the original height of this part of the building. Above this height, the stone detail changes (the stones are larger, but still coursed rubblestone) and the direction of the quoins is reversed). It is likely that the original cottage was built around the mid 17th C and this was extended at the end of that century. The height of the newer part was raised during the 18th C. This part has a 'taking in' door into the attic at road level. When this part was modified, it is plausible that the property was split into two cottages (hence the addition of the second ground floor entrance).

4 High Street **(Figure 8.260)**: This is another mid/late 17th C house, built gable end into the bank. It has recent additions to either side, so that only the S facing gable end of the original house is visible (from the canal). This shows that the original house has a lower ground floor, ground and first floors and an attic under a steeply pitched roof. There are two, three, two and two-light stone mullion windows on each floor passing up the gable end. All have rebated surrounds with plain chamfers and dripmoulds.

Valley Farm **(Figure 8.261)**: This has two-storeys and attic, under a steeply pitched roof. The walls are built of coursed rubblestone. There is a central ground floor entrance, with flanking three-light stone mullion windows and a continuous dripmould that rises over the entrance. This passes to the edge of the building and there is a small return on the W gable end wall. On the first floor, there are five, two-light windows, built directly under a deep, coved eaves cornice. The windows have plain surrounds and flat chamfers. The detail (the cornice and the continuous drips) show that the building was built at the very end of the 17th or beginning of the 18th C. A single storey wing projects to the lane from the front wall. This has a blocked 'taking in' door to the attic in the gable end wall (on the lane). There is also a rear wing.

Cottages in Chalford Valley

There are many cottages spread out along the S facing valley side. They are mostly built above the valley floor, presumably as a protection against damp. Only the newer houses are built on the actual floor. They are built along the High Street and on several higher levels, which are reached by a network of footpaths **(Figure 8.262)**. The uppermost cottages seem to be constructed on a shelf formed by the quarrying of the Inferior Oolite. Quarrying must have been an important industry here for several centuries. The lower cottages seem to be built on shelves, which have been excavated for the purpose of building the cottages. Retaining walls are used to support the excavated shelf, as is the cottage itself in many cases. These cottages share many of the details of those described in Chalford Hill and therefore, they are not described in detail. There are several that are built gable end into the valley side and these are the earliest and date from the latter part of the 17th or early 18th C **(Figure 8.263-266)**. They have gable end fireplaces backing onto the valley side, some have stone mullion windows with plain surrounds and dripmoulds, others have timber window frames (mainly replacements). All are constructed in coursed rubblestone and the roof pitches are fairly steep. The relatively low number of this type of cottage in the valley, shows that weaving was less important here than in Chalford Hill. There seems to be a clear distinction between the two settlements: the mill owners and clothiers in the valley and the weavers on the hill. By far the greatest number of stone built cottages in Chalf-

Vernacular Buildings of Chalford

ord valley date from the 18th and early part of the 19th C. There are some later cottages built in brick and they date from the latter part of the 19th C. Presumably by this time quarrying had ceased in the immediate area and it was cheaper and easier to transport bricks into the village using the canal. It is possible that the stone quarrying industry declined with the cloth industry, as the need for new buildings decreased, and as alternative materials were brought in via the canal. An indication of the date of the stone cottages of the 18th and 19th C can be gained from the window, stone, timber (beams and roof structure) and fireplace details. Most are aligned parallel to the slope and are simple in their design with the minimum of detail. A few have continuous dripmoulds and stone mullion windows, indicating a late 17th C date **(Figure 8.267)**. Some have stone mullion windows with the larger light area and without dripmoulds and these date from the 18th C **(Figure 8.268 and 269)**. Many of the cottages have segmented arch lintels in stone over the cottage casement window and door openings and original coal burning hearths **(Figure 8.270 and 271)**. These suggest an origin in the early 19th C and coincide with the period when many of the mills were rebuilt as cloth making factories. As in Chalford Hill, extra cottages have been added to the earlier cottages to increase the number of cottages available **(Figure 8.272)**. This shows they were built at a time of industrial expansion, as the local labour force was increasing. Many have now been combined to form larger properties. This is the same process of gentrification as has occurred in Chalford Hill over the last 40 or so years.

Overview of the Development of the Settlement in Chalford Valley

The valley was formed about 10000 years ago at the end of the last Ice Age. The flow of water in the River Frome is now small compared with the amount of water that must have been flowing at that time. Nevertheless, it still has sufficient energy in its current to power water mills and these have been sited in the valley for over 1000 years. The early mills were probably a mixture of both corn and fulling mills. None of the very early mills survive. Mills do survive in relatively large numbers, but these mainly date from the late 18th and early part of the 19th C, when the organisation of the local cloth making was changed. Prior to this time, the weaving was cottage based and the cloth was brought to the mill for fulling and subsequent processes. In the late 18th and early 19th C, the clothiers (who controlled the local industry), wanted to gain greater control of the whole manufacturing process and make it more competitive. They rebuilt the mills so that the weaving could take place in a factory environment, where it could take advantage of technical advances, which involved increased mechanisation. Some remnants of earlier mills remain in some of the surviving mills, but their dominant character is of the factory type mills. The mills are spaced along the valley floor, with some taking advantage of springs flowing off the valley side. The early mills seem to be based near the main river crossing points. Whether, the siting was next to an existing crossing point or whether it became a crossing point because it was near a mill is not known. As time progressed, the mills became spaced out along the whole valley at Chalford and there would have been competition for the water supply. The original clothiers lived close to their mills, so there are concentrations of early, larger houses near the earlier mills (e.g. St Mary's Mill and Chalford (Belvedere) Mill) and also some smaller houses and cottages. The larger houses contain cores that go back to at least the 16th C and possibly earlier. However, their external appearance (mainly at the front) was kept up to date with the current styles (presumably as a manifestation that the owner was doing alright)! Many of houses date from the later part of the 17th C, when there seems to have been a post Civil War boom. There are concentrations of these buildings at St Mary's, at the bottom of Hyde Hill, near the New Red Lion Inn in the High Street and at the bottom of Coppice Hill and these form the nuclei of the present larger settlement. In the

Chapter 8

18th and 19th C the mill owners still lived in the valley, but new clothier houses were built slightly above the valley floor.

There are some cottages in the valley that can be dated back to the late 17th C, but there are far fewer than in Chalford Hill. These are placed at random intervals along the valley side and close to the lower spring line. Chalford Hill therefore seems to be the weaving settlement that fed the mills with the unprocessed cloth. In the later part of the 18th and early 19th C, many more cottages were built and this seems to coincide with the rebuilding and perhaps increase in the number of mills.

Mixed in the developing settlement, new transport links along the valley were constructed in the late 18th C (canal), 1818 (turnpike road) and 1845 (railway).

VERNACULAR BUILDINGS OF CHALFORD

Figure 8.189. Dark Lane. *(1950's)*

Figure 8.190. Marle Hill. *(1950's)*

Figure 8.191. Coppice Hill. *(1916)*

Figure 8.192. Derelict building at St Mary's Mill. *(1980)*

Figure 8.193. St Mary's Mill: early 19th C factory mill. *(1980)*

Figure 8.194. Clayfields Mill. *(2006)*

315

CHAPTER 8

Figure 8.195. Iles Mill. *(2006)*

Figure 8.196. Iles Mill, without a roof. *(1930's)*

Figure 8.197. Belvedere Mill. *(2006)*

Figure 8.198. Belvedere Mill. *(2006)*

Figure 8.199. Bliss Mills. *(1930's)*

Figure 8.200. New Mill (Chalford Building Supplies). *(2006)*

VERNACULAR BUILDINGS OF CHALFORD

Figure 8.201. Smarts Mill. *(2006)*

Figure 8.202. Sevilles Mill, demolished in the 1960's. *(1907)*

Figure 8.203. Mortons Mill, demolished (mill on left, Valley Inn on right). *(1912)*

Figure 8.204. Ashmeads Mill (with the waterworks building in front). *(1912)*

Figure 8.205. St Marys Mill House. *(1991)*

Figure 8.206. St Marys Mill Cottages. *(1991)*

317

CHAPTER 8

Figure 8.207. Brookside. *(2006)*

Figure 8.208. Iles Mill Cottages. *(2006)*

Figure 8.209. Belvedere Mill House: front view, being stripped. *(mid 1980's)*

Figure 8.210. Belvedere Mill House: porch dated 1789. *(mid 1980's)*

Figure 8.211. Belvedere Mill House: rear view. *(mid 1980's)*

Figure 8.212. Belvedere Mill House: front view, taller roof being constructed. *(mid 1980's)*

VERNACULAR BUILDINGS OF CHALFORD

Figure 8.213. Belvedere Mill House: fanlight in façade modified in late 18th C. *(mid 1980's)*

Figure 8.214. Belvedere Mill House: blocked windows. *(mid 1980's)*

Figure 8.215. Belvedere Mill House: cross window. *(mid 1980's)*

Figure 8.216. Belvedere Mill House: removed timbers. *(mid 1980's)*

Figure 8.217. Belvedere Mill House: added fireplaces. *(mid 1980's)*

Figure 8.218. Belvedere Mill House: earlier roof structure. *(mid 1980's)*

319

CHAPTER 8

Figure 8.219. Belvedere Mill House: statue formerly in garden. *(mid 1980's)*

Figure 8.220. The Company's Arms. *(1930's)*

Figure 8.221. Chalford Place: N side. *(mid 1980's)*

Figure 8.222. Chalford Place: N side. *(mid 1980's)*

Figure 8.223. Chalford Place: rebuilt S side. *(2004)*

Figure 8.224. Chalford Place: unusual window. *(2004)*

Figure 8.225. Chalford Place: porch hood on brackets. *(2004)*

Figure 8.226. Chalford Place: S side, central section and E end. *(2004)*

Figure 8.227. 16th C house in Chalford Industrial Estate. *(2006)*

Figure 8.228. 8.227 in the 1930's with industrial wing to the front.

Figure 8.229. 16th C house: fine quality masonary. *(2006)*

Figure 8.230. 16th C house: three light window. *(2006)*

CHAPTER 8

Figure 8.231. 16th C house: four light window with king mullion. *(2006)*

Figure 8.232. 16th C house: projecting chimney breast on first floor. *(2006)*

Figure 8.233. 16th C House: E gable end with early 18th C windows. *(2006)*

Figure 8.234. This is thought to be a painting of 8.227 in the early 19th C

Figure 8.235. Sevillowes. *(2006)*

Figure 8.236. Wickham Grange. *(2006)*

Vernacular Buildings of Chalford

Figure 8.237. The Grove. *(2006)*

Figure 8.238. Smarts Mill House. *(2006)*

Figure 8.239. Vale House. *(2006)*

Figure 8.240. Springfield House, in the 1930's.

Figure 8.241. The Mount. *(2006)*

Figure 8.242. Green Court. *(2006)*

Chapter 8

Figure 8.243. Green Court. *(c 1920)*

Figure 8.244. The Old Valley Inn. *(2005)*

Figure 8.245. Mount Cottage. *(c.1985)*

Figure 8.246. Mount Cottage: structural ribs. *(c. 1985)*

Figure 8.247. The Mount: porch hood. *(2006)*

Figure 8.248. Mount Cottage: gable end chimney breast. *(c.1985)*

VERNACULAR BUILDINGS OF CHALFORD

Figure 8.249. Dark Lane House. *(2006)*

Figure 8.250. Thanet House. *(c.1990)*

Figure 8.251. The Bell Inn. *(c.1930)*

Figure 8.252. Cottage near New Red Lion. *(c. 1920)*

Figure 8.253. The New Red Lion Inn. *(2006)*

Figure 8.254. Tankard Spring House. *(c.1950)*

CHAPTER 8

Figure 8.255. Tankard House. *(2006)*

Figure 8.256. Cyprus Villa. *(2006)*

Figure 8.257. Anchor House. *(2006)*

Figure 8.258. Sevilles Mill House. *(2002)*

Figure 8.259. Bubblewell House. *(2006)*

Figure 8.260. 4 High Street. *(2006)*

VERNACULAR BUILDINGS OF CHALFORD

Figure 8.261. Valley Farm. *(2006)*

Figure 8.262. Cottages along the side of the valley. *(1930's)*

Figure 8.263. Late 17th/early18th C cottage in the valley: Old Red Lion Inn. *(2006)*

Figure 8.264. Late 17th/early18th C cottage on Rack Hill. *(2006)*

Figure 8.265. Late 17th/early18th C cottage in Dimmelsdale. *(2006)*

Figure 8.266. Late 17th/early18th C cottage on Coppice Hill. *(2006)*

CHAPTER 8

Figure 8.267. Cottage with a continuous dripmould on the High St. *(2006)*

Figure 8.268. Saratoga: middle part is 18th C. *(2006)*

Figure 8.269. Late 18th C cottage near the Valley Playing Field. *(2002)*

Figure 8.270. Early 19th C cottage on Rack Hill, now renovated. *(2002)*

Figure 8.271. Early 19th C cottages above the High St. *(2002)*

Figure 8.272. Additional cottage added to a late 17th C cottage on Rack Hill. *(2002)*

CHAPTER 9

COMPARISON OF THE SETTLEMENTS AT STROUD AND CHALFORD

Chalford- developed through industry

Stroud- developed as the commercial centre for the valleys

Both postcards c 1940

Comparison of the Settlements at Stroud and Chalford

The settlements are geographically close, but the drivers for the development of each are different. Stroud has an early root and grew along the highway to Bisley (the earliest local settlement identified in documents). Its growing importance was recognised by the construction of a Chapel of Ease in the 13th C and the presence of a market by the 16th C. Other local towns also had developed markets by this time (Tetbury, Painswick, Minchinhampton and Cirencester). Stroud developed its role as a commercial centre. The buildings in the core of the older part of the town reflect this role: they date from at least the 16th C and still retain some urban medieval detail, despite having been changed on a regular basis. The original core of the town became developed and it extended outwards. The first expansion occurred in the late 17th C, into the fields above the old part of the town. The character of this part is domestic and documents suggest it was inhabited by those associated with the cloth trade, together with masons, and all the other trades expected in a developing commercial centre. The original houses had generous plots of land, but over the coming centuries these were progressively infilled (particularly in the 19thC onwards), so that by the early 20th C this part of the town was regarded as a bit of a slum. In parallel with the latter developments here, Stroud also expanded in other directions. Development occurred to the S when the new turnpike road was constructed in the early 19th C. Lansdown was constructed in the mid 19th C to be followed by the Bisley Road, Horns Road and Uplands developments in the late 19th C. The impetus for these later developments must have originated in the coming of the railway to Stroud in the mid 19th C and the consequent economic development. By the time the railway came to Stroud, the cloth industry at Chalford had declined, but it continued in the Stroud area, although with many changes to maintain its competitiveness.

The settlements at Chalford have linked, but different origins. Both were sited in the outlying part of one of the manors of Bisley. The power in the river was used to drive water mills and documents mention a number of mills in the valley from the time of the Domesday Book. It was the availability of the reliable power supply, which stimulated the growth of the cloth industry and the settlement in the valley. No doubt the wealth being generated at Chalford (and in the other Stroud valleys) had a knock on effect for Stroud. The cloth industry grew from one serving local needs to one of national and international importance. This was accompanied by a great increase in the number of local clothiers and the number of mills. There were some early houses associated with the early mills and these, together with newer houses were the clothier houses of the developing cloth industry. They are sited close to the mills, presumably so the owner could keep an eye on his property and business. These houses range in date from the 16th to the early 19th C and many of these houses survive today. Clearly, they have been altered over the years to meet the changing needs, fortunes and aspirations of the owners. The mills themselves were also subject to a late 18th/early 19th C revolution in the way the industry was organised and most of the surviving mills date from this time. The cloth industry had declined at Chalford by the mid 19th C, to be replaced by a succession of 'new' industries, which used the established powered mill infrastructure. These industries include silk manufacture, production of walking sticks and engineering works. Chalford Valley is a settlement with industrial roots and this is reflected in the mixture of buildings dating from the 16th C to the mid 19th C that survive today. There is a mixture of mill buildings, clothier houses and smaller houses and cottages for those

Chapter 9

employed in the industry. The settlement in the valley has also been affected by the development of the transport links, which assisted in the later development of the industry. They are visually and audibly intrusive and together with the sites still in commercial and industrial use, maintain a busy feel to the valley.

Chalford Hill developed because there was power to drive mills in the valley. It grew as a settlement of handloom weavers. They produced the raw cloth that was then further processed in the mills in the valley. The settlement is random and developed as a squatters settlement of weavers on the fringes of the Bisley common land. Documents suggest that the cottages were built without permission, but inhabitants were allowed to keep them on payment of a fine. The developing settlement seems to have grown along existing tracks through the area, leading to the crossing points of the River Frome. These early cottages are simple and provided the basic human needs: somewhere to cook, keep warm, a degree of security and somewhere to sleep and work. Two main plan types are apparent, those with a ground floor and attic and those with two-storeys and attic. It is possible that the single storey houses are the earlier, with the two-storey type coming into favour in the latter part of the 17th C. The stone for the cottages was dug locally and local springs provided the water supply. These cottages are built without footings and generally without cellars. The early settlement must have been self-sufficient and each cottage had a large garden. The garden was surrounded by a dry stone wall to differentiate it from the remaining common and to protect growing crops. As the industry developed, so the population of weavers in Chalford Hill and the adjacent villages expanded. New cottages were built in the remaining common land and further cottages were added to the existing homes. This process continued through to the early 19th C and the village became fairly densely built up. By this time the village will have contained all the trades and professions needed to support a large population. It is difficult to imagine the impact of the factorisation of the weaving process in the early 19th C on the cottage based handloom weavers. There must have been great resentment to the change: the lucky ones found occupation in the factory mills, whilst the remainder became unemployed. The cloth industry then collapsed and the cloth mills had closed by the middle of the century, causing further hardship. The records show that local families were given assistance to move to other parts of the UK and abroad (particularly Canada and Australia). New industries replaced cloth manufacture and these maintained the need for a large local workforce living in the ridge villages, through to the mid 20thC.

CHAPTER 10

RECENT CHANGES AND THE FUTURE

Recent Changes and the Future

THERE WAS continuity in the use of the settlements at Stroud and Chalford through to the period ending in the 1940's: Stroud as the local urban centre, Chalford (and the valleys) being a centre for production (although what was produced changed markedly over the years). Homes for the working population were built along the lower valley slopes and in the ridge villages. In the first part of the 20th C, the old cottages became regarded as sub-standard and new homes began to be built to house the working population. Many of the early properties were allowed to fall into disrepair, rather than being updated and some, but by no means all, were demolished. This process had a more substantial impact on Stroud because it was the local urban centre and the District Council wanted to 'modernise' it. OK, what was done may be regretted now, but it was thought to be for the best at the time. It has however, had a negative impact on the subsequent development of the town (*my opinion*). Chalford was more remote and poorer, and was not subjected to the process of renewal. There were limited demolitions of structurally unsafe buildings, or where a builder spotted an opportunity to replace an old cottage, but in the main the buildings have survived fairly well from the pre 1940 period. They have been adapted and changed on many occasions, but their origins can still be traced. In the immediate post-war period the area was slumbering, to be awoken in the 1960's by the start of an influx of new people to the area. They did not necessarily come here to work in industry, but came because they liked the area and sensed the intrinsic value of the built and natural environment of this less popular end of the Cotswolds. Many were prepared to travel to work. This process has continued now for about 30 years and it has had a marked impact on the make-up of the population and on the character of the settlements. Changing attitudes have resulted in much expenditure on the preservation and restoration of the old vernacular buildings. Some of the earlier work was not done particularly well, but work now being done shows far greater sensitivity to the buildings. However, sometimes this can result in what could be called over 'gentrification'. The cottages are no longer the homes of local workers, but of professionals not necessarily working in the area and of entrepreneurs running their own companies. Property prices have risen dramatically and the area is seen as a popular place to move to from London. This means there is an economic incentive to keep the properties in good order, but it does have unforeseen effects. Land values are now high and there is an economic argument, which says more money can be made by demolishing a small cottage, in its large garden and re-developing with several detached 4/5 bedroom 'executive' houses. This particularly affects the ordinary cottage that is not listed. 'Property developers' are also active in the area. Programmes on the TV have encouraged people to make money by renovating and upgrading old properties. Quite often, say after a death, a house will be sold for what seems a reasonable value, only to re-appear on the market within a year or so, after a 'make-over' and at a greatly increased price. Cash buyers are waiting for the undone-up property and are favoured by the agents, as there is the potential for another and larger sale on the horizon. Nothing illegal in any of this, but it does represent a barrier to those who want to live in and contribute to the community of the area, rather than just make money out of it. It also tends to alter the social make-up of the villages. Property prices are now high and it has become difficult for first time buyers to purchase a property in many of the villages.

Change will continue and how the buildings survive will depend on how they are treated and

Chapter 10

respected by their owners. I hope this book will encourage the sympathetic and sustainable treatment of our built heritage as it moves forward in time. Remember, once gone, our historic buildings cannot be replaced.

A final important point is that large populations lived in these buildings for several centuries in a truly sustainable way. They were built with locally available resources (stone, earth and timber). They had no external power supplies and used biomass for heat, sunlight for light and water for industrial power. Food was grown locally and water bubbled-up from the ground. Sewage was disposed of in the gardens, where it enhanced soil fertility. There is much we can learn here for the future.

SOURCES OF INFORMATION

THE FOLLOWING books have been used in gathering some of the information for use in this book. They are recommended as sources of further information for those interested in particular parts of our local history.

GEOGRAPHY AND GEOLOGY

British Regional Geology, Bristol and Gloucester District, HMSO 1948

The Geology of Stroud and the Area Drained by the River Frome, E Witchell, published by James 1882

FEATURES OF LOCAL VERNACULAR BUILDINGS

The Georgian Group Book of the Georgian House by Steve Parissien, Aurum Press 1995. An excellent book for those owning /interested in 18th C houses.

House and Cottage Interiors (Do's and Don'ts) by Hugh Lander, Acanthus Books, Cornwall, 1982.

Firegrates and Kitchen Ranges (Shire Album 99) by David J Eveleigh, published by Shire Books.

Fixtures and Fittings in Dated Houses by Linda Hall and N W Alcock, published by the Council for British Archaeology in 1994.

Period House Fixtures and Fittings 1300-1900, by Linda Hall, published by Countryside Books in 2005.

LOCAL HISTORY

Notes and Recollections of Stroud, Gloucestershire by P H Fisher, first published in 1871 by J Elliot, High Street, Stroud, but republished several times since then.

Historical Records of Bisley with Lypiatt by Mary A Rudd. Published privately in 1937 and republished by A Sutton in 1977.

The Victoria County History of Gloucestershire Volume XI, edited by N M Herbert, published by the Oxford University Press in 1976.

Stroud, by Joan Tucker, published by Phillimore in 1991.

Bisley, a Cotswold Village Remembered, by Juliet Shipman, published by the Chantry Press in 1991.

Oakridge, A History, by Pat Carrick, Kay Rhodes and Juliet Shipman, published by Playne Books, in 2005.

Journal of the Society of Industrial Archaeology, various articles by Ian Mackintosh, 1984-1986.

Report on the Condition of the Handloom Weavers in Gloucestershire, 1837, copy in Stroud Reference Library.

Local Interest

Jerusalem on Chapel Street, words by Enid Airy, Claire Toy, Roger Yates, Sarah Lutyens, R Newman, pictures and photos by B Day and Roz Yates, published by Chapscorp in 1975.

The Plotter of Gloucester by Claire Toy, Matrix Design, Gloucester 1976.

The Cloth Industry

The Textile Industry of South West England by Marilyn Palmer and Peter Neaverson, published by Tempus 2005.

The Cloth Industry in the West of England by J DeL Mann, published by Alan Sutton 1971.

Gloucestershire Woollen Mills, Jennifer Tann, published by David and Charles, 1967.

The Mills of Gloucestershire, S Mills and P Riemer, published by Barracuda Books, 1989.

Vernacular Architecture

Old Cottages, Farmhouses and Other Stone Buildings in the Cotswold Region by W Galsworthy Davie and E Guy Dawber, published by Batsford in 1905.

The Buildings of England: Gloucestershire, The Cotswolds by David Verey and Alan Brooks, third edition, revised and reprinted in 2000, Penguin Books.

SOURCES OF INFORMATION

Cotswold Stone Homes (History, Conservation and Care) by Michael Hill and Sally Birch, published by Alan Sutton in 1994.

Illustrated Handbook of Vernacular Architecture by R W Brunskill, published by Faber in 1971

The Dry Stone Walls in the Chalford Area by Janet Gaskell and Nigel Paterson, issued by the Chalford Village Walls Project in 1999.

The Rural Houses of North Avon and South Gloucestershire (1400-1720) by Linda J Hall, published by City of Bristol Museum and Art Gallery, Monograph No 6, 1983.

RESTORATION OF STONE BUILDINGS

New Stone for Old: Techniques for Matching Historic Stone Finishes , by Jamie Vans (Stone Mason and Sculptor), Article written for Historic Churches, 1999 and available from Cathedral Communications Ltd, Tisbury, Wiltshire and on http://www.building conservation.com/articles.

Historic Buildings: A Guide to their Conservation and Repair, published by the Stroud District Council, 1998.

The Repair of Historic Buildings: Advice on Principles and Methods by Christopher Brereton, published by English Heritage in 1991.

PHOTOGRAPHS OF THE AREA

Cotswold Memories (recollections of rural life in the steam age) by Ron Pigram and Dennis F Edwards, published by Unicorn Books in 1990.

Stroud and the Five Valleys by S J Gardiner and L C Padin, published by Alan Sutton in 1984.

Stroud and the Five Valleys, a second selection, by S J Gardiner and L C Padin, published by Alan Sutton in 1987.

Stroud Road and Rail, by S J Gardiner and L C Padin, published by Alan Sutton in 1987.

Chalford to Sapperton, by Stanley Gardiner, published by The Chalford Publishing Co in 1995.

Pubs of the Old Stroud Brewery, by Wilfred Merret, published by The Chalford Publishing Co in 1996.

Stroudwater and Thames and Severn Canals by Edwin Cuss and Stanley Gardiner, published by Alan Sutton publishing in 1993.

MEMORIES LAST LONGER THAN DREAMS

The Author:

NIGEL PATERSON is an energy research scientist, who worked for British Coal, at the Coal Research Establishment (near Tewkesbury) and now at Imperial College London. He has maintained an interest in the historic buildings of the area, since moving to Stroud in 1974. He has restored several houses in Stroud and Chalford and has helped many owners understand the development of their buildings. He was one of the founder Directors of the Stroud Preservation Trust and a founder member of the Gloucestershire Buildings Recording Group. He is currently Chairman of both groups. He is married to Kathy (Head of the History Department at Marling School).

ISBN 1-41209951-X